Louis W. Daws.. W9-AZG-292

10TH MOUNTAIN HUT & TRAIL SYSTEM

Colorado 10th Mountain Trails

OFFICIAL GUIDE · SECOND EDITION

WHO PRESS · ASPEN COLORADO

DEDICATION

Dedicated to Billie Tagert, Alfred A. Braun,
and all those pioneer skiers who are long forgotten,
but on whose shoulders we stand.

PUBLISHED BY

WHO Press
P.O. Box 1920
Aspen, Colorado 81612

Library of Congress Catalog Card Number: 91-65946

ISBN 0-9620046-7-7

Second Edition 1991

Printed in the United States of America

All photos by Lou Dawson unless otherwise indicated

Book design by Curt Carpenter

Edited by Warren H. Ohlrich

Foreword

As I go through this busy life, I relish my time in places of solitude and beauty. Such places provide a kind of meditation, an escape from the humdrum world. I like to call it "the icing on the cake of life." The 10th Mountain hut and trail system has given me many such experiences. A couple of years ago one of my compadres on such a trip looked at me after floating through waist-deep powder and commented, "With snow like this anyone can feel like a ski god." I agree.

My first experience with the 10th Mountain system was with my wife and parents. We began our trip in Aspen, skied east to the McNamara and Margy's huts, then out to the Diamond J Guest Ranch. Looking back, this three-day trip was one of the best times I have ever had with my parents. But it was also an epic. Even though we were all intermediate or advanced skiers, we had problems such as underestimating travel times, carrying too much equipment, and having the wrong ski gear for the downhill sections of trail. Since this first trip I've used the 10th Mountain system regularly. I've learned how to cope with most problems, but one has continued to plague me: a lack of information about the trails. As a result, I stick with familiar pastures and ignore new and exciting options.

I met Lou Dawson when he did some writing for us at *Rocky Mountain Sports Magazine*. I was intrigued by the way he conveyed the excitement of backcountry travel while weaving good information on safety, navigation, and other factors into the fabric of his story. Recently, I met up with Lou in Telluride for some spring corn skiing on El Diente Peak. This was the first time I had skied with the man, and the trip was another memorable adventure. I was highly impressed by Lou's knowledge of backcountry skiing and his love for the sport. His reputation for being one of the finest ski mountaineers is well deserved.

Lou's previous guide *Colorado High Routes* covered some of the 10th Mountain huts and trails. However, the system has grown to the point where it needs a guide of its own, as shown by the book you hold in your hands. Speaking for myself, there will be no more skiing the trails over and over. As soon as I feel like something new, the information I need is right here, between these pages. Thus, I am ecstatic about *Colorado 10th Mountain Trails*. I'm certain that many other skiers will feel the same.

John Winsor
PUBLISHER, *Rocky Mountain Sports*

ACKNOWLEDGMENTS

One person could never provide all the facts in a book such as *Colorado 10th Mountain Trails*. Scott Messina, who has set trails for 10th Mountain for several years, was an invaluable help. Thanks also to the staff at 10th Mountain for answering my endless questions. I am grateful to Peter Looram, 10th Mountain Executive Director, for his timely decisions about official map and trailhead names. My wife Lisa deserves a special thanks for ignoring the long hours and weird schedule of a writer. I'd also like to acknowledge my late grandfather, L.W. Dawson, for his encouragement and support.

Thanks to Colorado Outdoor Sports in Denver and Summit Canyon Mountaineering in Glenwood Springs for help with my equipment. Kim Miller of Black Diamond also deserves thanks for his support. The Mountainsmith pack was terrific. The Kastle Tour Randonee ski is the perfect tool for my work — thanks to Kastle for supplying me with skis.

Berg Heil!

L. D. 1991

Preface

F or many years the world over, mountain huts have sheltered skiers and climbers. In the Alps, hundreds of huts hang from mountainsides, and many have been in use for over a century. In the 1940s in Colorado, a chain of shelters cut through what is now the Maroon Bells-Snowmass Wilderness. The first ski hut in Colorado was created in the late 1940s, when Billie Tagert and his friends fixed up an old miners cabin at the head of Castle Creek near Aspen. Tagert and his group loved ski mountaineering, but they knew that skiing with a load of camp gear could turn fun into plain toil.

Winter camping still makes for a pack that could break a mule. You spend hours on survival, with skiing last on your list. Backcountry ski shelters (huts) relieve those burdens. Since the old-timers skied Castle Creek, scores of huts have been built in Colorado. They range from primitive to palatial, but have one thing in common – popularity.

The most extensive of these ski hut systems is managed by the the 10th Mountain Trail Association (10th Mountain). A nonprofit corporation, 10th Mountain was formed in the early 1980s by several Aspen skiers who cherished the perfect ski touring between Vail and Aspen. From the beginning they set their sights on a trail with closely spaced huts, all accessible via intermediate ski touring trails.

The name "10th Mountain" honors the soldiers of the 10th Mountain Division of the U.S. Army. Fifty years ago, with the world at the brink of World War II, the U.S. War Department began experimenting with mountain troops. It was soon obvious that having troops trained for the mountains was necessary. A training site was chosen in Colorado's Eagle River Valley just to the north of Tennessee Pass. Known as Camp Hale, the site became home to 11,000 troops in December 1942.

The troops trained for about two years at Camp Hale, then moved to Washington and Texas. By January of 1945 the 10th Mountain Division was in Italy. Here, they had a crucial role in several battles. The men of the 10th developed a strong camaraderie, and many gained a love for Colorado as well. After the war, hundreds of 10th vets returned to Colorado to settle down. With their ski skills, many of these men were key figures in the development of Colorado's ski industry.

If there were a Hilton of wilderness skiing, the huts of the 10th Mountain Trail Association would qualify. In all, 10th Mountain books about 22 accommodations in the area bordered by Aspen, Vail, Leadville, and Crested Butte, Colorado. Thirteen of these huts and lodges form a loop north and east of Aspen, through the vicinity of Vail and Leadville. This is known as the 10th Mountain Hut and Trail System, and is the system covered in this guide. For the area south of Aspen, 10th Mountain books the Alfred A. Braun huts, Toklat Chalet, and the Friends Hut. Routes for this area can be found in *Colorado High Routes*.

The official 10th Mountain trails are approved by the Forest Service, and marked with blue plastic diamonds and tree blazes. As a convention in this book, these marked trails are called "10th Mountain suggested routes," as opposed to "branch routes" which explore terrain around the huts, and "alternate routes" which are simply routes that are not marked or Forest Service approved.

The 10th Mountain suggested routes are well marked and heavily traveled. Thus, experienced backcountry skiers will find navigation to the huts is fairly easy (given good weather and a modicum of map work). Yet after a few trips from trailheads to huts, many skiers realize that perhaps the greatest benefit of the 10th Mountain system is the access it gives to alternate routes. This is especially true of travel in the designated wilderness bordered by many of the huts. The 10th Mountain suggested route is like an interstate highway, with country roads and turnoffs that are not always obvious.

This guide will help you use the 10th Mountain suggested routes, the "Interstate." It will give you essential information on trailhead access, parking, trip planning, and actual navigation. *Colorado 10th Mountain Trails* will also help you turn from the "Interstate" onto the country roads. Enjoy.

How To Use This Book

CHAPTERS

The chapters in this book are organized around each 10th Mountain accommodation. For example, if you want routes for travel from the Peter Estin Hut to the Polar Star Inn, turn to the Peter Estin Hut chapter; for the reverse turn to the Polar Star Inn chapter. A glance at the table of contents will clarify this.

TRAILHEADS

The trailhead is where you begin nonmotorized travel, and where you usually park. The trailheads are marked on all the text maps. Directions to the trailheads are given in Chapter 1.

Most trailheads are well signed, but signs change. Another concern is unpredictable snow closures on access roads. Closure varies because of plowing policy and weather. For closure information try calling the county's road maintenance division or the Forest Service. General information about snow closure is included in the text.

ROUTE INFORMATION

ROUTE NUMBER AND NAME: Each route is numbered with a conjunction of chapter number and the route's consecutive number within the chapter; e.g., route 4.6 means Chapter 4, route 6. The routes are named using points of origin and destination. There are three types of routes:

• Routes between trailhead and hut.

• Routes from hut to hut.

• Branch routes from the hut to a destination other than a hut or trailhead.

DIFFICULTY RATING: To help you pick routes that match your skills, all the routes are rated for novice, intermediate, advanced, or expert skiers. (See pp. 16-17 for description of each skill level.) Since the 10th Mountain suggested routes are designed as intermediate routes, you'll notice a majority of intermediate routes in this guide.

TIME: The travel time is an estimate taken from an average of reported times. As such, it should only be used as a general guide. It assumes the trip was made by intermediate level skiers.

DISTANCE: Distances are one-way for the trailhead — hut and hut to hut routes; they are round trip for all branch routes.

ELEVATION GAIN AND LOSS: The elevation gain and loss figures include most of the smaller ups and downs. In the trailhead — hut routes, the elevation change is given for the trailhead to hut direction. In the hut to hut routes, the change is given for the direction of travel. In the branch routes, the elevation change is for the round trip.

MAPS: Three types of maps are listed in the data block:

• Text maps in this guide are similar to the commercially available 10th Mountain Maps. In most cases, the text maps should be all you need to navigate the trails described in this book.
• 10th Mountain Maps are published by the 10th Mountain Trail Association. They are composites of USGS 7.5-minute maps.
• USGS 7.5-minute (1:24,000 scale) maps are the "topo" maps familiar to backcountry users.

For "road-finding" use a Colorado road map and a USFS Forest Visitor map such as the White River National Forest Map. The USFS Forest Visitor maps are updated often, and cover large areas with a scale of ½ inch to a mile.

ROUTE DESCRIPTION: In the trailhead — hut routes, route descriptions are given for both directions. In the hut to hut routes, the descriptions start at that chapter's hut. The branch route descriptions are for round trip.

ATTENTION READERS

The information presented in this book is based upon the experience of the author and might not necessarily be perceived as accurate by other persons. Therefore, extreme care should be taken when following any of the routes described in this book. This book is not intended to be instructional in nature but rather a guide for backcountry users who already have the requisite training, experience, and knowledge for the activities they choose. An advanced level of expertise and physical conditioning is necessary for even the "easiest" of the routes described. Proper clothing and equipment is essential. Failure to have the necessary knowledge, equipment, and conditioning will subject you to extreme physical danger, injury, or death. Some routes have changed and others will change; avalanche hazards may have expanded or new hazards may have formed since this book's publication.

Table of Contents

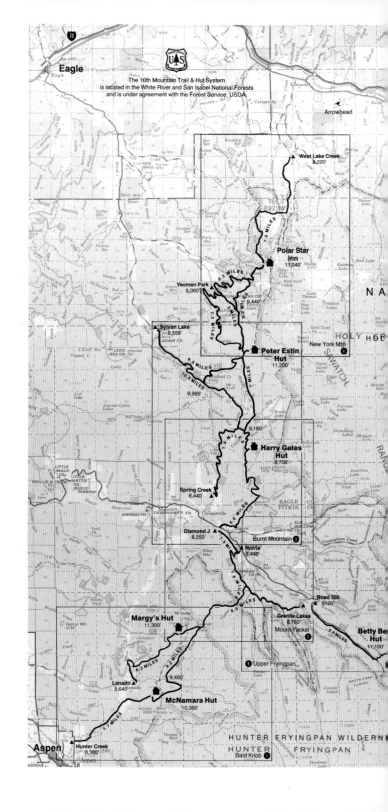

The 10th Mountain Trail & Hut System
is located in the White River and San Isabel National Forests
and is under agreement with the Forest Service, USDA.

Eagle

Arrowhead

West Lake Creek
8,220'

Polar Star
Inn
11,040'

Yeoman Park
9,060'

Sylvan Lake
8,558'
ADAM CG

Peter Estin
Hut
11,200'

New York Mtn

HOLY HO

SWATCH

NA

9,995'

9,180'

Harry Gates
Hut
9,700'

Spring Creek
8,440'

EAGLE
PITKIN

Diamond J
8,250'

Burnt Mountain

Norrie
8,440'

Road 505
9120'

Margy's Hut
11,300'

Granite Lakes
8,760'
Mount Yeckel

Betty Be
Hut
11,100'

Upper Fryingpan

Lenado
8,640'

9,450'

McNamara Hut
10,360'

Hunter Creek
8,380'

Aspen

HUNTER FRYINGPAN WILDERN

HUNTER
FRYINGPAN
Bald Knob

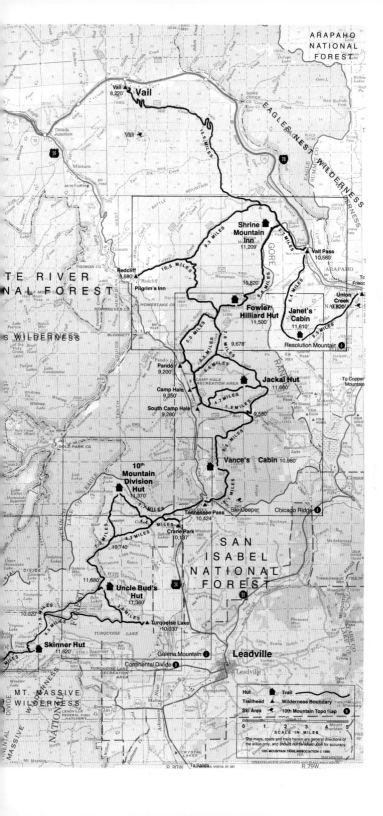

15

The 10th Mountain Huts & Trails

The 10th Mountain Trail Association provides backcountry lodging primarily for ski tourers. In summer, however, many of the privately owned accommodations in this guide stay open, and certain lodging owned by 10th Mountain is available as well. Summer lodging varies greatly from year to year, so call 10th Mountain before you make plans. The accommodations in this guide are often termed "huts" in backcountry parlance; yet these "huts" range from small cabins near timberline to lodges or inns that supply all the amenities from running water to catered meals. Reservations are required for all hut use.

Most of the huts in this book are booked by 10th Mountain, while several of the private accommodations do their own booking (see Directory). Most huts are booked well in advance, so plan ahead. You should remember that, though existing 10th Mountain owned lodging changes little from year to year, privately owned lodging can change drastically. Current information is available from 10th Mountain.

Who Should Use the Huts and Trails

Now that huts can make camping unnecessary, skiers with less skill and vigor are enjoying the winter wilds. Even so, you still need a level of skill and strength to travel safely on the trails in this book, and you must know your limits. Weather can make any tour an epic, and illness, injury, or navigation problems can force you into a bivouac. The alternate and branch routes in this guide run the gamut of winter challenge and risk.

Sure, these trails travel to and from cozy shelters; but these are full-bore treks, not "day trips." To ski any of these routes you could have to break trail in deep powder and navigate with zero visibility—all at altitudes over 8,000 feet. In short: no route in this book is an easy backcountry trail, no such thing exists! Thus, you should be at least an intermediate level backcountry skier to enjoy these trails without a guide.

Though only several routes in this book are suitable for beginners, most novices will find plenty of enjoyable skiing in the region, mostly by skiing within a short distance of the various trailheads. The several routes that are rated novice should only be attempted by novice skiers accompanied by skiers with backcountry experience. Also, novice skiers can always hire a guide service to insure a safe, fun hut trip.

Intermediate, advanced, and expert backcountry trails require the following skill levels:

Intermediate backcountry skiers can use a strong snowplow for downhill control. They can change direction with a parallel or telemark turn, though they may not be highly skilled in downhill skiing. They have done long tours with at least 2,000 feet of elevation gain, at altitudes over 8,000 feet. Intermediates know how to read a topographic map, compass, and altimeter. They have plenty of first-aid knowledge, and carry and know how to use bivouac gear. Avalanche safety is more theory than experience for an intermediate, as they need field practice to learn hazard recognition.

Advanced backcountry skiers have all the skills of an intermediate, with the addition of several years experience skiing to the huts, and better ski skills. They usually have their first-aid card and are well versed in emergency conduct. Their orienteering skills are impeccable, and they have the fitness to ski for long days with over 3,000 vertical feet elevation gain. They have taken an avalanche safety course, and continue to study avalanche safety.

Expert backcountry skiers combine superb avalanche safety knowledge and climbing skills with their expert skiing skills. They have at least eight years of solid experience, and have made the craft of wilderness skiing into an important hobby. Expert skiers are skilled enough to organize a rescue.

The spacious kitchen of the Fowler/Hilliard Hut

17

The Huts

Unlike many huts in Colorado, 10th Mountain's huts can sleep large numbers of people — usually 16 — and are often rented to several groups at a time. The whole hut can be rented for a flat fee.

Cooking is done by the hut users in communal kitchens. All the huts are stocked with eating and cooking utensils, and have gas burners. Most of the huts have no plumbing, so water is dipped or pumped from a spring, or melted from snow; the bathroom is an outhouse. The lodges and inns usually have plumbing and optional food service; many also supply full bedding. At the huts you'll find mattresses, but you'll have to bring your own sleeping bag. Since you'll be sleeping in a heated building, a lightweight sack will suffice. Pillows are available as well, so bring an oversized pillow case.

ETIQUETTE

In order to maintain the huts and the trails for everyone's enjoyment, a code of etiquette has been developed by 10th Mountain and the users. Civilized manners will help make the touring experience pleasant for all of the groups using the hut system. The following rules should always be observed.

Dogs are not allowed at the huts for several reasons. First, snow is melted for drinking water at many of the huts, and dogs contaminate the source snow. Second, dog tracks ruin packed trails, and skiing through dog feces is unpleasant at best. Finally, dogs harass wildlife.

Hut crashers (hut users without reservations) will be prosecuted as trespassers.

You must be quiet in the evening when other users go to bed. Though 10th Mountain has no set quiet time, most county noise ordinances are in effect from around 10:30 P.M. to 7:00 A.M.: these are good guidelines for hut users.

Smoking is not allowed in the huts, both for fire safety and consideration of nonsmoking users.

At no time is drunkenness, wild partying, or rude behavior acceptable.

It's common for day tourers without reservations to use the huts for tour destinations. At the 10th Mountain owned huts, people without reservations are allowed to use the outhouse and to have lunch on the porch. Use of cooking facilities is not allowed, and using the hut as a warming house is also discouraged.

The 10th Mountain roving hutkeepers keep their eye out for abuses, as should all hut users.

PROCEDURES

HEATING: Most of the huts are heated by woodburning stoves. The wood is bucked, split, and stocked in the summer. Since wood gathering costs money and volunteer hours, conservation is important. First, keep the hut at a reasonable temperature – don't turn the place into a sauna. Second, study the outline for stove use that you'll find at the hut, and adjust the stove controls for an efficient burn. Finally, if the hut has a wood cookstove, and you use it, plan on extra cooking time; otherwise you'll have to overstoke the stove to get enough heat.

Wood stoves are a fire hazard. For safety, the stove door should only be open while you're stoking or starting the fire. To build a fire, start with a small neat stack of paper and kindling, rather than a sloppy bonfire that can spill onto the floor or ignite the flue. Keep all inflammable material a good distance from the woodburner, including gear that you are drying. Many groups carry pack stoves for emergencies; keep these (and fuel) outside.

WATER: At many of the huts, you get water by melting snow on the woodburner. Several things can streamline this tedious chore. As soon as you get to the hut, light a fire. The snowmelt pot will be obvious; it's the biggest thing around, and is usually left on the stove. If the pot is empty take it outside, find some clean snow, and pack it densely. If the pot already has some water, leave it on the stove, and bring in the snow by shovel or plastic garbage bag. The key is to keep feeding snow to the pot while dipping out the melt. Finally, conserve water. Snow may look pure, but it's full of pollutants. It won't make you sick, but snowmelt can look and taste like three-day-old dishwater. Many skiers carry a filter pump for snow and stream water purification. Several huts have outside water sources. These are spring-sourced, and usually pure. If you have a sensitive stomach, you may still want to filter or treat the water.

Another water source common to several huts is a cistern and hand-pump system. The water in the cisterns is collected from roof melt, and should only be used for cleaning, unless filtered.

COOKING: Cooking at the 10th Mountain huts is done in communal kitchens. Thus, if there are several groups at the hut, they should stagger their kitchen work. Arranging this can test your diplomatic skills, but it will result in a nicer evening. It's a good idea to bring food with reasonable cooking time. Many a group has sat and grumbled while another took hours to create a multicourse feed worthy of the presidential dining room. Since wash water is scarce, plan meals that use a minimum of cookware.

You must carry out all your trash and uneaten food, so before you leave home, repackage foods that are in cans or jars. Eggs can be carried 'prescrambled' in a plastic bottle. In cold weather you can use tricks like carrying a frozen block of spaghetti sauce in a plastic bag. If you carry food that is only edible when cooked, be sure each person carries their own selection of trail food; you don't want to gnaw on frozen tomato sauce if you get separated from the group. Finally, plan your meals so that you don't haul extra food.

GENERAL HUT USE: If your group is the last to leave the hut, you'll be the ones doing the sweeping and general cleanup. Other parties leaving earlier could keep things fair by stocking some wood or cleaning the toilets. There is always plenty to do.

Your Trip

PLANNING

Backcountry skiing is complex. Food, gear, fitness, navigation, and group dynamics can overwhelm the best of us. Above all, keep it as simple as possible. Once you're in the field, you will regret lugging any more than the essentials. Grandiose route plans can sound good over cocktails at home, but you might have to set your sights lower if you're shooting for a fun, safe trip. Above all, remember that no book can make you an expert, but it can help you along the way. That's all *Colorado 10th Mountain Trails* will do. Put some thought into your travel style and transportation requirements. Most people leave from a trailhead go to one hut, then return to the same trailhead. With some 'base skiing' from the hut, this kind of trip can be simple and fun. More experienced skiers can plan a 'ski-through' that connects two or more huts. On a one-way trip you will cover more new territory by not retracing your steps to your original starting point, but you will also have to arrange some kind of car shuttle. If you don't have friends in the area, or if it's inconvenient to perform your own shuttle, make arrangements — well in advance — with one of the shuttle services listed in the directory in the appendices. It's usually most efficient to leave your car at the trailhead where you will be coming out, and have the shuttle take you and your party to the starting point of your trip.

TRAIL TECHNIQUE

Ask some questions at the trailhead. "Who's carrying the repair kit, the first aid kit? What if Joe's binding breaks, and he's behind in Sherwood Forest?" To prevent that kind of situation, leave the trailhead as a group and travel within sight of each other. Drink every hour and eat light carbohydrates at least every two hours. Take short, regular rests at least every two hours. Avoid charging up the trail as if you're running the hundred-yard dash; the key is a slow, steady pace.

Dress lightly in layers and make extra stops to adjust your clothing. Even on a cold winter day, you can get heat exhaustion from overdressing. For travel in a snowstorm, wear thin undergarments under a full waterproof, breathable shell. Keep your hair dry by pulling the shell hood loosely over your head, or by wearing a shelled hat.

Most of the time you'll be following a packed trail. However, after a storm someone will have to break trail. Breaking out a ski trail is one of the most arduous tasks in mountain skiing. To make trail breaking easier, change the lead often and keep a steady — albeit slow — pace. Even on the flats, skins really help the 'break-out'. On packed trails, use climbing skins for uphills, but take the time to remove them for all but the shortest downhills.

TRAIL MARKERS

While many fine routes lead to, from, and around the 10th Mountain lodging, only certain trails are designated by the Forest Service as 10th Mountain suggested routes. These routes are marked with 5-inch by 7-inch high blue plastic diamonds nailed to trees, or with blazes hacked into tree bark (the latter when laws preclude hanging plastic in designated wilderness). Some direction changes are indicated by blue plastic arrows. This guide covers the marked routes, as well as unmarked alternate and branch routes.

Trail markers are not a follow-the-dots system. They are difficult to place above timberline and in clearings, and common wisdom holds that a backcountry ski trail could easily be ruined by too many markers. Thus YOU CANNOT EXPECT TO ALWAYS SEE FROM ONE MARKER TO THE NEXT. Nevertheless, every year skiers try to "follow the dots" and get lost. Many experienced 10th Mountain skiers agree that the best attitude is to ignore markers and navigate from your maps. Then look for markers to verify your map work. You should be saying, "Ah, another marker, we must have read our map right," rather than, "Hey, I can't find a diamond, did you bring a map?"

You should know the general methodology behind the placement of 10th Mountain trail makers. The beginning of each trail is marked, and an effort is made to mark points of confusion such as switchbacks, forks, and clearings. In the latter case a marker will lead you into the clearing. To navigate the clearing, keep the same heading you had when you entered the clearing. A good rule of thumb is that most trails follow the path of least resistance, which in turn is often the obvious route. Indeed, many groups who lose the blue diamond trail just keep with their map reading and follow obvious lines – and soon see another blue diamond or arrive at the door of the hut. Finally, remember that blue diamonds and blazes are not the only signs of a trail; trimmed trees, sawed log ends, ski tracks, and the actual trail-cut are all signs you should look for.

SAFETY

Avalanche danger is the most well-known risk in backcountry skiing. Fortunately, slide danger is minimal – or nonexistent – on the 10th Mountain suggested routes. Yet skiers who venture from the beaten path are sure to encounter slide terrain. Once buried by an avalanche, you have less than a a 50 percent chance of survival up to the first half hour, and no chance after that. Even if the slide does not bury you, just the savage ride down a mountain is likely to kill you.

The most important part of avalanche safety is hazard recognition. You can easily identify slopes where snowslides are possible: basically, any treeless or sparsely timbered slope steeper than 25 degrees. By learning about snowslides, you can practice hazard recognition and avoidance, and safely travel through moderate avalanche terrain. Formal training through avalanche school is a good place to start learning. To supplement your schooling, use weather reports and local avalanche hazard forecasts. Speak with local mountaineers about current conditions. Finally, go out and practice. One rule bears constant emphasis: EXPOSE ONE PERSON AT A TIME TO HAZARD. You do this by traveling one at a time through exposed areas, or by spreading your group out on routes that have repeated exposure.

Avalanche danger varies with the season. Midwinter in Colorado is always very dangerous, but there is usually an eight to twelve week corn-snow season in the spring when danger is minimal and predictable. The spring season is the time to enjoy ski runs off the high peaks. To be safe, you have to get up early and ski before the late morning thaw. The 10th Mountain huts are closed during most of the alpine corn-snow season, but if you're lucky, you can catch a few days of 'hut corn' towards the end of April.

Though avalanches are a bewitching hazard, illness and ski falls account for most lost days and rescues on the routes in this book. At the altitude of the Colorado Plateau, you have about half the oxygen and humidity you get at sea level. For visitors from lower elevations these changes can cause sickness, even death from altitude sickness. The only sure way you can prevent altitude problems is by acclimating in steps. If you come from sea level, get to Colorado 48 hours before a hut trip. If you cannot schedule extra days, try to spend your first hut nights at some of the lower-elevation huts, such as the McNamara Hut, Diamond J Guest Ranch, Fryingpan River Ranch, or Harry Gates Hut.

If you must go high without acclimation, stay hydrated and don't exhaust yourself. Eat more carbohydrates for several days before you leave. Lower your salt intake and take iron pills. Above all, don't drink alcohol; it amplifies the effect of altitude. If you must have beer and wine, use low-alcohol brands.

If you're acclimated and fit, but still feel awful (headache and malaise) after a day on the trail, chances are you're dehydrated. In one day of ski touring you can lose more than a gallon of water from sweating, breathing dry air, and the diuretic effect of the cold. In addition, coffee and alcohol are diuretics. There are several ways to reduce dehydration. To begin, limit your morning coffee to one cup, and tank up on water before you hit the trail. Then, since humans are not camels, stop and drink several ounces of water at least once an hour. Try some of the athletic drink mixes that can be added to your water. These are quickly absorbed and supply some calories. Another trick is to put a quarter of a lemon in your water bottle. This will flavor fill-ups for about a week.

No matter how careful most people are, they will probably be slightly dehydrated when they arrive at the hut. Thus, it is critical to drink as you step in the door. All this begs the question: how do you know you are hydrated? The answer is crude but effective: the more yellow the snow, the more water you should drink.

IF YOU GET INTO TROUBLE • *An Emergency Checklist*

The mountains are a dangerous place for us fragile humans, and no matter how careful we are, human error can strike. Thus, you should always be ready to handle your or someone else's emergency. To do so, you should be skilled in first and secondary aid, as well as moving an injured person over snow. Gain these skills by taking first-aid courses and studying books.

In Colorado, all search and rescue is done by expert teams under the direction of the county sheriff. Organized rescue groups aside, you must remember that an expedient rescue begins in the field with the victim and their party. Follow these guidelines:

Before you leave on a trip, be sure someone in civilization knows of your route and schedule. This person should notify the county sheriff if you are overdue. Even with this arrangement, you will not get immediate help. Thus, you must handle things yourself.

In the case of an accident or illness, your first step in the field is to give the proper first aid. Next, move the person to a hut or bivouac. If you decide you need a rescue, send someone out for help. In a party of two, the victim will have to be left alone.

The person who goes for help should have a USGS map clearly marked with the location of the victim. He should ski with care to the nearest phone. To initiate the rescue, it's necessary to call the sheriff of the county in which the victim is located.

Avalanche rescue drill

If the sheriff decides you need a rescue, he may authorize a helicopter. If you're not staying at a hut, bivouac as close as you can to a likely landing site. Mark your location with a large figure stamped in the snow. An SOS or an arrow pointing to your exact location will do fine. A smoky fire can help by acting as a signal and showing wind direction. Anchor all your gear to withstand the hurricane winds of helicopter rotors. If you haven't had time to construct good markers, you'll have to signal the aircraft with your body. To do so, wear bright clothing, lay down in an open area, and wave your arms. Before nearing an operating helicopter, secure all your loose clothing, and carry skis at hip level horizontal to the ground.

EQUIPMENT

Gear — it's perplexing, expensive, and critical. Even after hours of shop clerk advice, and research worthy of a Greek scholar, many skiers still wonder exactly what equipment to use on the 10th Mountain trails. The problem is twofold: myriad choices, and trips that vary from the basic ones to mountain climbs on 13,000-foot peaks. The tips below will help you sort out the choices.

SKIS: 'Free-heel' gear refers to the 'three-pin' skis, boots, and bindings used by most skiers on the routes in this guide. Alpine touring (AT) gear means wider alpine style skis, plastic boots, and bindings with an optional heel latch.

Unlike many ski huts in the Alps, Canada, and other countries, the 10th Mountain huts can be reached via long, relatively flat trails. So, though downhill skiing is harder on free-heel gear than with AT gear, most people on the 10th Mountain suggested routes use free-heel ski gear.

AT gear, though less efficient on the flats, is used by many who venture higher into the mountains beyond the huts. Also, many people have found that an AT setup helps with the 'toboggan run downhills' on many of the hut – trailhead routes. Elderly skiers, for whom the consequences of a fall can be more severe, have found this to be especially true.

If you're deciding on free-heel skis, consider your main use. If you stick to the 10th Mountain suggested trails, use the slightly lighter weight 'trail' models. If you like to break out the alternate routes or ski powder, you may want a wider, heavier ski. In either case, be certain that you use true back-country free-heel skis, with steel edges, and at least 55 mm wide under the foot. By all means, do not use cross country track skis. AT skis are easier to pick; they are all wide enough and plenty strong. Choose them by the type of snow the skis are designed for – usually soft snow for 10th Mountain routes. As for length, shorter skis, both AT and free-heel, save weight and can be carried on your pack without catching your partner's chin or nipping your calves. But make sure your ski length is compatible with your weight while carrying a pack. Flex is a good clue to ski performance. As a rule of thumb, a softer flex will turn more easily in soft snow, while a stiffer flex gives you better edge hold on hard snow. Above all, weight is the enemy: you'll realize that every time you drag a ski through a stride. At least one equipment expert, when asked about the best and least expensive way to save weight, has pinched his paunch and smiled. Stay fit.

FOOTWEAR: As with skis, choosing touring boots can bemuse anyone. For touring on the 10th Mountain suggested routes, a medium weight free-heel boot will work well. But if your plans include ventures off the beaten path, look at boots that are designed with downhill turns in mind. If you plan on winter camping, or have the slightest problem with cold feet, buy double boots. While in the shop, be sure you can put on your double boot shells while you're wearing the inners. That's because the inners make nice hut slippers, or during a bivouac – it happens – you may want to sleep with them on. Single boots cost less, and some people say they're better for downhill skiing. Single boots are more likely to cause blisters, however, and are just not as comfortable as doubles. For distance touring, lean toward softer, lighter boots, but don't use track racing boots.

What do you look for in an AT boot? For long tours, use lighter, softer boots. Experts who ski steep spring corn snow like stiffer boots, but these usually compromise touring comfort. With all boots comfort is crucial. Too short, and they'll bruise and freeze your toes; too long, and they'll pinch and bind. Poor fit combined with lack of blister prevention on the trail can make your feet into hamburger. Start the boot-fit trail with buying your boots from a reputable shop. Boots by mail can be a disaster.

For boot accessories, super gaiters will do more to preserve your feet and boots than any other add-on. All super gaiters have one problem: boot attachment. The ones with a rubber rand are hard to fit, tend to pop off at the worst times, and if left on can ruin your boots by trapping moisture. Also the rubber instep yoke on these gaiters wears out quickly while boulder-hopping or scree-slogging. To get around these problems, many savvy trekers take the classic supergaiter – the one with nylon rather than rubber around the bottom – and simply screw the bottom edge of the gaiter to the boot welt with brass screws.

SKI BINDINGS: Free-heel bindings are simple. They come in two varieties: those with three pins that insert into your boot sole and those with a cable that latches around your boot heel. The latter weigh more, but they give more control and help your boots last longer. Since free-heel bindings cost so much less than other parts of a ski setup, and since they are so lightweight, simply buy the most durable ones you can find.

AT bindings differ from free-heel bindings in the complexity that allows them to perform two very different tasks. They provide a solid, yet releasable attachment of boot to ski for downhill skiing, as well as a walking mode that allows your heel to move up and down. For the routes in *Colorado 10th Mountain Trails*, choose AT bindings that are light and allow full freedom of movement for walking. Some AT bindings limit how high you can heel lift. Also, use AT bindings that allow you to change modes without removing them from your feet. That way you can latch your heels for short, scary downhills.

You can get good accessories for free-heel bindings. The *Voilé Plate* preserves your boots and enhances downhill performance. Another good option is the *Televate*, which lifts your heels for climbing. All AT bindings allow the use of ski crampons. These are a godsend for steep traverses or steep climbing. At least one version of ski crampons is made for free-heel skis.

SKI POLES: Every backcountry skier should have ski poles that convert to an avalanche probe. Even if you stay away from slide danger, you never know when a nearby accident will require your help. In addition to avalanche-probe capability, you have a choice of adjustable length or fixed length poles. Adjustable poles are good because they can be elongated for skating or diagonal striding, then shortened for downhill skiing. Adjustables are expensive, however, and they can be difficult to adjust in cold weather. Fixed length poles save a little weight, cost less, and are more reliable.

Your pole straps should be made of wide nylon webbing, and be easy to adjust with gloves. A larger basket is nice for powder snow. The snowflake plastic design is the best; it is designed not to snag on vegetation and such. Large powder rings are helpful for long slogs, but avoid these if you do much downhill skiing. They snag, add weight, and are tough to pull up out of the snow after a pole plant.

CLIMBING SKINS AND WAX: Climbing skins are useful — perhaps essential — for the 10th Mountain suggested routes. They are a must for all alternate and branch routes. Skins were invented long ago when a clever Nordic skier strapped animal pelts to the bottom of his skis for traction. If the natural lay of the fur was aligned with the ski, with the hair ends pointed back, the skins would slide forward yet provide traction by virtue of the hairs penetrating the snow. These evolved into modern strap-on skins. Now most skiers use strapless 'stick-ons' that glue to the ski bottoms with special adhesive. Stick-on skins are terrific. They go on and off quickly, glide better, and weigh less. Moreover, they prevent ice chunks from forming between skin and ski, and give better edge hold on icy hillsides.

Occasionally, stick-ons don't stick. Hooking the skin on the ski tip and just wrapping the end of the skin up over the ski tail is an invitation to disaster. Duct tape may work for a few miles, but it will likely end up as unsightly trail litter. It's best if you use a good tip and tail fix system. Also, refresh your glue often. Excellent products are available for doing this on the fly, but nothing refreshes like a fresh coat. When the temperature is below freezing, damp glue will freeze and not stick; take care while removing your skins to keep the glue dry, and consider keeping them warm under your jacket until the next application. The best way to protect the glue is to double each skin over and stick it to itself when it's not on the ski.

Climbing skins are available with three types of 'fur': mohair (real goat hair), nylon, and mixes of both. Nylon skins climb better and are less likely to form ice, but have poor glide. Mohair skins are not as durable, but weigh less and have better glide. Skins that mix the two types of fur can give good climb with very nice glide. Because most trails in the 10th Mountain region involve long distance travel on relatively low-angled terrain, choose skins with good glide.

As a general rule, use the widest skins you can without covering your edges. If you cover up your edges you won't be able to sidestep or snowplow. Skinny skins, though they glide well, require perfect technique for steep climbing.

Skins can be overkill on flat trails, and they take all control out of downhilling, though you can put them on backwards for "walking wounded" downhilling. For lower angled routes use Nordic wax. Any of the two-wax systems available will work fine. Apply wax in a thin layer so that it will be easy to remove before you put your skins back on.

PACKS: You can lump packs for hut skiing into two size categories. The smaller variety has little volume, a minimal internal frame or no frame at all. Medium-sized packs have around 3,000 cubic inches volume and an internal frame. Small packs will work for an overnight hut trip—given minimal gear and some sacrifice of comfort or vino. On the other hand, if your ski adventures require survival gear, a shovel, winter clothing, and camera gear, you should use a medium-sized pack.

Many trailheads, peak ascents, and dry sections on the trails require walking. Thus, some sort of ski attachment is a vital pack feature. Ski slots behind pockets work, as do compression straps, but both of these take time to rig. Lashing skis lengthwise over or under the top flap is favored by some people, especially those with shorter skis. Still another method is to put the ski tails down through the ice axe loops (many modern packs have two), then lash the upper portion of the skis to the pack. This works well because it angles the ski tails away from your legs.

Attaching a shovel to the pack can frustrate the most jolly mountaineer. Several packs are available with shovel holders, and are worth considering. If your pack lacks a dedicated shovel attachment, use extra lashing straps. Take care that your shovel blade will not hit you in the head if you fall, and be sure you can get it off quickly for avalanche rescue or sculpting a picnic table.

SHOVEL: Your shovel is as important as your clothing. It's mandatory for shelter building, avalanche rescue, and avalanche safety evaluation. A shovel can also serve as a stove platform, snow melter, or even part of a rescue sled. You have two choices in shovel materials: plastic and aluminum. Plastic is slightly lighter, and can bend repeatedly without breaking. Forces strong enough to bend aluminum will quickly break it, but aluminum shovels are easier to use in hard snow such as frozen avalanche debris.

A telescoping shovel shaft is nice but not essential. Be sure the shovel grip fits your mittened hands. The grip should have a lashing hole; this is handy for everything from lashing to your pack to improvising a sled.

AVALANCHE RESCUE GEAR: Though most 10th Mountain suggested routes avoid avalanche danger, many groups venture into avalanche terrain while using alternate routes, or base skiing from a hut. Without the help of an electronic rescue beacon, recovering a person alive from an avalanche burial is like a blind man finding a friend at a rock concert. In avalanche terrain, each party member must carry, and know how to use, an avalanche rescue beacon, compact shovel, and convertible probe ski poles.

NAVIGATION AIDS: Map, compass, and altimeter are the essentials for quality navigation. Though many intermediate skiers are unfamiliar with the altimeter, this simple device has been in use by mountaineers the world over for many years and is considered indispensable for safe, sure route finding in mountain terrain. Elevations are given in this book throughout all the route descriptions to aid your navigation. Avoid budget altimeters: they don't have the accuracy required for the backcountry.

The maps in this book are adequate for navigation on the 10th Mountain suggested routes, and are helpful for the alternate and branch routes. The 10th Mountain Trail Association sells topographic maps with the 10th Mountain suggested routes marked on them. If you plan on much exploring, or just want to get a broader view of things, you can also purchase USGS 7.5-minute topographic maps. These are available in local mountaineering stores, or by mail from the USGS.

The best compass is the kind with a clear plastic base and a dial that rotates on top of the base.

FIRST-AID KIT: In truth, few things you can carry in your first-aid kit will help with major medical problems. Indeed, the crucial items in this category are things such as sleeping bags, shovels, food, and some way of melting snow and heating water. Nonetheless, your kit should have supplies for splinting (such as some cravat bandages), one large-sized ace elastic wrap, and extra lash straps. For dressing wounds, bring athletic tape and some larger *Telfa* pads that you can cut to size. Include an antiseptic ointment and a small unbreakable bottle of *Betadine* soap.

More often than not, blisters are why you will dig into your kit. But don't wait until you are limping: prevention of blisters is the key to a good trip. For starters, everyone but those with the toughest feet and broken-in boots should pretape their heels. To do this, simply swab the bony rear point of the heel with tincture of benzoin, tape vertically for three inches or more with athletic tape, dust the area with talc powder, then roll the sock on with care so the tape stays on. You can also use duct tape for this, but duct tape can cause skin reactions, so only use it if you've tested it on your skin. Though pretaping helps, it is of limited value because blisters are caused by pressure as well as rubbing. Thus, many people will feel 'hot spots' even after pretaping.

As soon as you get a 'hot spot', remove your boot and sock and stick a thick moleskin donut around the spot. Do not remove the old tape, just attach the donut with more athletic tape. The idea is to leave the tender "preblister" skin intact under the first layer of tape. If the moleskin is cold, warm the glue with a lighter for better adhesion. So: for blisters, add benzoin, talc, and moleskin to your kit. Some people like *Spenco Second Skin*; this should only be used for blister repair, not prevention, as its thickness causes more pressure.

Medication supplies are simple. For minor discomforts, bring antacid and a pain killer. A small bottle of artificial tears to treat dry-eye or wash out the eye is also handy. Everyone should carry a good sun block — at least SPF 15 — and use it.

WATER CONTAINER: Hydration is so crucial in the mountains that the lowly canteen takes on a new meaning. Wide-mouth plastic bottles make the best water jars. Those available usually hold about a quart, so carry two if you plan on long days. Frozen water can be an acute problem during the colder winter months: sucking on a block of ice is no way to stay hydrated. To keep your water from freezing, fill your bottle up in the morning with hot water or tea, wrap the bottle in extra clothing, and stow it in your pack as close to your back as possible. Some people carry an unbreakable thermos, or one of the insulated jars available in mountaineering stores. The latter will cool sooner than a real thermos, but they never freeze.

HUT TRIP REPAIR KIT • *One Per Party*: Even the best equipment can fail, so carry a repair kit consisting of the following in a separate sack:

- Two three-pin bindings drilled with extra screw holes (you don't need a pair because left and right are interchangeable in a pinch).
- Extra oversize and regular-size binding screws, epoxy, and steel wool.
- Screwdriver for your binding screws — usually posidrive #3.
- Duct tape for taping your boot to your ski, or just about anything to anything else.
- Pliers with built-in wire cutter.
- Three yards malleable wire, like bailing wire.
- Two ski pole baskets.
- Three hose clamps for splicing broken poles.

- Thread, needle, and a few safety pins.
- Some strong nylon cord.
- Other repair items, as for stove repair.

CLOTHING: Bring clothing that's light, comfortable, and warm, even when damp. This rules out cotton. The new synthetic fabrics are a good choice, but wool still works well. Many people forget that very wet snow and rain are both possible during a Colorado winter, so your shell garments should keep out the wet, as well as the wind. The key to winter comfort is layering your clothes. Bring the following:

- Mediumweight long-underwear top and bottom for a foundation layer.
- Stretch tights for fair weather or to double as a foundation layer.
- Breathable nylon windshirt for a fair-weather outer layer.
- Pile jacket and side-zip pile pants for main insulation layer (these pants are also good for hut lounging).
- An additional upper layer in midwinter.
- Side-zip wind pants and a good shell jacket made with one of the breathable coatings like Gore-tex for a bad-weather outer layer.
- Gloves with wrist gauntlets for colder weather and lightweight synthetic gloves for warmer conditions.
- A thick pile hat, a neck gaiter, wool or polypro socks, and a good pair of boot gaiters.

(See the inside back cover for a complete equipment check list)

Remember that although using the huts allows you to carry a light pack, you should still carry the essentials for a night out. At a minimum that should be a gas stove, shovels, food, sleeping bags for each person, and some sort of bivouac shelter. Also, the best gear in the world will not help you unless it fits, functions, and you know how to use it.

Chapter 1 • Trailheads

The trailheads are arranged by region (highway or drainage), clockwise from Aspen. Finding trailheads can be frustrating and time consuming, so follow these directions carefully and allow extra time for false turns.

Aspen Area

Hunter Creek Trailhead

ELEVATION: 8,380 feet
10TH MTN MAP: Bald Knob
USGS MAP: Aspen

To reach the Hunter Creek Trailhead, start in Aspen. Follow Main Street in Aspen to Mill Street (the stoplight next to the Hotel Jerome). Turn N on Mill and drive a short distance down a hill, then across a bridge over the Roaring Fork River (.25 miles). Bear left after the bridge and follow the Red Mountain Road 1.2 miles to its second switchback. Just before the switchback, turn right and downhill on the Hunter Creek Road. Drive .25 miles on Hunter Creek Road, then take a hard left on an unpaved driveway that leads up past a water tank several hundred feet to a parking area. The actual trailhead is farther up the mountain, but this is the only parking.

You have several choices for foot travel to the actual trailhead. The simplest method is to walk back down the driveway to the Hunter Creek Road, turn left through two stone gate posts that are marked Private, and follow the paved Hunter Creek Road 1/3 mile around a hairpin switchback to the well-signed Hunter Creek Trailhead on the right side of the road. Your other choice for foot travel is to follow a poorly marked foot trail that traverses up the mountain from the parking area to the trailhead. Perhaps the best way to deal with this trailhead is to enlist the services of a friend or taxi, and get dropped off at the actual trailhead.

Lenado Trailhead

ELEVATION: 8,640 feet
10TH MTN MAP: Bald Knob
USGS MAP: Aspen

From Aspen drive 6 miles NW (downvalley) on Highway 82. At the sign for Woody Creek Canyon, turn right and follow Smith Way .35 miles down a steep hill and across the bridge over the Roaring Fork River. At the T intersection just past the bridge, turn left and follow the Upper River Road 1.59 miles downvalley to a hard right onto the Woody Creek Road (also known as the Lenado Road). Drive the Woody Creek Road 8 miles to Lenado, a small group of rustic homes, then continue a short distance to the plow turnaround for the winter trailhead.

The Woody Creek Road begins as a paved road, then becomes a narrow unpaved track. It is fine for 2-wheel drive in good conditions, but it is one of the last roads the county plows and can have some mighty slick mud, so beware after storms. In the summer you can drive on the road past the winter closure. It switchbacks about 5 miles to 10,910 feet, just below the summit of Larkspur Mountain. This is a good starting place for hikes and bike rides.

Lenado Alternate Trailhead

ELEVATION: 8,540 feet
10TH MTN MAP: Bald Knob
USGS MAP: Aspen

This trailhead is used for the Lenado Gulch route (2.3) from Lenado to the McNamara Hut. It is a hard trailhead to find; trailhead signs often disappear after a few weeks. The Forest Service has installed a few "no motor vehicle" stakes which may be there when you arrive, but don't count on it.

The best way to locate the trailhead is to use an odometer reading. The trailhead is located on the right side of the Woody Creek Road, exactly 8.2 miles from the Upper River Road. Of course, not all odometers are equal, so following is a verbal description: Follow the Woody Creek Road 8 miles to Lenado (see Lenado Trailhead description). Cross a bridge, drive a short way up a hill, then though the center of town (really just a few buildings on both sides of the road). Look for the first telephone pole on the left as soon as you pass the buildings. The trail starts exactly across the road from this telephone pole.

Fryingpan River Drainage

Fryingpan Drainage trailheads are located on or near the Fryingpan Road. To reach the Fryingpan Road, drive Highway 82 to Basalt from Aspen or Glenwood Springs. Drive E through Basalt on Midland Avenue (the main street), which soon becomes the Fryingpan Road (county road 104). All mileages below are measured from the Alpine Bank on Midland Avenue.

Spring Creek Trailhead

ELEVATION: 8,440 feet
10TH MTN MAPS: Mount Yeckel, Burnt Mountain
USGS MAP: Meredith

Follow the Fryingpan Road 25.2 miles from Basalt to the well-signed Eagle Road on the left. Turn off the Fryingpan Road onto the Eagle Road and follow it 2.7 miles to the plow turnaround at the Spring Creek Fish Hatchery. Parking here can be tricky, as you must allow for the plow and autos to turn around. The best way to do this is to park well to the side of the road a short ways back down the road from the turnaround. The Eagle Road is well maintained, but think twice about driving with 2-wheel drive if you get there before the county plow.

In the summer you can continue with 2-wheel drive all the way to Eagle. One caveat: do not attempt this road when it is wet — even with 4-wheel drive. Add a little rain or snow-melt and it becomes slicker than axle grease.

Diamond J Trailhead

ELEVATION: 8,250 feet
10TH MTN MAPS: Mount Yeckel, Burnt Mountain
USGS MAP: Meredith

From Basalt, follow the Fryingpan Road 26.1 miles to the Diamond J Guest Ranch driveway on the right (south) side of the road. Turn into the driveway, go over the bridge and up a short steep hill on the right to the ranch parking area. Be sure to check at the lodge inside as to the best place to leave your vehicle. The ski trail to the Norrie Trailhead heads SE from the main lodge through the cabin area. For the Montgomery Flats/Burnt Mountain Road trail, walk back on the driveway to the main road. The trail starts on the side of the road opposite the driveway. The first marker is usually atop the roadbank — so look up!

Burnt Mountain Road Trailhead

ELEVATION: 8,830 feet
10TH MTN MAP: Mount Yeckel, Burnt Mountain
USGS MAP: Nast, Meredith

From Basalt, follow the Fryingpan Road 26.6 miles to a Y fork in the road known as the Biglow Fork. A sign here says Mountain Haven. Take the left fork (North Fork Road) and drive 2.2 miles. Here the well-signed Burnt Mountain Road turns off to the left (north). In winter you should park at the Diamond J Guest Ranch and either walk or car shuttle to the Burnt Mountain Road. During summer the road is suitable for high-clearance 2-wheel drive, and parking is obvious.

Norrie Trailhead

ELEVATION: 8,440 feet
10TH MTN MAP: Mount Yeckel
USGS MAP: Meredith

This trailhead is short on parking space, so most people park at the Diamond J Guest Ranch and either ski, walk, or car shuttle to the Norrie Trailhead. For the ski option, a well-defined trail follows the south side of the valley from the Diamond J to the Norrie Trailhead.

From Basalt drive the Fryingpan Road 26.6 miles to the Biglow Fork, take the right fork (paved), and continue up the main Fryingpan Road 1.1 miles to a right turn off the main road. This turn is marked by a Norrie Colony sign and a Forest Service road sign 504. Park at the snowplow turnaround.

Granite Lakes Trailhead

ELEVATION: 8,760 feet
10TH MTN MAP: Mount Yeckel, Upper Fryingpan
USGS MAP: Nast

The Granite Lakes Trailhead is located at the privately owned Fryingpan River Ranch. Be aware that the name of this ranch can change.

To reach the Granite Lakes Trailhead from Basalt, drive the Fryingpan Road 26.5 miles to the Biglow Fork. Take the right fork and continue up the main paved road 5 miles to a well-signed right turnoff. You'll see signs here for Fryingpan River Ranch and for Nast Lake/Granite Lakes Trailhead. After the turnoff, a winding dirt road leads 1.1 miles to the obvious buildings of the ranch. This road has several steep switchbacks, so 4-wheel drive is recommended during snow season.

The Granite Lakes Trailhead is to the left just before the ranch buildings. For the trail to Twin Meadows and Margy's Hut: From the main lodge at the ranch, ski or walk (depending on snow cover) 500 feet SW on the ranch road to the last two cabins at the end of the road. The trail starts here in aspen trees between the two cabins. The trail-cut is not obvious.

Elk Wallow Campground and Cunningham Creek Road

ELEVATION: 8,827 feet (Elk Wallow Campground)
10TH MTN MAP: Mount Yeckel
USGS MAP: Nast

Drive the above description for the Burnt Mountain Road Trailhead. Do not stop or turn at Burnt Mountain Road. Instead continue upvalley .4 miles to Elk Wallow Campground. To reach Cunningham Creek Road, continue 1.3 miles past Elk Wallow to a Y fork. The well-signed Cunningham Creek Road takes the right (south) tine of the fork.

Road 505 Trailhead

ELEVATION: 9,120 feet winter; 10,040 feet summer
10TH MTN MAP: Upper Fryingpan
USGS MAP: Nast, Mt. Champion

Road 505 is a dirt spur off the paved Fryingpan Road. It was built for maintenance on the Fryingpan/Arkansas water diversion project. In winter it remains snow-covered and is shared by skiers and snowmobilers. Early in spring (usually mid-May) the road is plowed 5.8 miles into the Upper Fryingpan drainage, after which it's gated on occasion, but is usually open.

To reach Road 505 drive the Fryingpan Road from Basalt 26.6 miles to the Biglow Fork. Take the right fork and continue 5.8 miles. Here Road 505 takes an obvious right turn off the main paved road. A sign at the turn says Fryingpan Lakes. In winter park in the widened part of the main road.

Hagerman Pass Road Trailhead

ELEVATION: 9,200 feet
10TH MOUNTAIN MAP: Upper Fryingpan
USGS MAP: Nast

The Hagerman Pass Road Trailhead is simply the plow turnaround on the Hagerman Pass Road. The exact location of the turnaround varies from year to year. In the spring the road is plowed and opened in late May. It then connects with Leadville. Though an unimproved dirt road, the Hagerman Pass Road is navigable with high clearance 2-wheel drive.

To reach the Hagerman Pass Road drive the Fryingpan Road from Basalt 26.5 miles to the Biglow Fork. Take the right fork, and continue up the main paved road about 6 miles to the plow turnaround.

Eagle & Vail Area Off I-70

Sylvan Lake Trailhead

ELEVATION: 8,558 feet
10TH MTN MAP: Burnt Mountain
USGS MAP: Crooked Creek Pass

Sylvan Lake is a popular ice fishing and snowmobile area. The road to the lake is well maintained, but may be temporarily closed during heavy storms.

Drive I-70 29 miles W from Vail or 30 miles E from Glenwood Springs and turn off at the Eagle exit (Exit 147). Drive over the Eagle River, take a right on old Highway 6, and drive a short distance to Eagle. Turn left (S) on Broadway (the main street) in Eagle to 6th Street, turn left (E) on 6th, and drive one block to the Sylvan Lake (Brush Creek) Road. Good signs mark this route through Eagle.

Turn right (S) on the Sylvan Lake Road and follow it for 10.6 miles to a well-signed fork (pavement ends here). Take the right fork (West Brush Creek Road) and drive 4.6 miles to Sylvan Lake. In the winter do not block the plow turn when parking. Sylvan Lake is within a small state park. You'll find good car camping and bathrooms here (the park charges a small fee). You can fill up with tasty water at a spring .4 miles up the West Brush Creek Road.

Yeoman Park Trailhead

ELEVATION: 9,060 feet
10TH MTN MAP: New York Mountain
USGS MAP: Fulford

Follow the above directions for the Sylvan Lake Trailhead to get to the well-signed fork where the pavement ends on the Sylvan Lake Road. Take the left fork (East Brush Creek Road) and drive 5.8 miles to Yeoman Park. Turn right (SW) off the main road, and follow a spur a short distance down and over a bridge crossing East Brush Creek, then a few hundred feet to parking at snow closure in the campground. Summer parking is obvious.

West Lake Creek Trailhead

ELEVATION: 8,220 feet
10TH MTN MAP: New York Mountain
USGS MAP: Grouse Mountain

Because of poor signage the drive to the West Lake Creek Trailhead is more intricate than most. Drive I-70 13 miles W from Vail or about 46 miles E from Glenwood Springs, and turn off at the Edwards Exit (Exit 163). Drive S for a short distance across the Eagle River to a stop sign and T intersection with Highway 6. Turn right (W) and drive .7 miles to the

At the West Lake Creek Trailhead. The 10th Mountain suggested route follows the snow-covered road left of the fence.

poorly signed Lake Creek Road on the left (there may be a sign on a bus shelter here).

Drive the Lake Creek Road 1.9 miles to a well-signed Y intersection. Take a right (W) on the West Lake Creek Road and follow it 2.8 miles to a parking area where a switchback in the road makes a hard left. The Card Creek drainage trail follows a distinct snow-covered road S from the parking area. Four-wheel drive may be necessary to reach this trailhead.

Vail Trailhead for the Commando Run

ELEVATION: 8,220 feet
USGS MAP: Vail East

The Vail Trailhead for the Commando Run is not signed, but it's fairly easy to find. Follow I-70 to the main Vail Exit (Exit 176) at Vail Resort. Take the exit, then turn immediately right (S) into a 4-way stop intersection. Turn left (E) here on the frontage road and drive .4 miles E to an intersection marked with an oversized stop sign. Turn right (S) here and follow Vail Valley Drive .4 miles to parking at the Golden Peak Children's Skiing Center at the base of lifts 6 and 12. In the winter parking is highly regulated, so check the parking rules when you get there.

At any rate, you can skin up the ski area from here to start the Commando Run in Mill Creek. This is a grueling start for such a nice tour, so consider accessing the Commando Run from the Vail ski lifts. There has been talk for years of a one-ride ticket for just that purpose, so check for this option. To reach the Commando Run from the lifts you can get into Mill Creek from the top of lift 6; or take a more roundabout route, finally using the Orient Express Lift to reach the west ridge of Siberia Peak. In the summer you can ride the Vail Gondola most of the way up the mountain, then hike the ridge to Siberia Peak. Cyclists can take their bike up the Gondola and ride across the ski area to the Mill Creek Road.

Vail Pass Trailhead

ELEVATION: 10,580 feet
10TH MTN MAP: Resolution Mountain
USGS MAP: Vail Pass

As the second highest point on I-70, Vail Pass is known for its severe winter driving conditions. Take chain and snow tire laws seriously.

To reach the Vail Pass Trailhead, drive I-70 14 miles E from Vail or 5 miles W from Copper Mountain Resort. Take Exit 195 at the summit of the pass and park at the large parking area (the Vail Pass Rest Area) just east of the overpass. The Shrine Pass Road leaves from the parking area. It has good signage and is well used. Look out for snowmobiles.

Union Creek Trailhead

ELEVATION: 9,820 feet
10TH MTN MAP: Resolution Mountain
USGS MAP: Copper Mountain/Vail Pass

Drive to Copper Mountain Resort via Interstate 70 or Colorado Highway 91. Park behind the Transportation Center near the entrance to the resort (inquire at the Transportation Center for specifics, you may need to display a parking permit behind your windshield). From the Transportation Center catch the free shuttle to Union Creek, a base facility with several ski lifts, bathrooms, and a cafeteria.

Highway 24 & Leadville

United States Highway 24 (10th Mountain Division Memorial Highway) connects the towns of Minturn, Red Cliff, and Leadville. Leadville (10,152 feet) is the highest city of its size in the United States. This charismatic old mining town was created by the gold and silver boom in the late 1800s. Curiosity seekers will find several excellent museums and plenty of photogenic old buildings. Lodging and dining in the old mining town are fun and affordable. Harrison Avenue is the main street through the old part of town. Here you'll find the fabulous restored Hotel Delaware, as well as several affordable motels. For dining, don't miss authentic mexican food at The Grill on the west end of Elm Street. For breakfast, try the Golden Burro or Golden Rose cafés on Harrison Avenue.

Red Cliff Trailhead

ELEVATION: 8,680 feet
10TH MTN MAP: Resolution Mountain
USGS MAP: Red Cliff

Drive I-70 5 miles W from Vail Resort, or 55 miles E from Glenwood Springs, and take the Minturn Exit (Exit 171) onto U.S. Highway 24. Drive 11 miles S on Highway 24 to a poorly signed left turnoff that leads a short distance down into a canyon, then into Red Cliff. The Shrine Pass Road leaves from the northeast corner of Red Cliff. It is poorly signed, but fairly obvious. You can ask any local where it is, and the USGS map shows it clearly as the only road up Turkey Creek. For accommodations in Red Cliff, Pilgrim's Inn is located near the beginning of the Shrine Pass Road.

Once you find the Shrine Pass Road you have several choices for parking. The best place to park, both for snowplowing and safety from theft, is in Red Cliff on any side street. The curb across from Reno's Bar is a good bet, and so is the Mexican food at Reno's. If you are on a day trip, drive just over a mile up the Shrine Pass Road to the snowplow turnaround at a water tank. You can park here for the day, but don't park overnight (leave a note on your car).

Pando Trailhead • Elevation 9,200 feet
Camp Hale Trailhead • Elevation 9,250 feet
South Camp Hale Trailhead • Elevation 9,280 feet

10TH MTN MAP: Chicago Ridge
USGS MAP: Pando

These trailheads are located at the site of former Camp Hale — a huge, 3-mile long flat area on the Eagle River a few miles north of Tennessee Pass. Fifty years ago Camp Hale was home for two years to the men of the 10th Mountain Division of the U.S. Army, for which the 10th Mountain hut and trail system is named (see Preface). Only road-cuts and a few foundations remain.

Drive I-70 5 miles W from Vail Resort or 55 miles E from Glenwood Springs and turn off at the Minturn Exit (Exit 171) onto Highway 24. At 16 miles from the exit you will broach the huge flat area of Camp Hale. Look for a railroad siding to your right (the Pando siding) and a distinct parking area to your left with a sign reading Resolution Road. This is the Pando Trailhead.

To reach the Camp Hale Trailhead, continue from the Pando Trailhead 1.6 miles S on Highway 24. Look to your left for two stone gate posts and a plaque. Again, parking is straightforward.There is no bridge across the Eagle River from the Camp Hale Trailhead; you might find a snow bridge, but don't count on it. For reliability, you may want to forgo using this trailhead and use the Pando Trailhead.

For the South Camp Hale Trailhead, continue S on Highway 24 for .7 miles past the Camp Hale Trailhead. Look to your left for another distinct parking area. Again, you won't find a bridge over the river, but due to the distance this trailhead can save you, it might be worth looking for a snow bridge.

41

If you drive from Leadville and Tennessee Pass, the South Camp Hale Trailhead is 5 miles north of Tennessee Pass on Highway 24. Use the connection mileages above to find the other two trailheads.

Tennessee Pass Trailhead

ELEVATION: 10,424 feet
10TH MTN MAP: Chicago Ridge, Galena Mountain
USGS MAP: Leadville North

To reach the Tennessee Pass Trailhead from the north (I-70), follow the above directions for Pando Trailhead and Camp Hale. From Camp Hale continue S on highway Highway 24 for 7.3 miles to the well-signed Tennessee Pass. Parking is obvious on the west side of the road (opposite the turnoff to Ski Cooper).

From the south ("old town" in Leadville), follow Harrison Avenue (Highway 24) N, then follow signs for Highway 24. You'll pass through the strip development on the north side of Leadville and come to an obvious, well-signed left turn onto Highway 24 to Tennessee Pass. It's about 1 mile from "old town" to this turn. Take the turn and follow Highway 24 for 8.8 miles to Tennessee Pass.

Crane Park Trailhead

ELEVATION: 10,137 feet
10TH MTN MAP: Chicago Ridge, Continental Divide, Galena Mountain
USGS MAP: Leadville North

From the north, follow the directions above to the Tennessee Pass Trailhead. Stay on Highway 24, and 1.6 miles past Tennessee Pass turn right (W) off the highway onto a dirt road. There is a sign here mounted on an antique road-grader for Webster's Sand and Gravel. The most reliable and secure parking is in an obvious plowed area within sight of the main road. If the gravel pit is operating, the road will be plowed to there. In this case, it's possible to eliminate some walking if you park at the well-signed intersection of the Wurts Ditch Road .9 miles from Highway 24. This option, however, leaves your car more vulnerable.

To reach the Crane Park Trailhead from Leadville, follow the directions above for Tennessee Pass Trailhead from Leadville via Highway 24. About 2.5 miles from Leadville you'll broach impressive Tennessee Park, with good views to the west of Galena Mountain and Homestake Peak. At about 7.5 miles from Leadville take a left onto the aforementioned road with the sign for Webster's Sand and Gravel.

Turquoise Lake Trailhead

ELEVATION: 10,030 feet
10TH MTN MAP: Galena Mountain, Continental Divide
USGS MAP: Leadville North

Turquoise Lake is a beautiful reservoir several miles west of Leadville. It is a popular snowmobile recreation area. Thus, you'll have to share the parking and portions of trail with snow machines. Most importantly, if you park in a turnaround area, do so in a way that allows people with trailers to use it.

The trailheads around Turquoise Lake are simply snow closures on a continuous loop road. They vary with the season and the severity of storms, so you might find the road open several miles farther than the closures described below. If so, use your USGS map to reduce confusion.

To reach the Turquoise Lake Trailhead, start from Leadville's Harrison Avenue in the historic "old town". Turn W onto West 6th Street and drive .8 miles to a T intersection with an obvious sign pointing right to the Turquoise Lake Recreation Area. Turn right and drive Lake County 4 to another well-signed right turn (1.8 miles from Harrison Avenue). A sign here points right and says Turquoise Lake North Portal (you are now on Lake County 9). Drive N then W over railroad tracks (3.4 miles from Harrison Ave.), then uphill to another T intersection (3.9 miles from Harrison Ave). If this is snow closure, it is your trailhead. If not, turn right and continue to snow closure, which is often at 5.3 miles from Harrison Ave., where the spur for the Tabor Boat Ramp turns left off the main road. Most often the plow turns around here. At times the main road is plowed .4 mile past the Tabor Boat Ramp spur to another parking area (10,030 feet). This is the official Turquoise Lake Trailhead and is marked on the text map as such.

During summer the paved road leads around Turquoise Lake, with turnoffs for various dirt roads and pack trails.

Chapter 2 • McNamara Hut

The McNamara Hut, built in 1982, was one of the original two huts in the 10th Mountain system. The hut is a memorial to Margy McNamara (as Margy's Hut is as well). Funds to build the hut were donated by Margy's husband

ELEVATION: 10,360 feet
COUNTY: Pitkin
TEXT MAP: pp. 46-47
10TH MTN MAP: Bald Knob
USGS MAP: Thimble Rock
TRAILHEADS: Hunter Creek, Lenado, Lenado Alternate

Robert, who served as secretary of defense. Located in Burnt Hole deep in the forest on the north side of Bald Knob (11,092 feet), the McNamara Hut has a cozy secluded feeling that lends itself to sipping tea by the wood burner or exploring the nearby forest. You'll find good intermediate ski touring on Bald Knob, and experts can strike out on long tours east towards the Continental Divide. The hut is owned by 10th Mountain and is only open during the winter season due to a nearby elk herd.

Back during the silver boom in the late 1800s, lumber for fuel, mine timbers, and building was a valuable commodity. As a result, the entire area around Burnt Hole, from Red Mountain to Bald Knob and east to Hunter Flats, was stripped of trees. Many sawmills operated in the area, including a Burnt Hole sawmill, the remains of which can still be seen east of the hut. During this period of logging, forest fires burned many acres; one such fire created Burnt Hole.

According to one old-timer, Widow Gulch (the watered drainage above the trail just west of Lenado Gulch) is named after widow Jennie Adair

who operated a sawmill in the gulch. By all reports, she was quite a character. For food, she would cut down a quarter of beef just large enough to fit in the cook stove oven (probably similar to the stove in the McNamara Hut). After some roasting of the beef, she would trim away the done parts for a meal, put the roast back in the oven to supply the next day's meal, and so on. Her two bull dogs would clean up what was left. In those days women wore dresses even while doing manual labor. While firing the sawmill boiler, Jennie's skirt would sometimes catch fire; she would just dunk it in a nearby water tub and keep on working.

Compared to many other huts, the McNamara has limited choices for ski routes. For ski-throughs, use route 2.4 north to Margy's Hut, or route 2.1 west to the Hunter Creek Trailhead. For branch routes, an ascent of Bald Knob makes a nice jaunt, but one that can lack interest for experts. Hardcore bushwhackers can try route 2.6 — it is quite a challenge. For quick ascents to the hut, route 2.1 is the most popular, mostly because it is near Aspen. Route 2.2 is slightly shorter, but leaves from a remote trailhead.

2.1

Hunter Creek Trailhead — McNamara Hut via Van Horn Park

DIFFICULTY: Intermediate
TIME: 6 hours up, 4 hours down
DISTANCE: 6 miles
ELEVATION GAIN: 2,000 feet; loss: 20 feet

TEXT MAP: p. 46
10TH MTN MAP: Bald Knob
USGS MAP: Aspen, Thimble Rock

This 10th Mountain suggested route is the only practical way to get to the McNamara Hut from Aspen. Going the opposite direction as a route from the hut to Aspen, it is usually the route of choice, though experts can ski to Aspen via Midway Pass (see *Colorado High Routes*). The Van Horn Park route follows old, well-defined logging roads and is well marked with signs and blue diamonds. There are, however, several confusing junctions, and finding the trailhead can be trying. Use your maps. If you start from the Hunter Creek Trailhead you'll soon need climbing skins, so put them on before you start.

ROUTE DESCRIPTION: For travel from Aspen to the hut, leave from the Hunter Creek Trailhead. Ski a fairly level trail NE through scrub oak ⅛ mile, then across the Benedict Bridge over Hunter Creek. From here the trail climbs steeply for ¾ mile on the south side of Hunter Creek, then breaks out into an open area at 8,600 feet elevation. Continue NE through lower angled open areas for ¼ mile, then turn N and cross the 10th Mountain Bridge over Hunter Creek (8,640 feet). This bridge is well marked and easy to spot, but could be elusive in poor visibility. In that case, stay close to the stream past 8,600 feet elevation and you'll bump into the bridge.

After you cross the 10th Mountain Bridge, continue N for a few hundred feet, then make a climbing traverse W (downvalley) to within sight of a sturdy fence and private home. Staying about 100 feet E from the fence, begin climbing N again and you will intersect a clearly visible snow-covered jeep

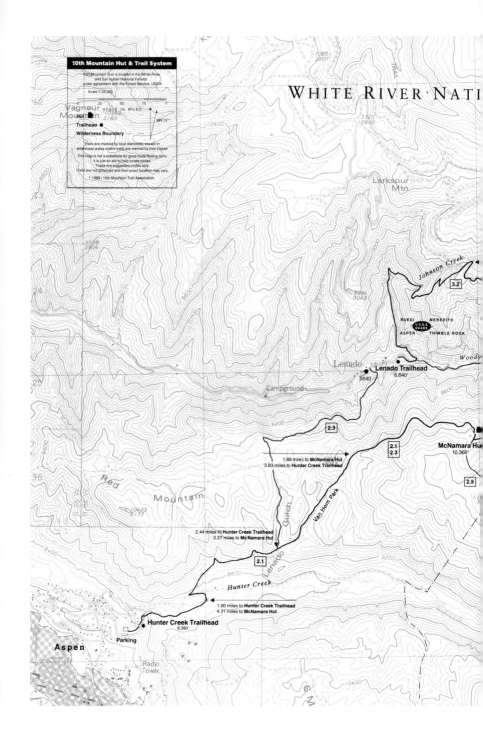

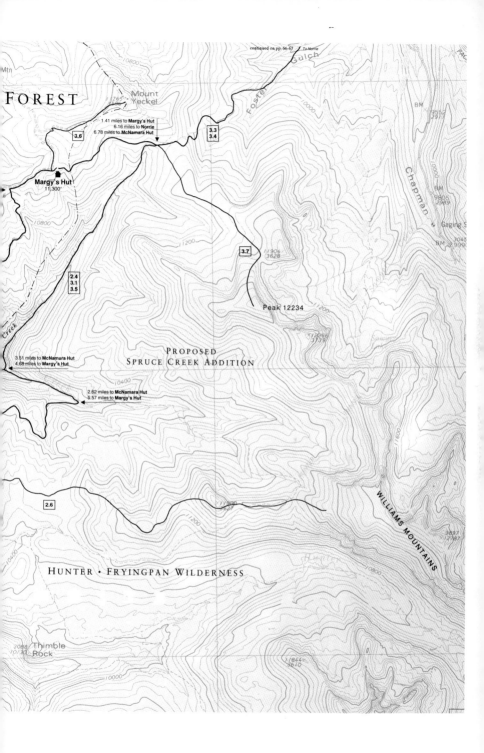

FOREST

Mtn

Mount Yeckel

continued on pp. 66-67   To Norrie

Foster Gulch

1.41 miles to **Margy's Hut**
6.16 miles to **Norrie**
6.78 miles to **McNamara Hut**

3.6

3.3
3.4

BM

Margy's Hut
11,300'

Chapman

BM
9905

Gaging S

BM 9599

3045

11,200

3.7

11,906
3628

Peak 12234

Creek

2.4
3.1
3.5

12266
3739

11,200

PROPOSED
SPRUCE CREEK ADDITION

3.51 miles to **McNamara Hut**
4.68 miles to **Margy's Hut**

10,400

2.62 miles to **McNamara Hut**
5.57 miles to **Margy's Hut**

11,600

WILLIAMS MOUNTAINS

2.6

11,200

9897
12,467

HUNTER · FRYINGPAN WILDERNESS

Hunter

10,800

10,400

Thimble Rock

10,000

11,844
3610

47

trail at about 8,720 feet. Now the real climbing begins. Follow the jeep trail as it takes you on a 1 ⅓-mile climbing traverse to Lower Van Horn Park at Lenado Gulch. Take care not to turn left into Lenado Gulch. Just continue on an easterly tack across Lower Van Horn Park, through a gate (usually open), then climb NE through another aspen forest into Van Horn Park—a classic alpine "open space."

Read your map with care and ski up the north side of Van Horn Park to Lower Van Horn Saddle (really just a low-angled shelf) at 9,760 feet. Continue along the north side of the park to Upper Van Horn Park, then Upper Van Horn Saddle, a more definitive saddle at 9,925 feet, just E of point 10,097.

From Upper Van Horn Saddle, ski easterly up a well-marked, narrow roadcut through the forest. This road gradually climbs 2 miles to the McNamara Hut. Generally, this trail is easy to follow. If you happen to catch it unbroken, use your compass and altimeter, and take care to not drop N down into the dense timber and steep terrain of the Woody Creek drainage. You'll usually smell wood smoke before you see the hut, as it is hidden by trees until you are within a few hundred feet.

REVERSE ROUTE DESCRIPTION: Reversing the route above is fairly simple. The crux is to get on the trail as you leave the cabin, as myriad ski tracks can be confusing. To be certain, take a compass bearing before you leave. It also helps to ask directions from new arrivals; but remember, they may be more bewildered than you are. After you're on the trail, you'll find a fast downhill traverse to Upper Van Horn Saddle. From there ski the fall line down through Upper Van Horn Park. At the lower end of the park swing slightly left (S) and drop through trees into Lower Van Horn Park.

Just entering Van Horn Park on the way to McNamara Hut.

Ski W across Lower Van Horn Park, re-enter the trees at the west end of the park, and find a distinct road-cut that takes you on a "flying downhill" traverse into Hunter Creek. Cross the 10th Mountain Bridge over Hunter Creek, then continue downhill, gliding on a distinct trail that loosely follows the south side of the creek to the Benedict Bridge. Cross the Benedict Bridge and follow a short, low-angled trail through scrub oak to the Hunter Creek Trailhead and Hunter Creek Road. Enjoy Aspen.

SAFETY NOTES: This route has almost no avalanche danger and is defiantly at the easier end of the intermediate rating. The steepest slopes in Upper Van Horn Park could avalanche, given extremely unstable snow. The downhills force you into some pretty narrow slots, so ski in control.

SUMMER: This route is an excellent hike, horse, or bike ride.

2.2

Lenado Trailhead—McNamara Hut via Woody Creek

DIFFICULTY: Intermediate
TIME: 5 ½ hours up, 5 hours down
DISTANCE: 5 ¼ miles
ELEVATION GAIN: 1,720 feet

TEXT MAP: pp. 46-47
10TH MTN MAP: Bald Knob
USGS MAP: Aspen, Thimble Rock

As a route between trailhead and hut, this alternate trail is less popular than route 2.1, mostly because most people like the convenience of a trailhead closer to Aspen, but also because the lower 1 ½ miles of trail is not marked by 10th Mountain and not open enough for easy skiing. Yet for just those reasons, you'll find more wilderness solitude on this route and better map reading practice. Most skiers should use climbing skins for the ascent.

ROUTE DESCRIPTION: From the Lenado Trailhead, ski about ¼ mile up the road from the trailhead to a point just before an automobile bridge crossing Woody Creek (8,680 feet). On the right side of the road you'll see some Forest Service trailhead signs. Leave the road here and ski past the signs and up the Woody Creek drainage. Basically, the best route follows that of the pack trail marked on the USGS Thimble Rock map. Snow cover and low branches, however, may dictate some custom route-finding. Your exact route up the drainage is not important, while drainage identification is. Using map, compass, and altimeter as you travel, spot Cliff Creek's confluence with Woody Creek. Continue up Woody Creek, and at the next confluence, that of Spruce Creek and Woody Creek, find the marked 10th Mountain trail on the north side of Woody Creek (9,440 feet). Note that a 10th Mountain suggested route leading to Margy's Hut (route 3.1) follows the Spruce Creek drainage from here.

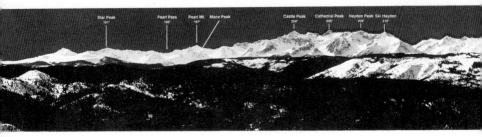

View from Bald Knob to the southwest.

Due to the well-maintained and marked 10th Mountain suggested route from here to the McNamara Hut, orienteering is easier above this point. One note, however: you won't see blue diamonds — this section of trail is marked with tree blazes. From the Spruce Creek confluence follow the 10th Mountain marked trail another mile along the north side of Woody Creek. Stay on the trail as it crosses to the south side of Woody Creek (9,900 feet), then makes a switchback to the W, climbing up the south side of the Woody Creek drainage. This is perhaps the most critical juncture of the route, but it can be easily identified by careful altimeter use. Follow the switchback ½ mile W into a shallow gulch, then turn S and continue on the marked trail as it climbs the gulch to 10,240 feet. Here the trail turns and begins a westerly, gradually climbing traverse 2 miles to the McNamara Hut. The hut is visible from several hundred yards away.

REVERSE ROUTE DESCRIPTION: Leaving from the front porch of the Mc-Namara Hut, ski directly SW a few hundred feet, then swing E and follow a gradually dropping contour for 2 miles to 10,240 feet at a shallow gulch. Turn N and ski down the gulch (this can be difficult, use caution) to 9,960 feet. Stay on the trail as it turns and follows a dropping traverse E into the Woody Creek drainage, crosses Woody Creek, then follows the north side of the creek to Woody Creek's intersection with Spruce Creek. Here, the marked 10th Mountain suggested route continues up Spruce Creek to Margy's Hut (route 3.1).

To continue to the Lenado Trailhead, stay in the Woody Creek drainage. Ski the north side of Woody Creek for another mile or so, then cross the stream and ski the south side the next ½ mile to the automobile bridge mentioned above, then continue a short distance down the main road to the plow turnaround. Again, remember that the 10th Mountain suggested portion of this route is mostly marked with tree blazes, while the portion in lower Woody Creek has few markers of any sort.

SAFETY NOTES: With extremely unstable snow, bank sluffs are possible on the steep sides of the Woody Creek drainage. These areas are easy to avoid, but pay attention. Be careful as you ski down into Woody Creek, as many tempting runs have stumps and rocks just under the snow's surface.

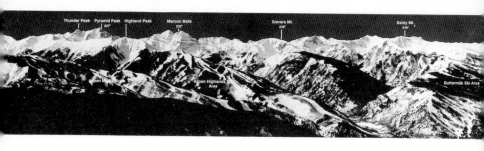

SUMMER: This route is a fine hike, but horses should avoid the section from Woody Creek to the hut, as this trail is mostly just a marked winter route with no real path. Cyclists should note the wilderness boundary a short distance up Woody Creek from the trailhead.

2.3

Lenado Alternate Trailhead — McNamara Hut via Lenado Gulch

DIFFICULTY: Advanced
TIME: 7 hours up, 6 hours down
DISTANCE: 6 ½ miles
ELEVATION GAIN: 2,300 feet;loss: 480 feet

TEXT MAP: p. 46
10TH MTN MAP: Bald Knob
USGS MAP: Aspen, Thimble Rock

This alternate route follows classic, old-fashioned logging roads. Usually these are the perfect angle for hiking, horses, cycling, or mellow skiing — this one is no exception. Due to it's lack of "official" status, this is another lightly traveled trail that allows more solitude and requires more map work.

ROUTE DESCRIPTION: As it is with many routes from trailhead to hut, the crux of this trip is finding the start of the trail. Use the description in Chapter 1 for "Lenado Alternate Trailhead."

On the trail the going is mostly straightforward, but a few tricky spots can catch the unwary. Put your skins on at the start. From the road, follow the trail for several hundred feet S, stay on the trail as it makes a left, then climbs E, then S, and switchbacks W. The trail then makes a long 2-mile climbing traverse W along the side of the Woody Creek valley, winding in and out of numerous small gulches to a turn left (S) around a shoulder at 9,700 feet. From here turn S and follow the trail ⅓ mile as it passes first though open forest, then through a few open areas to a meadow at 9,800 feet. This meadow is called Four Corners, and has a good sign (which may be covered by snow). Continue S downhill from Four Corners on a distinct road-cut for 1 mile to a grove of aspen at the lower (W) end of Lower Van Horn Park (9,360 feet). Here you intersect route 2.1, which you follow to the McNamara Hut.

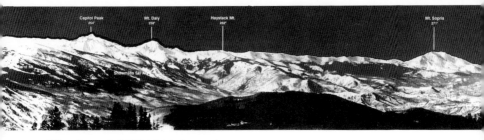

View from Bald Knob to the west.

REVERSE ROUTE DESCRIPTION: To follow this route from the Mc-Namara Hut, take route 2.1 (reverse route) to the aspen grove at the lower (west) end of Lower Van Horn Park. Leave the marked route here and turn right (N) onto the Lenado Gulch road-cut. Climb 1 mile and 440 vertical feet to Four Corners. Start down the hill N from Four Corners and identify the trail as it swings E to the side of the Woody Creek drainage. Stay on the trail as it takes a wild downhill traverse E into the Woody Creek valley, eventually dropping you onto the Woody Creek Road a short distance downvalley from the winter plow turn.

SAFETY NOTES: See route 2.1. Take care at Four Corners to use your orienteering skills, many groups have become a bit bewildered here.

SUMMER: This route is terrific for all nonmotorized use.

2.4

McNamara Hut to Margy's Hut via Spruce Creek

DIFFICULTY: Intermediate	**TEXT MAP:** pp. 46-47
TIME: 8 hours	**10TH MTN MAP:** Bald Knob
DISTANCE: 8 1/4 miles	**USGS MAP:** Thimble Rock, Meredith
ELEVATION GAIN: 1.860 feet; loss: 920 feet	

This is the 10th Mountain suggested route from the McNamara Hut to Margy's Hut. For most of the tour you'll be in dense conifer forest.

ROUTE DESCRIPTION: From McNamara Hut follow route 2.2 (reverse route) to the Spruce Creek/Woody Creek confluence, where the Spruce Creek Trail intersects the Woody Creek Trail (9,400 feet). Keep a careful eye out for this junction, it's marked by 10th Mountain, but that's no reason to shirk your map duties. At the junction put on your skins and ski N then NE up the well-defined, well-marked Spruce Creek Trail. You have a long pull ahead of you, as the trail follows the Spruce Creek drainage 3 1/4 miles and 1,560 vertical feet to the west end of Sawmill Park (11,000 feet).

As soon as you enter Sawmill Park keep a sharp eye out for another trail fork on your left. Many groups miss this junction – the trick is to identify Sawmill Park with adroit map reading, then stay at the lower (west) end of the park and carefully search out the 10th Mountain junction markers on a couple of medium-sized evergreens. An altimeter can really help here. If you've skied more than 50 feet into the open park, you have gone too far. Once you find the junction, leave the main trail and follow a spur W then SW as it makes a long 1 ¾-mile climbing traverse up to the hut. The hut is usually visible from several hundred yards away, but it may be hidden by snow on heavy snow years, with just the upper front windows visible.

SAFETY NOTES: Be careful on the downhill into Woody Creek. Use care identifying the junction in Sawmill Park.

SUMMER: This route is a good hike, but most equestrians will find too much brush and deadfall for fun horse travel. Cyclists are not allowed on this wilderness trail.

2.5

Bald Knob from McNamara Hut

DIFFICULTY: Intermediate
TIME: Several hours round trip
DISTANCE: 2 miles round trip
ELEVATION GAIN: 732 feet round trip

TEXT MAP: p. 46
10TH MTN MAP: Bald Knob
USGS MAP: Thimble Rock

This is the most popular branch from the McNamara Hut. The spectacular view of the Elk Mountains from Bald Knob (11,092 feet) makes up for the McNamara Hut's lack thereof, and the skiing is terrific.

ROUTE DESCRIPTION: From the hut's front porch ski to the water hole, then continue SW up the left side of the intermittent stream shown on the USGS Thimble Rock map. At about ¼ mile swing left and climb S up open areas with burnt trees, then through a grove of evergreens to Bald Knob's summit. Enjoy the view of the spectacular Elk Mountains and try to spot Margy's Hut which is visible from several spots near the Bald Knob summit. For downhill skiing check out the aforementioned open areas, or explore glades to the east of the summit, taking care to traverse back to the hut before dropping into Slab Park.

SAFETY NOTES: Remember that Bald Knob is not a maintained ski resort! Hidden obstacles and sudden drop-offs exist. Ski in control.

SUMMER: This is a beautiful wildflower hike. No real trail exists for bikes or horses. The wilderness boundary runs north/south through the summit.

2.6

Williams Mountains from McNamara Hut

DIFFICULTY: Expert
TIME: Very long day
DISTANCE: 14 miles round trip
ELEVATION GAIN: 2,890 feet round trip

TEXT MAP: p. 46-47
10TH MTN MAP: Bald Knob
USGS MAP: Thimble Rock

Few peak climbs are possible from the McNamara Hut. The alpine ridge nearest the hut is miles away, with an approach through heavy timber that can make the best orienteer weep. Skilled ski mountaineers still enjoy trying this route — and some make it. All groups attempting this route should have a map, compass, altimeter, and avalanche transceivers.

ROUTE DESCRIPTION: To begin, take route 2.5 to the summit of Bald Knob. Get out your map on the summit and do some careful planning, with the following description as a guideline. Ski E than NE down Bald Knob into the upper end of Slab Park (10,600 feet). Put skins on here, then climb E into Horse Park, then ski to the far east end of Horse Park. Use compass and map here to climb E onto a bumpy, timber-studded ridge that climbs 2 miles to the summit of point 11,900 (a good goal in itself), then drops another ¾ miles E to a saddle at 11,500 feet. Take care with your orienteering on this ridge, as you'll be in some dense timber. It may be possible to save some work by contouring the south side of point 11,900.

Climb E from the saddle and you'll soon break timberline and be on a beautiful west face dropping from the Williams Mountains ridge. Before you climb to the ridge, spend some time doing your avalanche evaluation. This slope is often wind-scoured and safe, but it can be loaded with unstable snow. Depending on conditions, hike or ski the 650 vertical feet from timberline to the ridge top. The return is via the same route, perhaps with a traverse below Bald Knob to save energy.

SAFETY NOTES: This route requires expertise in all aspects of winter mountaineering, hence its expert rating. You'll find little problem with avalanche danger until the final open slope on the Williams Mountains ridge, where you should use extreme caution. Turn back if you have doubts.

SUMMER: This route begins in heavy timber that makes for difficult hiking. The Williams Mountains ridge, however, is a worthy summer objective. To avoid some of the timber, use the pack trail shown dropping from the 11,500-foot saddle. With either choice the route is long and strenuous.

Chapter 3 • Margy's Hut

Built in 1982, Margy's Hut (along with the Mc-Namara Hut) was one of the first two huts in the 10th Mountain system. The building of these two huts represented a major step for the fledgling organization, which had to

ELEVATION: 11,300 feet
COUNTY: Pitkin
TEXT MAP: pp. 46-47, 66-67
10TH MTN MAP: Bald Knob, Mt. Yeckel
USGS MAP: Meredith
TRAILHEADS: Lenado, Norrie, Granite Lakes

promise the Forest Service that the huts would be razed if they were not used.

Located on a lightly treed hillside just below timberline, Margy's Hut has beautiful views of the Elk Mountains to the south. The area around the hut was heavily logged in the mid 1900s, but virgin timber still stands east of the hut. Margy's was built with funds given by Robert McNamara (former secretary of defense) and friends, in memorial to Margy McNamara, Robert's wife.

You'll find good downhill skiing close to this hut, and several fine branch routes lead into the surrounding mountains. Mount Yeckel (route 3.6) is the most popular place for downhill skiing, and there is a good run from

the front porch of the hut. For ski-throughs to the north, most skiers use the Twin Meadows route (3.3/3.4) which drops into the Fryingpan River drainage. See Chapter 4 for information on the Fryingpan River drainage. Ski-throughs south from Margy's usually follow Spruce Creek (route 3.5). The shortest route from a trailhead to Margy's Hut climbs from Lenado via Johnson Creek (route 3.2).

3.1

Lenado Trailhead — Margy's Hut via Spruce Creek

DIFFICULTY: Intermediate
TIME: 6 hours up, 4 hours down
DISTANCE: 6 ½ miles
ELEVATION GAIN: 2,660 feet

TEXT MAP: pp. 46-47
10TH MTN MAP: Bald Knob
USGS MAP: Aspen, Thimble Rock,
    Meredith

As a route between trailhead and hut, this alternate trail is less popular than route 3.2, mostly because the lower 1 ½ miles of trail is not marked by 10th Mountain and not cleared for skiing. Yet, for just those reasons, you'll find more wilderness solitude on this route, and you'll get better map reading practice. Use climbing skins for the ascent.

ROUTE DESCRIPTION: From the Lenado Trailhead ski about ⅓ mile up the road to a point just before an automobile bridge crosses Woody Creek (8,680 feet). On the right side of the road you'll see some Forest Service trailhead signs. Leave the road here and ski past the signs and up the Woody Creek drainage. Basically, the best route follows that of the pack trail marked on the USGS Thimble Rock map. Snow cover and low branches, however, may dictate custom route-finding. Your exact route up the drainage is not important, while drainage identification is. Using map, compass, and altimeter as you travel, spot Cliff Creek's confluence with Woody Creek. Continue up Woody Creek, and at the next confluence, that of Spruce Creek and Woody Creek (9,440 feet), find the marked 10th Mountain trail junction on the north side of Woody Creek.

Keep a careful eye out for this junction; it is marked by 10th Mountain, but that's no reason to shirk your map duties. From the junction ski N then NE up the well-defined and marked Spruce Creek Trail. You have a long pull ahead of you, as the trail follows the Spruce Creek drainage 3 ¼ miles and 1,560 vertical feet to 11,000 feet in the west end of Sawmill Park.

When you enter Sawmill Park, keep a sharp eye out for another trail fork to the left. Many parties miss this fork. If you have trouble, the trick is to identify Sawmill Park with adroit map reading. Stay at the lower (west) end of the park and carefully search out the 10th Mountain junction markers on a couple of medium-sized evergreens. Your altimeter can really help here as well. If you ski more than 50 feet into Sawmill Park, you are past the junction. Once you find the junction, follow the spur W then SW as it makes a long 1 ¾-mile climbing traverse up to the hut. The hut is usually visible several hundred yards before you reach it, but it may be hidden by snow on heavy snow years, with just the upper front windows showing.

REVERSE ROUTE DESCRIPTION: Follow route 3.5 (reverse route) from Margy's Hut down Spruce Creek to Woody Creek. Descend on the north side of Woody Creek. At the Cliff Creek confluence cross to the south side of Woody Creek and continue down Woody Creek to the road and auto bridge mentioned above. Take a left at the road and ski the road to the Lenado Trailhead.

SAFETY NOTES: Bank sluffs are possible on the steep sides of the Woody Creek drainage; however, these slopes are easy to skirt. This route includes two major junctions on what has been called the "Hidden Marker Trail" by frustrated skiers. Remember that, due to its location within designated wilderness, the trail is marked with tree blazes.

SUMMER: This route is fine for horseback riding or hiking. Most of the route is within designated wilderness, so cyclists should use other trails such as the Larkspur Mountain Road (see Chapter 1, Lenado Trailhead).

3.2

Lenado Trailhead — Margy's Hut via Johnson Creek Trail

DIFFICULTY: Intermediate   **TEXT MAP:** pp. 46-47
TIME: 5 ½ hours up, 4 hours down   **10TH MTN MAP:** Bald Knob
DISTANCE: 6 miles   **USGS MAP:** Aspen, Meredith
ELEVATION GAIN: 2,660 feet

This 10th Mountain suggested route is the "Interstate Highway" to Margy's Hut. It is well marked and follows distinct road-cuts and trails.

ROUTE DESCRIPTION: From the Lenado Trailhead at the road's snow closure, ski up the main road ⅓ mile across an automobile bridge over Woody Creek. Stay on the wide road-cut of the main road for 1 mile to a distinct left switchback (9,068 feet). Put your skins on here. Just before the switchback turn right off the main road and climb a steep hill. You will be following a more ill-defined road-cut on the east side of Silver Creek. At 9,270 feet turn right (E) out of the Silver Creek drainage and follow a sidehill trail that climbs (with several switchbacks) 1 ½ miles up Johnson Creek to another distinct snow-covered road at 10,480 feet.

Turn right (S) on this obvious road which leads slightly downhill and level for ¼ mile (leave your skins on) around a shoulder, then gradually climbs for 2 miles to 11,040 feet. Here the 10th Mountain suggested route takes a left fork (switchback) and climbs N 180 vertical feet to a timbered saddle. From the saddle ski several hundred feet N and intersect another snow-covered road on the north side of the saddle.

Turn right (E) on this road and follow it for ½ mile as it traverses north-facing terrain. Just before the road makes a turn N, leave the road and ski SE through a clearing, then a short distance downhill to the hut. The hut is not visible until you are several hundred feet away.

Many skiers like to take a more direct route from the 11,040-foot elevation. To do so, simply stay on the jeep trail as marked on the USGS Meredith map, then deviate slightly to contour the south side of the bump west of the hut, then traverse to the hut. Take care not to drop below the hut. (Use your altimeter).

REVERSE ROUTE DESCRIPTION: From the back of Margy's Hut ski NW up a short hill, then continue a few hundred feet to intersect a distinct snow-covered road. Follow this road SW for ½ mile, then turn left to leave the road and climb over a low saddle. Ski 180 vertical feet down the south side of the saddle. Try to stay on the 10th Mountain marked route. If your downhill speed forces you to deviate, just be sure to get back on the trail as it turns S then W, then gradually drops (with a few level sections and a short uphill) 2 miles to the head of Johnson Creek. Ski the trail down Johnson Creek into Silver Creek, then to the Lenado Trailhead.

SAFETY NOTES: This is a well-marked trail. Nevertheless, you will be traversing steep, heavily timbered mountainsides, where losing the route could be grim. Pay attention. While most of the trail is free of avalanche danger, there is one obvious steep gulch you cross while in the Johnson Creek drainage. Avalanches are rare here, but parties should still use standard precautions.

SUMMER: These trails provide good cycling, hiking, and horse riding. Cycling up the Johnson Creek route is quite strenuous, but it is a terrific advanced downhill. Cyclists should consider using the Larkspur Mountain Road for the trip up.

3.3

Norrie Trailhead — Margy's Hut via Twin Meadows

DIFFICULTY: Intermediate
TIME: 8 hours up, 6 ½ hours down
DISTANCE: 7 ½ miles
ELEVATION GAIN: 2,917 feet; loss: 57 feet

TEXT MAP: p. 67
10TH MTN MAP: Mount Yeckel
USGS MAP: Meredith

While adventurous skiers might find other routes from the Fryingpan drainage to Margy's Hut, this 10th Mountain suggested route is certainly the most popular line. You can also begin this route at the Diamond J and Granite Lakes trailheads (see Chapter 4).

ROUTE DESCRIPTION: From snow closure at the Norrie Trailhead ski up the well-defined cut of the Twin Meadows Road. It makes two switchbacks, then a 1 ¾-mile climbing traverse to 9,300 feet. Leave the road here and turn right (SE) onto a fairly narrow, marked trail that leads to the north end of Twin Meadows at 9,465 feet. Many skiers use wax up to this point, then put on their skins.

Follow a marked trail-cut along the west side of Twin Meadows. Stay on the trail as it leads out of Twin Meadows on the north side of Deeds Creek, then crosses Deeds Creek and climbs into Foster Gulch. The trail next parallels Foster Creek for ½ mile, then begins to turn W away from Foster Creek at 9,920 feet, and climbs W to 10,240 feet. From here you swing S then W to meadows at 10,400 feet.

From the meadows a steep climb leads over a divide (11,057 feet) and into Sawmill Park. Enjoy the view of the Elk Mountains from Sawmill Park and ski down to the lower (west) end of the park. At the lower end of the park (11,000 feet) keep a sharp eye out for another trail fork to the right. It is easy to miss this fork, as many people can attest. If you have trouble, the trick is to identify Sawmill Park with adroit map reading, then stay on the north side of the park and ski to the west end where you search out the 10th Mountain junction markers on a couple of medium-sized evergreens. Your altimeter can really help here.

Once you find the junction, leave the main trail and follow a spur W then SW as it makes a long 1 ¾-mile climbing traverse up to the hut. The hut is usually visible several hundred yards before you reach it, but it may be hidden by snow on heavy snow years, with just the upper front windows visible.

REVERSE ROUTE DESCRIPTION: Skiing this route from Margy's to the trailhead is simple. The traverse from Margy's Hut drops you into Sawmill Park, where you can find the marked trail by simply skiing to the saddle at the upper (east) end of the park. You then ski a well-marked trail down Foster Gulch and along Deeds Creek to Twin Meadows. Ski NE then N along the west side of Twin Meadows, then N through trees until you hit the distinct snow-covered road that traverses N to the Norrie Trailhead.

SAFETY NOTES: Most trail markers on this route are tree blazes. There is no avalanche danger. The long walk through the forest can lull you into a trance, so take extra care in Sawmill Park to find the correct route.

SUMMER: Hikers and equestrians will enjoy this route. Cyclists are not permitted due to designated wilderness.

3.4

Granite Lakes Trailhead — Margy's Hut

DIFFICULTY: Intermediate
TIME: 9 hours up, 7 hours down
DISTANCE: 8 ¾ miles
ELEVATION GAIN: 2,740 feet; loss: 200 feet

TEXT MAP: p. 67
10TH MTN MAP: Mount Yeckel
USGS MAP: Nast, Meredith

This 10th Mountain suggested route uses most of the same trail as route 3.3 from the Norrie Trailhead. It has slightly less elevation gain, but more miles.

ROUTE DESCRIPTION: Begin at the Granite Lakes Trailhead with skins. From the main lodge at the ranch, ski or walk (depending on snow cover) 500 feet SW on the ranch road to the last two cabins at the end of the road. The trail starts here in aspen trees between the two cabins. The trail-cut is not obvious.

Ski the trail SW another 500 feet to a foot bridge over a small creek (8,800 feet). Cross the creek, then swing W and climb ¼ mile up a steep gulch to a flat area (9,010 feet). The South Fork of the Fryingpan River will be directly in front of you at the bottom of a shallow gulch. Turn left (S then SW) and follow a trail-cut that parallels the South Fork for just under ¼ mile to cross the South Fork (no bridge) at 9,050 feet.

After crossing the South Fork, the trail winds W then SW for several hundred yards to a vague Y split. Here one trail continues up the South Fork of the Fryingpan, while the one you want climbs to the right (W) up a small hill, then winds ⅓ mile (light uphill) through conifer and aspen to a major road (9,150 feet). If you lose the trail here, just continue W and you'll intersect the road. Once you're on the road (road number 504.1), you simply follow snow-covered roads W for 3 ¼ miles to intersect route 3.3 at Twin Meadows.

In detail: from the trail/road intersection ski NW and W as the road climbs gradually for 1 mile, then drops slightly and swings around a shoulder to a T intersection with road 504.1A and 504. Turn right (W) on road 504 and follow it as it climbs gradually for ¾ mile around another shoulder, then drops gradually ¼ mile to another intersection at 9,500 feet. Be sure you take the left road at this intersection; it leads ⅛ mile and about 100 vertical feet down into the north end of Twin Meadows. Ski W across the north end of Twin Meadows and find 10th Mountain suggested route 3.3 that follows the west side of the meadows. Take a left (S) and follow route 3.3 to Margy's Hut.

REVERSE ROUTE DESCRIPTION: Start without skins at Margy's Hut. Follow route 3.3 (reverse route) to Twin Meadows. At the north end of the meadows, ski to the east side of the meadows, then up a road-cut that climbs ⅛ mile up through timber to intersect the major road-cut of road 504. Ski road 504 1 mile to another major intersection. Take a left (N) on road 504.1 and ski the road gradually uphill around a shoulder, then down a long gradual downhill 1 mile to 9,160 feet.

Here the trick is to find a not-so-obvious pack trail that drops into a forest of small aspen trees from the east side of the road. There might be 10th Mountain trail markers here, but use these to verify your careful orienteering, rather than blindly searching for markers.

This trail leads downhill SE then E to cross the South Fork of the Fryingpan River at 9,050 feet. You then parallel the river on your left for ¼ mile to a small flat opening (9,010 feet). Here, you must swing right (E) and ski into a small subsidiary gulch. This gulch steepens and leads you to a foot bridge over a small creek (8,800 feet). Cross the bridge (can be obscured by snow) and ski N 500 feet through aspen forest to the guest ranch at the Granite Lakes Trailhead. Enjoy your dinner!

SAFETY NOTES: There are no overt dangers on this route, but skiers should note the length of the trail and plan accordingly.

SUMMER: This route is a fine hike or horse ride. The section of trail from road 504.1 down to the ranch is a rough bicycle downhill, and mostly a portage in the opposite direction. The network of dirt roads makes for fabulous cycling. Cyclists should note the wilderness boundaries.

3.5

Margy's Hut to McNamara Hut via Spruce Creek

DIFFICULTY: Intermediate   **TEXT MAP:** pp. 46-47
TIME: 6 hours   **10TH MTN MAP:** Bald Knob
DISTANCE: 8 miles   **USGS MAP:** Meredith, Thimble Rock
ELEVATION GAIN: 920 feet; loss: 1,860 feet

For good downhill skiers, this 10th Mountain suggested route is one of the quicker hut to hut routes. Novice downhillers, however, should plan on some slow movement down Spruce Creek.

ROUTE DESCRIPTION: From the east side of Margy's Hut, climb NE up a short hill and follow the marked (tree blazes) 10th Mountain suggested route as it makes a long traverse into Sawmill Park. Expert parties have reported skiing directly SE from the hut down into the Spruce Creek drainage, but they encountered difficult timber towards the bottom. Anyone but the most expert skier should stick to the trail.

When you enter Sawmill Park, turn immediately right (W) and begin your descent SW down Spruce Creek on a 10th Mountain suggested route with standard tree-blaze markings. This section of trail is relatively straightforward. Ski 3 miles down Spruce Creek to the intersection with the Woody Creek Trail (9,440 feet). Take care to identify this junction. Turn left (E) onto the Woody Creek Trail (still marked by blazes) and follow the north side of Woody Creek 1 mile to 9,900 feet. Cross Woody Creek.

Due to the well-maintained and marked 10th Mountain suggested route from here to the McNamara Hut, orienteering is easier above this point, but skiers addicted to blue diamonds will still have to squint as they look for tree blazes. After crossing Woody Creek, stay on the trail as it makes a switchback to the W, climbing up the south side of the Woody Creek drainage. Follow the switchback ½ mile W into a shallow gulch, then turn S and continue on the marked trail as it climbs the gulch to 10,240 feet. Here the trail turns and begins a westerly, gradually climbing traverse 2 miles to the McNamara Hut. The hut is visible from several hundred yards away.

SAFETY NOTES: Watch for possible bank-sluff danger on the steep sides of the Woody Creek drainage. Ski in control while descending Spruce Creek.

SUMMER: Because of wilderness designation, cyclists are not allowed on this route. Hikers will find all the trails described above to be good, but they should note that the section between the McNamara Hut and Woody

Creek is not really a path, it is just a marked route for winter skiing. Horse riders should note the same.

3.6

Mount Yeckel from Margy's Hut

DIFFICULTY: Int./Advanced
TIME: 1/2 day round trip
DISTANCE: 2 1/4 miles round trip
ELEVATION GAIN: 465 feet round trip

TEXT MAP: p. 47
10TH MTN MAP: Mount Yeckel
USGS MAP: Meredith

Good views, plenty of downhill skiing, close to a hut: could you ask for more? This is the most popular branch route from Margy's Hut, and it includes something for everyone. Don't miss this route.

Touring to Mount Yeckel

ROUTE DESCRIPTION: From the back of Margy's Hut ski the 10th Mountain marked trail about 200 yards to a distinct snow-covered road. Instead of following the 10th Mountain route left, turn right and travel the general route of the road N through an open area, then E over point 11,648. From here follow a snow-covered jeep trail NE down a short hill, then up to the summit of Mount Yeckel. The return is via the same route.

You'll find excellent downhill skiing in the north-facing bowl of point 11,648; this is known as Yeckel Bowl. There is also good skiing off the summit of Mount Yeckel down the open west face; this is called the West Face of Yeckel.

SAFETY NOTES: There is ski touring on this route for any ability level. All downhillers should ski with care; avalanches are common in Yeckel Bowl. The West Face is slightly less avalanche prone. Stay away from Yeckel's steep, cliff-studded northeast face.

SUMMER: This is a good hike and horseback ride. Expert cyclists will enjoy it as well, but they should note the wilderness boundary just a few feet south of the jeep trail. The summit of Yeckel is also within wilderness, so be sure to leave your bike behind for the last hundred feet to the summit.

3.7

Peak 12,234 from Margy's Hut

DIFFICULTY: Advanced
TIME: 5 hours round trip
DISTANCE: 7 miles round trip
ELEVATION GAIN: 1,534 feet round trip

TEXT MAP: p. 47
10TH MTN MAP: Mount Yeckel
USGS MAP: Meredith

While enjoying the view from the Margy's Hut picture window (or outhouse), many a mountaineer has pondered Peak 12,234. Every year several groups make the ascent, and by all reports it is a worthwhile objective. While not the accessible ski area that Mount Yeckel is, Peak 12,234 has good views, a bit of turning on the way back down, and plenty of navigation practice.

ROUTE DESCRIPTION: To begin, ski from Margy's Hut to Sawmill Park (route 3.3). Put your skins on here. From the park use your map and compass to ski SE to point 11,250. This area is densely timbered, so don't expect any definitive landmarks. From point 11,250 climb SE up a broad timbered ridge; your goal is the large meadows northwest of peak 11,904. Again, pay attention to your map, compass, and altimeter. Ski to 11,400 feet at the bottom of the meadows. Next, climb the southwest edge of the meadows to the 11,650-foot saddle west of point 11,904. Climb the ridge to the summit of Peak 12,234. Return is via the same route.

SAFETY NOTES: Though the route above has little or no avalanche danger, there is plenty of slide terrain on the sides of Peak 12,234. Thus, groups planning on "adult" skiing should carry avalanche transceivers and know their avalanche safety techniques. This is a branch route with no trail markers.

SUMMER:

Due to heavy timber with no trail-cut or tread, this route would be a poor choice in the summer.

Chapter 4 • Fryingpan Drainage

The Fryingpan River drainage is the major east/west drainage that separates the Aspen area from the Eagle area to the north. Many routes connect the Fryingpan drainage with 10th Mountain huts. In the past the traditional stopover in the drainage was the Diamond J Guest Ranch. Now other lodging is available as well. You can also find lodging in the gateway town of Basalt. If you

ELEVATION: 8,000' average
COUNTY: Pitkin
TEXT MAP: pp. 66-67, 76-77, 196-197
10TH MTN MAP: Mt. Yeckel, Burnt Mt., Upper Fryingpan
USGS MAP: Meredith, Nast
TRAILHEADS: Diamond J, Granite Lakes, Hagerman Pass Road, Road 505, Elk Wallow Campground, Spring Creek, Norrie, Burnt Mountain Road

need supplies or 10th Mountain information while in the Upper Fryingpan valley, stop at the General Store in Meredith.

Since the Fryingpan drainage lodging is not in the backcountry, but on a road, most of the routes described in this chapter leave from trailheads near the lodging. Information about reaching trailheads from the lodging can be found below, while most routes are cross-referenced to other chapters. If you are staying in any of the Fryingpan valley accommodations, your lodge manager will know the best way to your required trailhead.

You have myriad choices for routes out of "The Fryingpan." If you're headed north to the Harry Gates Hut use route 4.2; it is shorter than route 4.3 and used by fewer snowmobiles. The most expedient route south to Margy's Hut is 4.1 from the Norrie Trailhead. For branch routes try 4.8, 4.9, or the first few miles of 4.4 and 4.5 to explore the country at the head of the drainage.

Most of the Fryingpan lodging is open year around. So hikers, cyclists, and equestrians should consider staying in the valley and exploring the surrounding backcountry. You can climb one of Colorado's famous 14,000-foot peaks from this drainage (see route 15.4), and the Fryingpan River has some of the best fly-fishing in the United States.

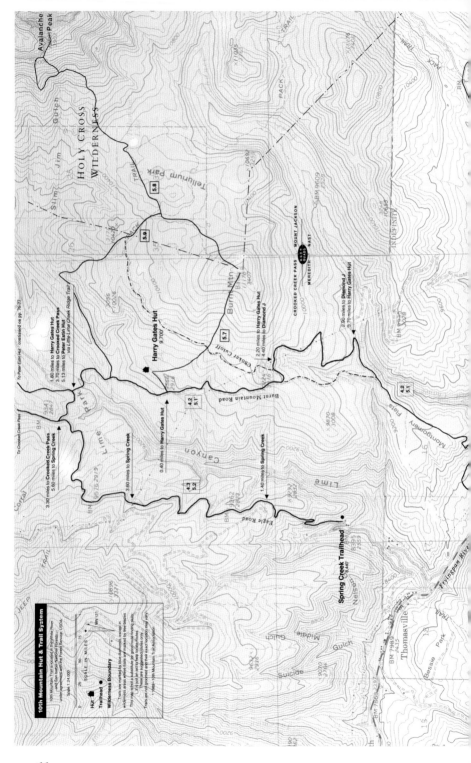

10th Mountain Hut & Trail System

10th Mountain Trail is located in the White River National Forest and is maintained and operated under agreement with the Forest Service, USDA.

Scale 1:24,000

SCALE IN MILES

Min 127

● Hut
▲ Trailhead
– – – Wilderness Boundary

Trails are marked by blue diamonds, except in wilderness areas, where trails are marked by tree blazes.

This map is not a substitute for good route-finding skills. It is just an aid to help locate routes. Trails and their suggested routes are approximate. Trails are not groomed and their exact location may vary.

1988 – 10th Mountain Trail Association

Holy Cross Wilderness

Avalanche Peak

Jim Gulch

Slim Jim Trail

Tellurium Park

5.8

5.9

Burnt Mtn

Harry Gates Hut
9,700'

Choker Cutoff

5.7

2.20 miles to Harry Gates Hut
4.40 miles to Diamond J

Mount Jackson

Crooked Creek Pass

Meredith Mast

2.90 miles to Diamond J
3.70 miles to Harry Gates Hut

4.2
5.1

Burnt Mountain Road

4.2
5.1

0.40 miles to Harry Gates Hut

4.3
5.2

1.40 miles to Spring Creek

Eagle Road

Lime Canyon

3.60 miles to Spring Creek

3.30 miles to Crooked Creek Pass
5.60 miles to Spring Creek

Lime Park

Corral Trail

To Crooked Creek Pass

To Peter Estin Hut   continued on pp. 76-77

1.80 miles to Harry Gates Hut
3.70 miles to Crooked Creek Pass
5.13 miles to Peter Estin Hut
via Little Creek Ridge Trail

Jeep Trail

Spring Creek Trailhead
8,440'

Nelson Gulch

Middle Gulch

Suicide Gulch

Bessie Park

Thomasville

Frying Pan River

66

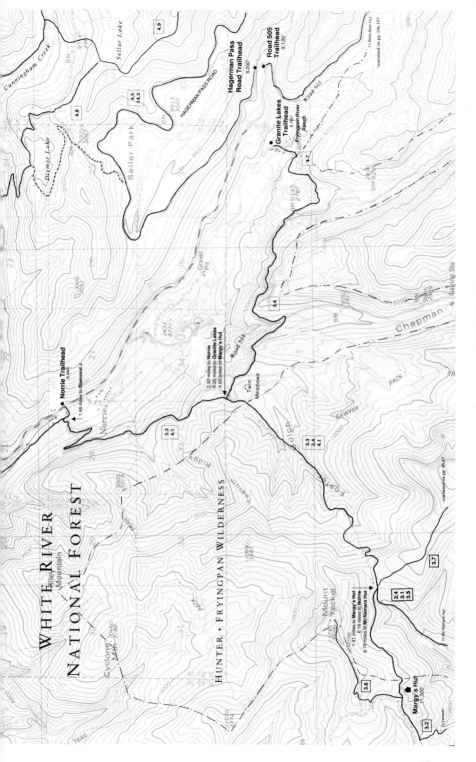

WHITE RIVER NATIONAL FOREST

HUNTER • FRYINGPAN WILDERNESS

Cunningham Creek

Sellar Lake

Diemer Lake

Sellar Park

HAGERMAN PASS ROAD

Hagerman Pass Road Trailhead
9,200

Road 505 Trailhead
9,120

Granite Lakes Trailhead
8,760

Fryingpan River Ranch

Road 505

Gravel Pit

Norrie Trailhead
8,440
1.45 miles to Diamond J

Norrie

Burnt Mountain

2.92 miles to Norrie
4.25 miles to Granite Lakes
4.65 miles to Margy's Hut

Road 504

Twin Meadows

Foster Gulch

Yeckel Ridge

Chapman

SAWYER

PACK

Cyclone

PACK

Mount Yeckel

1.41 miles to Margy's Hut
6.16 miles to Norrie
6.79 miles to McNamara Hut

Margy's Hut
11,300

continued on pp. 196-197

continued on pp. 46-47

To McNamara Hut

To Betty Bear Hut

4.9

4.5
14.3

4.8

3.4

3.3
4.1

3.3
3.4
4.1

4.7

3.7

2.4
3.1
3.5

3.6

3.2

4.1

Norrie Trailhead to Margy's Hut via Twin Meadows

DIFFICULTY: Intermediate   TEXT MAP: p. 67
TIME: 8 hours up, 6 ½ hours down   10TH MTN MAP: Mount Yeckel
DISTANCE: 7 ½ miles   USGS MAP: Meredith
ELEVATION GAIN: 2,917 feet; loss: 57 feet

While adventurous skiers might find other routes from the Fryingpan drainage to Margy's Hut, this 10th Mountain suggested route is certainly the most popular line.

ROUTE DESCRIPTION: See route 3.3.

4.2

Diamond J Trailhead to Harry Gates Hut via Montgomery Flats

DIFFICULTY: Novice   TEXT MAP: pp. 66-67, 77
TIME: 6 hours up, 5 hours down   10TH MTN MAP: Burnt Mt., Mt. Yeckel
DISTANCE: 6 ¾ miles   USGS MAP: Meredith, Crooked Creek
ELEVATION GAIN: 1,914 feet; loss: 464 feet   Pass

This 10th Mountain suggested route is the shortest and easiest route to the Harry Gates Hut. It is mostly a walk through the forest and on a logging road that passes under a major power line several times (helps with map work). Several good glimpses of the Elk Mountains to the south liven up the trip. Climbing skins are useful for the first 4 ½ miles of travel to the high point on the Burnt Mountain Road. You can strip skins there, wax the next 1 ¾ miles, then herringbone a short hill to the hut.

ROUTE DESCRIPTION: Follow the Fryingpan Road to the Diamond J Trailhead (see Chapter 1). For a description of the remainder of the trip to the hut see route 5.1.

4.3

Spring Creek Trailhead to Harry Gates Hut via Lime Park

DIFFICULTY: Novice   TEXT MAP: pp. 66-67, 76-77
TIME: 8 hours up, 5 hours down   10TH MTN MAP: Burnt Mt., Mt. Yeckel
DISTANCE: 8 miles   USGS MAP: Meredith, Crooked Creek
ELEVATION GAIN: 1,630 feet; loss: 370 feet   Pass

This long route follows a popular snowmobile trail on the Eagle Road which connects the Fryingpan drainage with Sylvan Lake and Eagle. With suitable snow you can use cross country wax. Some of the "fit and fleet" use skins for the initial climb, then skate the flats through Lime Park.

ROUTE DESCRIPTION: Follow the directions in Chapter 1 to the Spring Creek Trailhead. See route 5.2 for the trail description.

4.4

Road 505 Trailhead to Betty Bear Hut via Road 505

DIFFICULTY: Intermediate
TIME: 7 hours up, 6 hours down
DISTANCE: 6 ¾ miles
ELEVATION GAIN: 2,020 feet; loss: 40 feet

TEXT MAP: pp. 196-197
10TH MTN MAP: Upper Fryingpan
USGS MAP: Nast

This is the standard ski route to the Betty Bear Hut.

ROUTE DESCRIPTION: See route 15.1.

At Hell Gate (10,440 feet) on the Hagerman Pass Road route to the Skinner Hut from the Fryingpan drainage.

4.5

Hagerman Pass Road Trailhead to Skinner Hut via Hagerman Pass Road

DIFFICULTY: Advanced
TIME: 12 hours up, 8 hours down
DISTANCE: 16 miles
ELEVATION GAIN: 2,785 feet; loss: 365 feet

TEXT MAP: pp. 196-197
10TH MTN MAP: Upper Fryingpan
USGS MAP: Nast, Homestake Res.

This alternate trail connects the Leadville 10th Mountain huts with the Fryingpan drainage via a long trip up Hagerman Pass Road. Most of the road stays packed by snowmobile and snowcat. Thus, though long on miles, this trip can be used as a one-day route to the Skinner Hut. Use lightweight gear and cross country wax, with skins for the last climb to the pass.

ROUTE DESCRIPTION: Follow directions to the Hagerman Pass Road Trailhead (Chapter 1). Refer to route 14.3 for a detailed route description.

4.6

Diamond J Guest Ranch

ELEVATION: 8,250 feet
TEXT MAP: pp. 66-67, 77
10TH MTN MAP: Mount Yeckel, Burnt Mountain
USGS MAP: Meredith

The Diamond J Guest Ranch (see Diamond J Trailhead) is the oldest lodging in the Fryingpan drainage. In the Colorado Midland Railroad days of the late 1800s, the ranch location was known as Muckawanago, after a Ute Indian word meaning "where the bear walks." A nearby creek is still called Muckawanago Creek. A ticket office and rail station were built beside the creek. Intended as a shorter line in competition with the Denver and Rio Grande Railroad, this section of the Midland stretched from Basalt, up the Fryingpan valley, and over Hagerman Pass to the Leadville area. The line was famed for the "big trestle," an incredible span built completely with wooden timber; just to house the service people, a whole town existed under the trestle.

The Colorado Midland Railroad closed down in 1918, and Muckawanago was bought in 1927 by Delbert and Thelma Bowles. They registered the brand and operated several guest cabins. Presently the ranch is owned by a group of stockholders. The Muckawanago station building is now the hay barn. In the tradition of the great Colorado guest ranches, the Diamond J offers full-service lodging with all-season road access. For 10th Mountain hut skiers the lodge rents several rustic cabins. Amenities include showers, sauna, and jacuzzi. Meals and a shuttle service are also available.

To drive to the Diamond J Guest Ranch take Colorado Highway 82 to Basalt. Drive east through Basalt on Midland Avenue (the main street); Midland soon takes you out of Basalt and becomes the Fryingpan Road (County Road 104). Drive the Fryingpan Road 26.1 miles to the Diamond J Guest Ranch on the right side of the road. The ranch is well signed and easy to spot.

From the Diamond J Guest Ranch (Diamond J Trailhead) you can walk the ranch driveway to the start of the Montgomery Flats trail to the Harry Gates Hut (route 4.2/5.1). To reach the Norrie Trailhead you can ski via a well-defined trail on the opposite side of the river from the road, or take a car up the road. Other trailheads are best reached by car. Inquire at the ranch for shuttle service.

4.7
Fryingpan River Ranch

ELEVATION: 8,760 feet
TEXT MAP: pp. 67, 196
10TH MTN MAP: Mt. Yeckel, Upper Fryingpan
USGS MAP: Nast

Open year around, the Fryingpan River Ranch is located at 8,760 feet in the Upper Fryingpan River valley. The ranch consists of a main lodge and a number of outbuildings. Skiers stay in the main lodge. Meals, showers, and bedding are provided. A network of nearby trails and dirt roads provide winter ski touring and summer cycling, hiking, and horse riding. In the summer these dirt roads provide terrific access to the alpine backcountry.

To reach the Fryingpan River Ranch, drive the Fryingpan Road 26.5 miles from Basalt to a Y fork in the road. Take the right fork and continue up the main paved road 5 miles to a well-signed right turnoff. You'll see a sign here for Fryingpan River Ranch, as well as one for Nast Lake and Granite Lakes Trailhead. (Remember, the Granite Lakes Trailhead is located at the ranch). After the turnoff, a winding dirt road leads 1.1 miles to the obvious buildings of the Fryingpan River Ranch. This road has several steep switchbacks, so 4-wheel drive is recommended in snow or mud.

For skiing from the ranch to Margy's Hut via Twin Meadows, you must ski a trail and connector road to Twin Meadows, where you intersect the trail leading from the Norrie Trailhead to the hut. See route 3.4 for a detailed description of this trail.

If you're headed to the Betty Bear Hut use route 15.1 via nearby Road 505. Walk up the Fryingpan Road or use a car shuttle to reach the Road 505 Trailhead. For routes to the Harry Gates Hut, Peter Estin Hut, and Skinner Hut see those hut's respective chapters. Trailheads for these huts are best reached via car shuttle.

4.8

Sellar Lake from Elk Wallow Campground

DIFFICULTY: Novice
TIME: 6 hours round trip
DISTANCE: 7 miles round trip
ELEVATION GAIN: 1,370 feet round trip

TEXT MAP: pp. 66-67
10TH MTN MAP: Mount Yeckel
USGS MAP: Nast

This short branch route is a fine jaunt. Go for a picnic, or practice your winter camping close to civilization.

ROUTE DESCRIPTION: From the Elk Wallow Campground Trailhead ski S ¼ mile across the bottom land to the point where obvious power lines start up the mountainside. Put your skins on here and ski up the well-defined road-cut that begins a few feet south of the power lines. After about a mile of snow-covered road you will reach Diemer Lake.

From the north side of Diemer Lake follow an obvious road-cut E as it switchbacks under the power lines a few times and leads you to the top of a timbered shoulder at 10,050 feet. From here continue a gradual climb on the snow-covered road for another mile to Sellar Lake (10,210 feet). Return via the same route.

SAFETY NOTES: There is no avalanche danger on this route. Yet, do not let the novice rating lead you into a bad situation. Even a novice ski touring route requires some map reading, the correct timing, and proper equipment, not to mention a minimum overall skill level.

SUMMER: The roads in the vicinity of these lakes make good bicycle, horse, and hiking routes. Also, try for some trout if you like.

4.9

Sellar Peaks Traverse from Elk Wallow Campground/ Cunningham Creek Road

DIFFICULTY: Expert
TIME: 9 hours round trip
DISTANCE: 13 miles round trip
ELEVATION GAIN: 3,015 feet round trip

TEXT MAP: pp. 66-67, 196
10TH MTN MAP: Mt. Yeckel, U. Fry.
USGS MAP: Nast

This long branch route is perfect for a day in April or early May. It includes two summits, enjoyable and safe downhill skiing, and one of the best views in the Sawatch Mountains. It is a good choice if you are staying in the Fryingpan drainage.

ROUTE DESCRIPTION: You can start the Sellar Peaks Traverse two ways; your choice depends on whether the North Fork Road (Chapter 1, Elk Wallow Campground Trailhead) is open only as far as Elk Wallow Campground, or another 1.25 miles to its intersection with the Cunningham Creek Road.

(Start number 1) From Elk Wallow Campground follow route 4.6 to Sellar Lake, then connect with the route described below. Though not as direct as start number 2, you can do this any time of year.

(Start number 2) This option saves you about 380 feet of elevation gain and about two miles, but depends on your being able to drive up from Elk Wallow Campground to the Cunningham Creek Road. This section of road opens up sometime in late April or early May, depending on the year's snowfall.

From the intersection of the North Fork Road and the Cunningham Creek Road (9,210 feet), follow the Cunningham Creek Road 1 ¾ miles to 9,520 feet. Leave the road here, cross Cunningham Creek (can be a wade in the spring), then head up the hill about 680 vertical feet to Sellar Lake. Due to heavy timber it can be hard to navigate directly to the lake. Don't worry about this, because as long as you're in the general area of the lake you can continue climbing to the next part of the route—the 10,441-foot saddle on the ridge that divides the Cunningham drainage from the Fryingpan drainage. From the saddle stay on the ridge and climb through medium density timber to timberline, then to the summit of West Sellar Peak (12,074 feet).

At the summit enjoy the awesome views of Mt. Massive, Avalanche Ridge, the Red Tables, and the Elk Range. Then, if you're ambitious, make a short ski run SW for six or seven hundred vertical feet. Regain the ridge between the two summits and use it as your route (1 mile) to the east summit.

Near the summit of Sellar Peak. Looking southeast at Mt. Massive, 14,421 ft.

For an excellent downhill run from the east summit, ski down the southeast shoulder for about 600 vertical feet (stay away from the cornice), then take a northerly contour to the 11,320-foot saddle that the power lines pass through.

From the saddle, ski the line-cut and nearby glades all the way down to the dogleg turn in the lines (10,560 feet). Be careful of avalanches in a couple of the steeper parts of the line-cut. You can bypass these by skiing the glades to the east.

After the dogleg, continue down the power line to the low point just before the line crosses Middle Cunningham Creek. Take a right (N) turn out of the low point and travel an obvious road-cut down to the Cunningham Creek Road. Travel back down the Cunningham Creek Road to the North Fork Road.

SAFETY NOTES: Watch for low hanging power lines during heavy snow years. There may be pocket slide danger in several gullies on the descent. You can avoid these with simple traverses.

SUMMER: The Sellar Peaks are a worthy destination, but the routes described above require too much bushwhacking for summer use. You can hike Sellar Peak from the Hagerman Pass Road.

Chapter 5 • Harry Gates Hut

Built in 1986, the Harry Gates Hut was the fourth structure added to the 10th Mountain system. It is the largest of the 10th Mountain owned huts, with three floors that can sleep 20 people (reservations limited to 16). Indeed,

ELEVATION: 9,700 feet
COUNTY: Eagle
TEXT MAP: pp. 66-67, 76-77
10TH MTN MAP: Mt. Yeckel, Burnt Mt.
USGS MAP: Crooked Creek Pass
TRAILHEADS: Spring Creek, Sylvan Lake, Diamond J

many people feel it is too big, and more recent 10th Mountain huts have been scaled down. Inside, you'll find two kitchens: the main kitchen and one reserved for guided groups and hut maintenance people. Plenty of windows look out on the sunsets and the spectacular Avalanche Ridge. The hut was built with funds from the Gates Foundation in memorial to the late Harry F. Gates, who was an outdoorsman with a deep love for the mountains.

The hut is located in a clearing on a small wooded knoll, at the lowest elevation of any 10th Mountain hut. This makes the cabin easy to get to, but curtails access to the higher mountains east and northeast of the hut. Nonetheless, those skiers with the skill and endurance will find the Avalanche Ridge east of the hut to be a worthy objective (route 5.8). If you like to explore, the Tellurium Park area (route 5.9) is also an attractive branch trip. Skiers who want to stay closer to the hut, and novices, can use Burnt Mountain (route 5.7) as an accessible playground. The trip to the summit of Burnt Mountain is a terrific initiation into ski climbing.

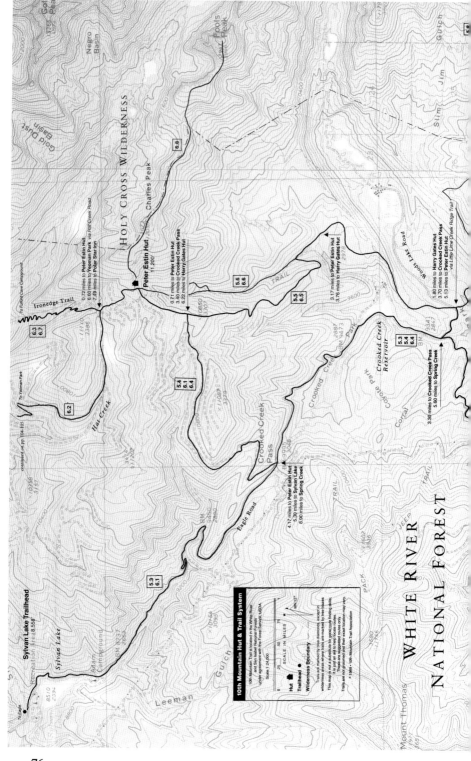

WHITE RIVER

NATIONAL FOREST

HOLY CROSS WILDERNESS

Sylvan Lake Trailhead
Recreation Area 8,558'

Peter Estin Hut 11,200'

Charles Peak

Fools Peak

Gold Dust Basin

Negro Basin

Gold Peak

Slim Jim Gulch

Crooked Creek Reservoir

Crooked Creek Pass

Ironedge Trail

Hat Creek

Woods Lake Road

Eagle Road

Leeman Gulch

Mount Thomas

To Eagle

To Sylvan Pass

To Yeoman Park

Continued on p. 104-105

0.72 miles to Peter Estin Hut
6.60 miles to Yeoman Park via Fall Creek Road
7.89 miles to Polar Star Inn

0.71 miles to Peter Estin Hut
3.40 miles to Crooked Creek Pass
6.22 miles to Harry Gates Hut

3.17 miles to Peter Estin Hut
3.76 miles to Harry Gates Hut

1.80 miles to Harry Gates Hut
3.70 miles to Crooked Creek Pass
5.13 miles to Peter Estin Hut
via Little Lime Creek Ridge Trail

3.30 miles to Crooked Creek Pass
5.60 miles to Spring Creek

4.17 miles to Peter Estin Hut
5.38 miles to Sylvan Lake
8.90 miles to Spring Creek

6.8

6.3
6.7

6.2

5.4
6.1
6.4

5.4
6.1
6.4

5.5
6.6

5.5
6.5

5.3
5.4
6.4

5.3
6.1

10th Mountain Hut & Trail System

SCALE IN MILES
0   .25   .50   .75

Scale 1:24,000

● Hut

▲ Trailhead

— — — Wilderness Boundary

Trails are marked by blue diamonds, except in
wilderness areas where blue diamonds are illegal.
and Sun Valley National Forests
under agreement with the Forest Service, USDA.

This map is not a substitute for good route finding skills.
It is just an aid to help locate routes.
Trails are suggested routes only.
Trails and routes and their exact location may vary.

© 1989 - 10th Mountain Trail Association

76

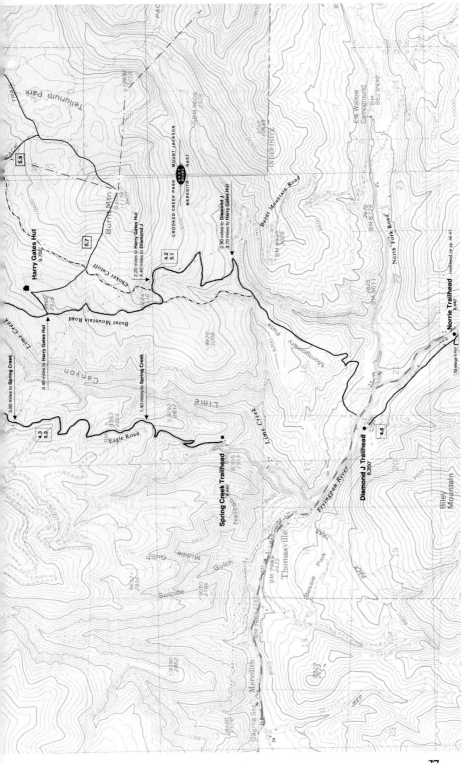

Telurium Park

5.9

Harry Gates Hut
9,700'

Choker Cutoff

5.7

Burro Mtn
BM 11178
3407

2.20 miles to Harry Gates Hut
4.40 miles to Diamond J

Burnt Mountain Road

4.2
5.1

CROOKED CREEK PASS
MEREDITH
NAST

MOUNT JACKSON
BM 9609
2929

SBM 9609
2929

2.90 miles to Diamond J
3.70 miles to Harry Gates Hut

Elk Wallow
Campground

BM
88272690

Burnt Mountain Road

North Fork Road

3.60 miles to Spring Creek

0.40 miles to Harry Gates Hut

Lime Creek

Lime Canyon

1.40 miles to Spring Creek

Lime Creek

Norrie Trailhead
8,440'

To Margy's Hut

4.3
5.2

BM 9262
2822

Eagle Road

Spring Creek Trailhead
9,440'

Diamond J Trailhead
8,250'

4.6

Nelson Gulch

Lime Creek

Fryingpan River

Riley Mountain

Middle Gulch

Suicide Gulch

Thomasville

Bessie Park

BM 7989
2435

Gaging Sta. Meredith

continued on pp. 66-67

77

With the exception of the Lime Ridge Trail to the Peter Estin Hut (route 5.5), the 10th Mountain suggested routes connecting the Harry Gates Hut to other huts and trailheads use snow-covered roads. Since these roads are heavily used by snowmobiles they are usually packed, so bring some picnic food and your lightweight skis—you're bound to have a good time. So far, snowmobilers and skiers have co-recreated with few problems. This will continue if people practice a few common courtesies. Simply put, snowmobilers should slow down while in the vicinity ot skiers, and skiers should step to the side to let them by.

The quickest route to the Harry Gates Hut is via the Montgomery Flats connection to the Burnt Mountain Road (route 5.1). The long, scenic route is the ski from Sylvan Lake (route 5.3)—a tour recommended only for the hearty.

If you're pushing towards Aspen from the Harry Gates Hut, you have a choice of spending a night at the Diamond J Ranch (Chapter 4) or continuing to Margy's Hut. The Diamond J is so close via a downhill of route 5.1 that, with the ranch your goal, you have time for a morning tour at the hut or some route variations on the way down. If you're on a long trip, this is an opportunity for an "active rest day." If you plan on skiing through the Fryingpan drainage to Margy's Hut, you're looking at more than 16 miles of skiing with almost 4,000 feet of elevation gain.

To reach the Peter Estin Hut from the Harry Gates Hut, use the Lime Ridge Trail (route 5.5) for the fastest 10th Mountain suggested route. For an even more direct route advanced skiers can use the Lime Drainage Trail (route 5.6). For a scenic cruise use route 5.4, but start early.

5.1

Diamond J Trailhead—Harry Gates Hut via Montgomery Flats

DIFFICULTY: Novice
TIME: 6 hours up, 5 hours down
DISTANCE: 6 3/4 miles
ELEVATION GAIN: 1,914 feet; loss: 464 feet

TEXT MAP: pp. 66-67, 77
10TH MTN MAP: Mt. Yeckel, Burnt Mt.
USGS MAP: Crooked Creek Pass, Meredith

This 10th Mountain suggested route is the shortest and easiest route to the Harry Gates Hut. It is mostly a walk on a logging road through the forest. The road passes under a major power line several times (good for map reading), while good views of the Elk Mountains to the south keep things interesting. Climbing skins are useful for the first 4 1/2 miles of travel to the high point on the Burnt Mountain Road. You can strip skins here and wax the next 1 3/4 miles, then herringbone a short hill to the hut.

Aerial view of the Harry Gates Hut from the west.

ROUTE DESCRIPTION: Park at the Diamond J Guest Ranch (see Diamond J Trailhead and Chapter 4). Walk back on the driveway to the Fryingpan Road, cross the road, and locate the 10th Mountain trailhead markers opposite the Diamond J driveway entrance. Hike N up the road-bank, cross the fence, then click into your skis (with skins). Head NE (cross under a power line) ¼ mile through an open area. Enter the aspen forest, and take care to intersect the first switchback (8,400 feet) of a logging road. This is an important junction, since the road takes you up an efficient route that avoids several steep gulches.

Climb the road to Montgomery Flats (9,100 feet). Stay on the road NE through Montgomery Flats for 1 ½ miles to a junction with the Burnt Mountain Road at 9,450 feet. The Burnt Mountain Road is a wide, distinct road-cut. Use your altimeter and the power lines for precise navigation.

From the junction the 10th Mountain suggested route follows the Burnt Mountain Road as it takes a northerly tack with several switchbacks for 1 ½ miles to the road summit at 10,030 feet. You can navigate by how many times you pass under the power lines—four times to the road summit. However, if you use skins it makes sense to cut the two main switchbacks on the way up. In fact, with good snow conditions and skilled orienteering, savvy skiers have found that a more direct ascent route and better downhill skiing can be had by using the general route of the pack trail to the west of Silver Creek, as marked on the USGS Meredith map.

From the road summit (10,030 feet) the 10th Mountain suggested route continues along the Burnt Mountain Road for another 1 ¾ miles to a clearing at 9,566 feet. Consider removing your skins at the road summit and applying some wax for this glide through the beautiful evergreen forest. At the clearing, turn right (NE) off the road and ski ¼ mile (134 vertical feet) up the hill to the northeast of the road, unlock the door of the hut, and make tea.

One major variation on this route makes sense for advanced skiers traveling to the hut. From the road summit mentioned above, leave your skins on, stay on the road, and ski from the summit down a short hill and around the shoulder of point 10,224. Just as the Burnt Mountain Road begins to head N, leave the Burnt Mountain Road and ski up an obvious logging road that cuts through the trees NE. The Choker Cutoff, as this shortcut is called, traverses for a mile to skiable glades on the west side of Burnt Mountain. Strip your skins here. Good skiers can make turns most of the way from here to the Harry Gates Hut. Be careful not to get lost in the woods. Most likely you'll find ski tracks leading to the hut from the glades.

REVERSE ROUTE DESCRIPTION: For travel from the Harry Gates Hut to the trailhead, it's easy to reverse the above directions. The whole trip can be done using cross country wax. You can get some turns by cutting the switchbacks on the Burnt Mountain Road. Farther down, hold a strong snowplow through the last steep section.

SAFETY NOTES: This route has no avalanche danger. Ski in control on the descent, as any wild falling will put you into a tree. Orienteering on the 10th Mountain suggested route is relatively easy. Variations should only be navigated by experts.

SUMMER: Cyclists should avoid Montgomery Flats by using the entire Burnt Mountain Road (see Burnt Mountain Road Trailhead). Hikers and horse riders will enjoy the route described above, but should check with 10th Mountain about private land at the start of the Montgomery Flats. With private land problems, the Burnt Mountain Road route should be substituted.

5.2

Spring Creek Trailhead — Harry Gates Hut via Lime Park

DIFFICULTY: Novice	**TEXT MAP:** pp. 66, 76-77
TIME: 8 hours up, 5 hours down	**10TH MTN MAP:** Mt. Yeckel, Burnt Mt.
DISTANCE: 8 miles	**USGS MAP:** Crooked Creek Pass,
ELEVATION GAIN: 1,630 feet; loss: 370 feet	Meredith

This long route follows a well-used snowmobile trail on the Eagle Road (see route 5.3) which connects the Fryingpan drainage with Sylvan Lake and Eagle. With suitable snow you can easily use cross country wax for the whole trip. Some of the "fit and fleet" use skins for the initial climb, then skate the flats through Lime Park.

ROUTE DESCRIPTION: Start at the Spring Creek Trailhead. Ski N up the obvious road-cut 3 ½ miles and 1,090 vertical feet to the huge open area of Lime Park (9,560 feet). You can identify your entrance into Lime Park by passage under the power line shown on the USGS Crooked Creek map.

Skirt the west edge of Lime Park for another ½ mile past the power line (still on the road). If you're using skins, remove them here, then swing E and follow the road down a wide ravine to 9,313 feet. Continue on the road as it turns N to its intersection with the Burnt Mountain Road. Take care to identify this intersection; there is a sign, but it may be covered by snow.

To continue to the Gates Hut (you're still in Lime Park) turn SE onto the Burnt Mountain Road. The road will lead you across a short flat area for about ¼ mile, then down a hill to the intersection with the Woods Lake Road at 9,270 feet. Again, whatever your direction of travel, use this intersection as a critical destination in your navigation. Stay on the Burnt Mountain Road as it takes you downhill another ⅛ mile and crosses Lime Creek at 9,190 feet.

At the crossing apply some cross country wax or skins if needed, and climb the Burnt Mountain Road a short distance E, then ½ mile S to a clearing at Slim Jim Gulch. Follow the road S another ¼ mile to a smaller clearing at 9,566 feet. At this point, turn left off the Burnt Mountain Road and ski NE 134 vertical feet up a hill to the hut. You cannot see the hut from the road, so pay attention!

REVERSE ROUTE DESCRIPTION: If you are heading from the hut to Lime Park, the Burnt Mountain Road is obvious at first, but can be hard to find in Lime Park. When you exit from the west side of Lime Park be sure to use the road, as a false trail could lead you into dangerous Lime Creek Canyon. The power line and an altimeter reading will set you on the correct track.

SAFETY NOTES: Keep your ears open for snowmobiles. (See route 5.3)

SUMMER: The road from the Spring Creek Fish Hatchery is a fine mountain bike ride. This whole area is beautiful for hiking, biking, or horseback riding. The Eagle Road, from the Hatchery to Sylvan Lake (and beyond), is passable for 2-wheel drive autos with high clearance when it is dry. Even 4-wheel drive vehicles have been stuck on this road when it gets wet.

5.3

Sylvan Lake Trailhead — Harry Gates Hut via Crooked Creek Pass

DIFFICULTY: Intermediate
TIME: 11 hours up, 7 hours down
DISTANCE: 10 ½ miles
ELEVATION GAIN: 1,952 feet; loss: 810 feet

TEXT MAP: pp. 76-77
10TH MTN MAP: Burnt Mountain
USGS MAP: Crooked Creek Pass

This gorgeous 10th Mountain suggested route is probably the least used trail to the Harry Gates Hut, simply because it is longer than other routes and the trailhead is farther from population centers. Wait until late winter or early spring, click into your light touring rig, and spend a day on this trail. You will be rewarded by a pleasant cruise through the forests, good views from Crooked Creek Pass, and downhill turns in Lime Park. The trail is almost always packed by snowmobilers.

ROUTE DESCRIPTION: To begin, drive to the Sylvan Lake Trailhead. From your parking at snow closure, ski up the distinct snow-covered West Brush Creek road-cut for a mile around the north and east sides of the lake, then up into the Brush Creek valley for 4 ¼ miles to Crooked Creek Pass. Use your altimeter to identify the switchbacks at 9,220 feet and 9,260 feet, then the turn at 9,450 feet. From here be certain to stay on the road as it climbs S then SE around a timbered ridge dividing Spine Creek from Brush Creek, and then continues paralleling Brush Creek to Crooked Creek Pass (10,005 feet). Crooked Creek Pass is fairly obvious, but an altimeter check is always a good idea.

From Crooked Creek Pass ski the road 1 mile SE to Crooked Creek Park. Ski into Crooked Creek Park (you may get a few turns here), then follow the Crooked Creek drainage (stay on the road if in doubt) to the obvious dam, buildings, and flat expanse of Crooked Creek Reservoir. Ski the road on the dam along the west side of the reservoir, then about ¾ of a mile down the Little Lime Creek drainage (still on the road) to Lime Park and a well-signed, obvious road junction (9,280 feet). Pay attention to your compass and altimeter to navigate to this point.

Now you will be standing at the north edge of Lime Park, a vast clearing that can make for confusing navigation on the best of days. The way to handle Lime Park is to look for the road-cuts and signs at road junctions, but continue to heed your compass and altimeter.

From the 9,280-foot junction, ski the road SE across Lime Park to its intersection with the Woods Lake Road, then downhill S to cross Lime Creek at 9,190 feet. Next, take care to identify and follow the Burnt Mountain

Road as it climbs into the timber after crossing Lime Creek.

Ski up the Burnt Mountain Road ½ mile to a large clearing at the base of Slim Jim Gulch (9,440 feet). Ski the road S across the clearing, then nip through the trees (still on the road) for another ¼ mile to a smaller clearing at 9,566 feet. Turn left (NE) off the road here and climb several hundred yards NE up a knoll to the Harry Gates Hut. The hut is visible from about halfway up the knoll.

REVERSE ROUTE DESCRIPTION: The crux is navigating across Lime Park up to Crooked Creek Reservoir. The road-cut from the reservoir up to Crooked Creek Pass is easy to find. Once you are on Crooked Creek Pass, the snow-covered road is obvious all the way to the Sylvan Lake Trailhead. If you get off the road, the drainage will still lead you to the lake.

SAFETY NOTES: You'll find little avalanche danger on this route. Some of the steeper slopes in Lime Park have avalanched during very unstable conditions. Bank sluffs have been observed along the road from Crooked Creek Reservoir to Lime Park. Take care with navigation through Lime Park, and by all means stay out of Lime Creek Canyon.

SUMMER: All the roads used by this route provide fabulous cycling, hiking, and running. Avoid holiday weekends or you will be coughing up dust for months. A good bike ride takes the power-line road from Crooked Creek Pass back S to its intersection with the Eagle Road (see route 5.2).

5.4

Harry Gates Hut to Peter Estin Hut via Crooked Creek Pass

DIFFICULTY: Expert	**TEXT MAP:** pp. 76-77
TIME: 10 ½ hours	**10TH MTN MAP:** Burnt Mountain
DISTANCE: 10 miles	**USGS MAP:** Crooked Creek Pass
ELEVATION GAIN: 2,275 feet; loss: 775 feet	

Arduous miles, intricate route-finding, rewarding vistas, and the sense of really covering the country—that sums up this fabulous hut to hut ski tour (10th Mountain suggested route).

ROUTE DESCRIPTION: Get an early start from the Harry Gates Hut and ski the 10th Mountain suggested route ¼ mile SW to the Burnt Mountain Road, or ski down the hill behind the hut N to the Slim Jim Gulch clearing and the Burnt Mountain Road. The latter route saves time for good downhill skiers.

Follow the Burnt Mountain Road downhill to the Lime Creek stream crossing at 9,190 feet elevation. You will now be in the midst of Lime Park, a huge open area that has confounded the best navigators. The best route through the park follows the road (portions may be obscured by snow) as it climbs and winds about ⅛ mile NW to the intersection with the Woods Lake Road. Do not take the Woods Lake Road. Stay on the Burnt Mountain Road another ½ mile W then NW to its intersection with the Eagle Road (9,300 feet). This is your critical intersection. Both intersections are marked by good signs, but the signs could be covered by snow. Your compass, map, and altimeter will insure positive identification.

Turn N and follow the Eagle Road as it leads up Little Lime Creek to the dam and obvious flat area of the Crooked Creek Reservoir. Stay on the road as it climbs past the reservoir up the north side of Crooked Creek Park, then enters the aspen trees at 9,650 feet, and continues 1 ½ miles to Crooked Creek Pass (10,005 feet).

Now the real climbing begins. Leave the Eagle Road at the summit of the pass by heading NW up an obvious road-cut (starts on the west side of a fence) that climbs just over ¼ mile to a switchback, then SE to another switchback, then around the west shoulder of point 11,087. The road, still an obvious cut, then follows a long traverse on the north side of point 11,087, then drops 260 vertical feet to a saddle near the head of Spine Creek (10,700 feet).

Stay on the road from the saddle for another ⅛ mile NE to the switchback as shown on the USGS Crooked Creek Pass map (10,760 feet). Leave the road here and climb E ¼ mile and 90 vertical feet to the top of the ridge separating Spine Creek from Little Lime Creek. Here your route converges with the Lime Ridge Trail (route 5.5) and continues N up a well-marked route through a sparsely timbered logged area to Hat Creek Saddle (11,120 feet). This is the broad saddle just west of the Peter Estin Hut. You cannot see the Peter Estin Hut from Hat Creek Saddle, and you can ski past the hut if you are not paying attention. To guard against this, use your altimeter and map to identify Hat Creek Saddle. Swing E here, and when you break through a grove of pines the hut will be obvious.

SAFETY NOTES: At many points along this route a navigation mistake will send you down the wrong drainage. So be certain that at least one member of your party is a good orienteer. Some of the steeper slopes in Lime Park avalanche on rare occasions, and bank sluffs have been observed on the road-cuts. Whiteout conditions are common in Lime Park.

SUMMER: The Eagle Road is easy cycling, while the road from Crooked Creek Pass up into Spine Creek is strenuous but ridable. A good bike ride leaves from Crooked Creek Pass, then takes the Spine Creek road up to the three-trail confluence just west of the Peter Estin Hut, then down the Hat Creek logging roads (see route 6.2). The Ironedge Trail (route 6.3) is a perfect downhill ride for mountain cycling experts. All the trails in this area are fine for running, hiking, and equestrian use. The Eagle Road is also a popular drive.

5.5

Harry Gates Hut to Peter Estin Hut via Lime Ridge Trail

DIFFICULTY: Intermediate
TIME: 8 hours
DISTANCE: 7 miles
ELEVATION GAIN: 2,130 feet; loss: 630 feet

TEXT MAP: pp. 76-77
10TH MTN MAP: Burnt Mountain
USGS MAP: Crooked Creek Pass

This is the most scenic and direct 10th Mountain suggested route between the Harry Gates Hut and Peter Estin Hut.

ROUTE DESCRIPTION: From the Harry Gates Hut follow route 5.4 to the Woods Lake Road intersection (9,270 feet) in Lime Park. The road here may be obscured by snow, but the signs and fence break are usually obvious. Put your skins on here. Use your compass to follow the trail (marked on the USGS Crooked Creek Pass map) that climbs N up through a clearing, then through timber to the crest of the ridge separating Lime Park from Crooked Creek Reservoir. Follow the trail NE along the ridge (the trail-cut is not obvious) for ¾ mile. Turn N and travel through timber, then down into the Little Lime Creek drainage. This circuitous route avoids private land around Crooked Creek Reservoir.

Cross the east fork of Little Lime Creek at 9,680 feet, take a perpendicular course from the creek, and contour ½ mile NW up the west fork of Little Lime Creek. At about 9,700 feet cross the creek and switchback S up to the crest of the ridge (Lime Ridge) separating Middle Creek from the west fork of Little Lime Creek. Once you gain the crest of Lime Ridge, follow a well-marked and fairly distinct trail-cut that leads through intermittent clearings and timber to 10,150 feet.

Continue up the ridge as the timber thickens, and follow a well-defined trail-cut through Sherwood Forest to a low-angled area with mature aspen trees. Look for interesting old initials carved in these trees. Continue N, switchback, then climb steeply through clearings and dark timber to another low-angled area at 10,850 feet. From here continue N ¾ mile through a sparsely timbered logged area to Hat Creek Saddle (11,120 feet), a nondescript divide between the Hat Creek drainage and west fork of Little Lime Creek. Travel E from the saddle several hundred yards to the hut. It is not visible directly from the saddle, but soon becomes obvious.

SAFETY NOTES: This trail is usually safe from snowslides, though steep slopes on the ridge sides could be dangerous during extremely unstable periods. Route-finding and the length of the trip should be of more concern.

SUMMER: This trail is not recommended for cycling. Equestrians and hikers will find much to explore in this area, but the actual Lime Ridge Trail was cut several years ago only for winter use. Thus, there is no real path to follow (see route 5.6).

5.6

Harry Gates Hut to Peter Estin Hut via Lime Drainage Trail

DIFFICULTY: Advanced	**TEXT MAP:** pp. 76-77
TIME: 7 hours	**10TH MTN MAP:** Burnt Mountain
DISTANCE: 6 1/4 miles	**USGS MAP:** Crooked Creek Pass
ELEVATION GAIN: 2,130 feet; loss: 630 feet	

Though best as a descent from Peter Estin Hut to Harry Gates Hut (route 6.6), this route also serves as a direct climbing route for the glycogen depletion crowd (it cuts 3/4 mile off the 10th Mountain suggested route 5.5). If that puts fire in your quads, bear in mind the fact that this is not a 10th Mountain suggested route, and thus is less likely to be broken out. If you have to, it's easy to abandon this trail and use route 5.5.

ROUTE DESCRIPTION: To begin, follow route 5.5 to the west fork of Little Lime Creek (9,700 feet). For the Lime Drainage Trail, simply stay on the route of the pack trail that follows the gut of the drainage, rather than switchbacking up onto Lime Ridge (see route 5.5). Stay in the drainage (veer to either side of the creek for easiest travel lines) for about 1 1/2 miles and 900 vertical feet to the bottom of steep open slopes at 10,600 feet. Head left (W) into the trees if you suspect avalanche danger and follow the edge of the timber or route 5.5 the remainder of the way to the Peter Estin Hut. With minimal avalanche danger you can stay on the open slopes and climb the crest of an obvious rib to a point directly below the hut.

SAFETY NOTES: Heed the possibility of avalanche danger on the slopes just below the Peter Estin Hut and on steeper sections of open glades lower in the drainage.

SUMMER: Hikers and equestrians can use the pack trail as marked on the USGS Crooked Creek Pass map. Cyclists will find this trail too steep and inconsistent for good riding.

5.7

Burnt Mountain from Harry Gates Hut

DIFFICULTY: Intermediate
TIME: 3 hours round trip
DISTANCE: 4 miles round trip
ELEVATION GAIN: 1,558 feet round trip

TEXT MAP: pp. 66, 77
10TH MTN MAP: Mt. Yeckel, Burnt Mt.
USGS MAP: Crooked Creek Pass,
   Mt. Jackson

Some say that the only thing better than skiing this branch route to the summit of Burnt Mountain would be a night in a hut on top—what a location! With a full panorama of views, perfect ski glades, and beautiful gnarled stumps and trees, this place is a "must see." Catch a sunrise or sunset if you can (bring a headlamp for the latter).

ROUTE DESCRIPTION: Start with skins. From the Harry Gates Hut, ski directly SE a few hundred feet and down into a ravine. Ski into the forest on the southeast side of the ravine, then ski almost due S to the toe of a long Y-shaped clearing that leads up the west side of Burnt Mountain. Optionally, you can stay in the forest to the NE of the clearing until you hit the pack trail (called Choker Cutoff) that contours at 10,200 feet. Choker Cutoff is easily identified by its cut through the trees and a well-defined trail shelf that shows through the snow cover (can be obscured during heavy snow years).

From Choker Cutoff the route is simple. Climb the Y clearing to its top at 10,600 feet, continue up for a few hundred yards through light timber to the summit clearing, then continue up through the summit clearing to the summit at 11,178 feet.

You can get some good skiing by heading down the ascent route, or try some tree skiing to either side of the clearings. Trap crust is common on these exposures. If you encounter this dread condition, try the slopes on the north and northeast side of the summit. If you're more into covering ground than making turns, try a high orbit of the summit at about 10,800 feet or do the Tellurium Park Loop (route 5.9).

SAFETY NOTES: Take care to ski in control while skiing the trees. There can be avalanche danger on the steeper slopes dropping from the summit, and cornices do form on occasion.

SUMMER: Burnt Mountain is an excellent summer hike. You'll encounter light bushwhacking if you leave directly from the Harry Gates Hut. For an easier route, take Choker Cutoff from the Burnt Mountain Road, then ascend the pack trail as marked on the USGS Crooked Creek Pass map. The first few miles of Choker Cutoff from the Burnt Mountain Road are actual-ly a logging trail and can be ridden on a mountain bike. The summit pack trail is too steep and inconsistent for cycling.

5.8

Avalanche Peak from the Harry Gates Hut

DIFFICULTY: Expert
TIME: 12 hours round trip
DISTANCE: 13 miles round trip
ELEVATION GAIN: 3,741 feet round trip

TEXT MAP: p. 66
10TH MTN MAP: Mount Yeckel
USGS MAP: Crooked Creek Pass,
Mt. Jackson

While many mountain skiers feel the pull of ascent fever as they ponder Avalanche Peak (12,803 feet) from the comfort of the Harry Gates Hut, few go to the summit. Only experts should attempt this long, involved tour. Even hardened mountaineers should only attempt the peak during very low avalanche hazard, preferably in the late winter or spring when the snowpack has consolidated. The route requires detailed orienteering through the Tellurium Park area. You'll get in plenty of downhill skiing as well as a real summit on this route.

View of Avalanche Ridge from the southwest, Avalanche Peak to the left.

ROUTE DESCRIPTION: The route has two starts; both end up at Tellurium Lake. If you want the best views and skiing, follow route 5.7 to the summit of Burnt Mountain, ski the glades on the northeast face of Burnt Mountain down to Tellurium Park, then swing through the park to Tellurium Lake. Navigation in this area is tricky, but taking time with compass, map, and altimeter will get you there. Using the other start, climb Burnt Mountain to Choker Cutoff at 10,200 feet (see route 5.7), then ski Choker Cutoff to the pack trail leading up into Tellurium Park and on to Tellurium Lake. The intersection of Choker Cutoff and the pack trail (10,240 feet) is not obvious, so pay close attention to your orienteering.

The real fun begins at Tellurium Lake. From the north end of the lake head N for about ¼ mile, then climb E to a small clearing starting at 10,660 feet. Climb to the top of this clearing, then continue climbing up a poorly defined shoulder and through several more clearings to timberline at about 11,500 feet. You may find discouraging bushwhacking up to this point, but stick with it. The idea is to get to timberline so you can travel through sparser trees and see where you're going. Once at timberline be careful of avalanche exposure as you contour N along the trim line for ½ to ¾ mile to the west shoulder that drops from the peak's summit. There is no obvious ridge line, so take care to identify the best route to follow the shoulder to the summit. In times of low avalanche danger (probably best in spring) you can wander up the west face.

For your descent, ski the west face if avalanche conditions allow, or follow ridges and ribs for an avalanche avoidance route down to timberline. Retrace your route to Tellurium Park, then take Choker Cutoff or Slim Jim Gulch (see route 5.9) back to the Harry Gates Hut. It is tempting to descend Slim Jim Gulch from the peak, but only the most expert skiers will be able to handle the dense bushwhacking that this requires.

SAFETY NOTES: Start early, bring a headlamp, and remember your emergency bivouac gear. Be very careful of avalanche danger on the above-timberline portion of this route. There is no ridge-line route that totally avoids potential avalanche slopes.

SUMMER: This is a fairly good hike, though there is no real trail between Tellurium Lake and the summit.

5.9

Tellurium Park Loop from Harry Gates Hut

DIFFICULTY: Intermediate
TIME: Full day round trip
DISTANCE: 7 miles round trip
ELEVATION GAIN: 1,800 feet round trip

TEXT MAP: pp. 66, 76-77
10TH MTN MAP: Mt. Yeckel, Burnt Mt.
USGS MAP: Crooked Creek Pass,
   Mt. Jackson

If you like to explore, variations on this branch route could keep you busy for days. This area is especially good for orienteering practice. You'll find a draconian lack of navigable ridges and valleys, and plenty of dense forest alternating with vast clearings.

ROUTE DESCRIPTION: To begin, climb Burnt Mountain (route 5.7). Remove your skins at the summit and enjoy a run NE off the summit into the sprawling (and somewhat confusing) meadows of Tellurium Park.

Ski to the area just west of the point 10,690 (you can see this from the summit of Burnt Mountain) and then to the north end of the clearing where three pack trails come together. Ski through timber NW to the next meadow (use the trail-cut to avoid dense timber) and ski to the north end of this long clearing. For a good landmark use the "weird hole" in the middle of the meadow. Next, follow the pack trail N down into Slim Jim Gulch. Then take Slim Jim Gulch 1 ¼ miles down to the Burnt Mountain Road, where you follow the later part of 10th Mountain suggested route 5.2 up to the Harry Gates Hut. With adroit compass, altimeter, and map work you can take a shortcut directly to the Gates from the lower end of Slim Jim.

For a shorter return to the hut, use the pack trail (Choker Cutoff) that circles the northwest slope of Burnt Mountain between 10,000 and 10,300 feet elevation. Follow Choker Cutoff to the Burnt Mountain ascent route, then ski down to the hut. Finding this trail can be hard, but it's easy to follow once you locate it.

SAFETY NOTES: Use proper avalanche safety procedures while skiing into Slim Jim Gulch, and off the summit of Burnt Mountain.

SUMMER: The network of trails in the Tellurium Park area are great for hiking and horses. Because of the close proximity of the Holy Cross Wilderness, cyclists should use routes closer to Lime Park.

Chapter 6 • Peter Estin Hut

B uilt in 1985, the Peter
Estin Hut was the third
publicly funded hut added to
the 10th Mountain system.
Funds were donated by the
Estin family in memory of
Peter Estin. The hut is located
in a clearing on a timbered sad-

ELEVATION: 11,200 feet
COUNTY: Eagle
TEXT MAP: pp. 76-77, 104-105
10TH MTN MAP: Burnt Mt., N.Y. Mt.
USGS MAP: Crooked Creek Pass
TRAILHEADS: Sylvan Lake, Yeoman
Park

dle, just northwest of Charles Peak (12,050 feet), with a clear view of the
Elk and Williams mountains to the south. Centered in a vast forested area,
the hut provides access to myriad trails, dirt roads, and one alpine ridge.

If you have used other "standard" 10th Mountain huts, the Peter Estin will
look familiar. It stands two stories high with a commodious deck jutting
from the front door. Inside you'll find sun-powered electric lights, a gas
stove, wood heat, and berths for 16 travelers. Plenty of windows face the
south views.

In the past the Peter Estin Hut has been open in the summer. A call to
10th Mountain will get you the latest information concerning the current
summer policy. Summer is a terrific season for enjoying this hut. Cyclists
can use hundreds of miles of low-angled logging roads that surround the
hut, and there are plenty of options for hikers and equestrians.

Building the Peter Estin Hut began 10th Mountain's trend of building huts closer to timberline, with access to terrain that varies from forest walks to technical climbing. To that end, alpine access from the Estin Hut is available via the Charles Ridge (route 6.8). For powder skiers the face of Charles Ridge just above the hut is a fine playground with minimal avalanche danger. Terrain that's more radical is available outside the front door of the hut (see route 6.6). For ski-throughs use route 6.5 or 6.6 to the Harry Gates Hut, and route 6.2 or 6.3 to descend north into the Yeoman Park and Fulford area.

6.1

Sylvan Lake Trailhead – Peter Estin Hut via Crooked Creek Pass

DIFFICULTY: Intermediate
TIME: 11 hours up, 8 hours down
DISTANCE: 9 ½ miles
ELEVATION GAIN: 2,907 feet; loss: 265 feet

TEXT MAP: p. 76
10TH MTN MAP: Burnt Mountain
USGS MAP: Crooked Creek Pass

This 10th Mountain suggested route is a long trail that uses miles of popular snowmobile track. Thus, it might prove attractive after a new snow which could mean strenuous trailbreaking on a lesser used trail. For a shorter and less mechanized route to the hut use the Ironedge Trail (route 6.3).

Aerial view of the Peter Estin Hut from the southwest.

ROUTE DESCRIPTION: To begin, drive to the Sylvan Lake Trailhead. Start with cross country wax. From your parking place at snow closure, ski up the distinct snow-covered West Brush Creek road-cut (also called the Eagle Road) around the north and east sides of the lake, then up into the Brush Creek valley for 4 ¾ miles to Crooked Creek Pass. In detail: use your altimeter to identify the switchbacks at 9,220 feet and 9,260 feet, then the turn at 9,450 feet. After this turn, be extra careful to stay on the road as it climbs around a timbered ridge dividing Spine Creek from Brush Creek and then continues paralleling Brush Creek to Crooked Creek Pass (10,005 feet).

Now the real climbing begins (consider skins). Leave the West Brush Creek (Eagle) Road at the summit of the pass and turn NW (on the west side of an obvious fence) up a road-cut that climbs just over ¼ mile to a switchback, then SE to another switchback, then around the west shoulder of point 11,087. The road, still an obvious cut, follows a long traverse on the north side of point 11,087, then drops 260 vertical feet to a saddle near the head of Spine Creek (10,700 feet).

Stay on the road from the saddle for another ⅛ mile NE to the switchback as shown on the USGS Crooked Creek Pass map. Leave the road here and climb E ¼ mile and 90 vertical feet to the top of the ridge separating Spine Creek from Little Lime Creek. Here your route converges with the Lime Ridge Trail (route 5.5) and continues N up a well-marked route through aspen and conifer, then through a sparsely timbered logging area. Look for interesting tree inscriptions on the aspen trees along the trail.

Like many other huts, the Peter Estin is slightly hidden from the trail, and you can ski past it if you are not paying attention. To prevent this mistake, as you ski through the forest use your altimeter and map to identify the three-trail confluence that you hit at a broad saddle (Hat Creek Saddle) just west of the hut. Swing E at the saddle, and when you break through a grove of pines the hut will be in front of you. Sniffing for wood smoke can help too, but your compass is more reliable than your nose.

REVERSE ROUTE DESCRIPTION: Follow route 6.4 to Crooked Creek Pass, where you intersect the Eagle Road. Turn right (NW) onto the Eagle Road and follow it down the Brush Creek valley 4 ¾ miles to the Sylvan Lake Trailhead.

SAFETY NOTES: Take care with route-finding in Spine Creek, since the trail only uses the upper part of the drainage.

SUMMER: All these roads make fine equestrian, bicycle, and hiking routes.

6.2

Yeoman Park Trailhead — Peter Estin Hut via Hat Creek

DIFFICULTY: Intermediate
TIME: 8 hours up, 6 hours down
DISTANCE: 7 ½ miles
ELEVATION GAIN: 2,140 feet

TEXT MAP: p. 105
10TH MTN MAP: New York Mountain
USGS MAP: Crooked Creek Pass,
    Fulford

As an ascent route many skiers will find this 10th Mountain suggested route to be quite tedious, but it is a perfect descent for those with minimal ski skills. The steeper alternative is the Ironedge Trail (route 6.3).

ROUTE DESCRIPTION: To ski the Hat Creek route, begin at the Yeoman Park Trailhead. Start with cross country wax but keep your skins handy. From your parking spot, carefully identify the start of the Hat Creek Road. It begins just west of the actual campground and follows a distinct road-cut up a SE-climbing traverse. Follow the road to the first switchback and continue climbing NW through several more switchbacks. Stay on the road; at 9,400 feet you'll swing S into the Hat Creek drainage.

Once in Hat Creek, the route continues to be obvious and well marked. Basically, you stay on the main logging road as it parallels Hat Creek. The only deviation from the creek takes some switchbacks starting at 9,800 feet elevation. At a 10,820-foot saddle (Ironedge Saddle) at the head of the Hat Creek drainage, the logging road makes a turn to the south. Leave the road here, ski several hundred feet farther E, and intersect the continuation of the Ironedge Trail that 10th Mountain has marked. Climb this trail ¾ mile SE up through timber to the Peter Estin Hut. This section of trail is less obvious than the logging roads, so pay attention.

REVERSE ROUTE DESCRIPTION: For the reverse, ski fifty feet W of the hut, then N downhill through timber to the 10,820-foot saddle (Ironedge Saddle). Though this route is marked by 10th Mountain, the pull of cutting turns could lead you past the saddle and down the Ironedge Trail (route 6.3). This will be fine for good skiers, since "all roads lead to Rome." Intermediate skiers, however, should make an effort to stay in Hat Creek — the icy toboggan run downhills on the Ironedge require legs of iron and an edge of courage.

SAFETY NOTES: This is a very safe, mellow route. Beware of "blue diamond dependency," or you could end up in the Ironedge treatment center.

SUMMER: The Hat Creek Road is a fine bicycle, equestrian, and hiking route. Summer users should take the road all the way to Hat Creek Saddle

(see text map), as the 10th Mountain route up from Ironedge Saddle does
not follow a summer path—it is just a marked route through the forest.

6.3

Yeoman Park Trailhead—Peter Estin Hut via Ironedge Trail

DIFFICULTY: Intermediate/advanced   **TEXT MAP:** p. 105
TIME: 6 hours up, 4 hours down   **10TH MTN MAP:** New York Mountain
DISTANCE: 4 1/2 miles   **USGS MAP:** Crooked Creek Pass,
ELEVATION GAIN: 2,140 feet   Fulford

This 10th Mountain suggested route follows a fine single track trail that is
closed to snowmobiles. It is an efficient ascent route, but can be a hairy
downhill. Those with minimal turn skill should consider descending Hat
Creek (route 6.2).

ROUTE DESCRIPTION: From the Yeoman Park Trailhead at the
campground ski (or walk depending on snow cover) N back across the
bridge over East Brush Creek, then turn right (E) onto the East Brush
Creek Road. The first part of this route uses the snow-covered East Brush
Creek (Eagle) Road for 1 1/2 miles to road's end at Fulford Cave
Campground. As you ski up the road, you'll pass two left turns onto other
10th Mountain suggested trails: the Fulford Road (route 7.1) at just under
1/2 mile and the Newcomer Spring Trail (route 7.2) after another 3/4 mile at
9,280 feet. Be sure not to turn onto these trails.

At Fulford Cave Campground swing around the east end of a small lake,
then angle back W for a few hundred feet to a distinct trail-cut that heads
through private property. Stay on the trail as it leads past several buildings
and begins to climb—and climb. The switchbacks start at 9,560 feet, and
they keep you breathing hard to the Ironedge Saddle at 10,820 feet.

Take care at Ironedge Saddle to identify the marked 10th Mountain suggested route that leads SE then S up through timber to the Peter Estin
Hut. If you get confused here you could easily end up skiing on the Hat
Creek Road up to Hat Creek Saddle (see text map). If this happens, just
ski E to the hut from Hat Creek Saddle. To prevent confusion, use your
compass at Ironedge Saddle.

REVERSE ROUTE DESCRIPTION: To descend the Ironedge Trail, ski a few
hundred feet W of the Peter Estin Hut, then take care to turn N onto the
10th Mountain suggested route down through timber to the Ironedge Saddle. Some map work in the hut will help you get a good start. From the
Ironedge Saddle ski the fall line for a short distance to a dropping traverse
to the left. This traverse leads to the famous Ironedge switchbacks. Ski

down the switchbacks and reverse the route above to the Yeoman Park Trailhead.

SAFETY NOTES: This route has no slide danger. Ski in control.

SUMMER: The Ironedge Trail is a good horse and hiking route. Expert mountain bike riders love it as a descent route, but find it an impossible ascent. Cyclists should use Hat Creek to gain their vertical. A good loop goes up Hat Creek then down the Ironedge.

Old tree writing on route 6.2, circa 1948.

6.4

Peter Estin Hut to Harry Gates Hut via Crooked Creek Pass

DIFFICULTY: Intermediate **TEXT MAP:** pp. 76-77
TIME: 7 hours **10TH MTN MAP:** Burnt Mountain
DISTANCE: 9 ½ miles **USGS MAP:** Crooked Creek Pass
ELEVATION GAIN: 775 feet; loss: 2,275 feet

This 10th Mountain suggested route wanders, but it is an excellent choice if you prefer mellow downhills. Leave your skins in your pack and use cross country wax.

ROUTE DESCRIPTION: Get out your map and compass while you're still in the hut, review this route, and remember to calibrate your altimeter. From the front steps of the Peter Estin Hut ski W about 600 feet to Hat Creek Saddle. From Hat Creek Saddle travel S down through a sparsely timbered logging area, then through dense conifer and aspen. At 10,850 feet take a crucial right (W) turn into the Spine Creek drainage and drop 90 vertical feet to the Spine Creek logging road (10,760 feet) at the head of the Spine Creek drainage.

Take care here as the route follows the logging road which, instead of descending the drainage, takes a climbing traverse W along the south side of the drainage. The climb takes you ¾ mile to 10,965 feet where the road begins to drop, then takes an obvious left (S) turn, and drops via two switchbacks to Crooked Creek Pass. From here follow route 5.3 to the Harry Gates Hut.

SAFETY NOTES: Take care with route-finding so that you drop into Spine Creek. Be sure to find the logging road out of Spine Creek, since an inadvertent descent of Spine Creek will place you far down the Brush Creek Road on the wrong side of Crooked Creek Pass.

SUMMER: Hikers, bikers, and horseback riders can use this route. At the head of Spine Creek deviate from the 10th Mountain suggested route and use the logging road and trail as marked on the USGS Crooked Creek Pass map.

6.5

Peter Estin Hut to Harry Gates Hut via Lime Ridge Trail

DIFFICULTY: Intermediate	**TEXT MAP:** pp. 76-77
TIME: 6 hours	**10TH MTN MAP:** Burnt Mountain
DISTANCE: 7 miles	**USGS MAP:** Crooked Creek Pass
ELEVATION GAIN: 630 feet; loss: 2,130 feet	

This is certainly the most efficient 10th Mountain suggested route between the Peter Estin Hut and Harry Gates Hut. It has some fast downhill sections, so be sure you can push a strong snowplow. The first half of the route descends the ridge separating Little Lime Creek from Middle Creek. Keep this in mind while navigating.

ROUTE DESCRIPTION: While still inside the hut, enjoy a cup of tea while you do a map check and set your altimeter. Keep your skins in your pack. From the front steps of the Peter Estin Hut ski W about 600 feet to Hat Creek Saddle. From Hat Creek Saddle travel S down through a sparsely timbered logging area, past the right turn (route 6.4) into Spine Creek, and into the trees on the east side of the ridge (10,845 feet). Continue down the ridge and around one switchback to a flat area at 10,200 feet. Just below the switchback examine old inscriptions on the mature aspen trees.

From the flat area continue S ¼ mile down the ridge, through the dense evergreens of Sherwood Forest, and to the meadows at 10,150 feet. Ski the marked trail as it uses intermittent clearings to descend the ridge crest down to the end of the ridge. Here, instead of dropping off the steep end of the ridge, the trail switchbacks left (N) and takes a descending traverse ¼ mile to cross Little Lime Creek at 9,700 feet.

Ski ½ mile down the east side of Little Lime Creek, cross the east fork of Little Lime Creek, then begin a gradual climb S then W for 1 mile to an indistinct jeep trail on top of the ridge. Descend this jeep trail ¾ mile SW along the ridge crest, then drop S into Lime Park and continue S across Lime Park to the bridge crossing Lime Creek at 9,190 feet. The route across Lime Park follows dirt roads. These are usually obscured by the snow cover, but the junctions are well signed and several fence breaks show where the road goes.

Lime Park can be a sublime place for ski touring, with Avalanche Peak looming to the east, and the sculpted snowscape of the park. But the place is so vast that navigating in poor visibility can be a nightmare. The danger is that you'll miss the crossing of Lime Creek and descend into Lime Creek Canyon, a narrow trap. You must find the bridge crossing Lime Creek at 9,190 feet, and the only way to do that in a whiteout is with compass and altimeter, and perhaps the occasional blue diamond.

From the bridge over Lime Creek follow the snow-covered Burnt Mountain Road as it climbs E than S up to a band of timber, then breaks out into another open area at Slim Jim Gulch. Stay on the road and continue S ¾ mile to 9,566 feet on the Burnt Mountain Road. Leave the road here. Take a left (E) turn and climb a hill ¼ mile NE to the Harry Gates Hut. You can't see the hut when you turn from the road—it comes into sight when you're about halfway up the hill. This climb is too short to warrant skins, but you may have to use a few herringbone steps.

SAFETY NOTES: Ski in control on the downhills. Pay attention to route-finding in Lime Park. Be courteous to snowmobiles in Lime Park and they will return in-kind.

SUMMER: The Lime Ridge portion of this route is only a marked route with no tread. Thus, hikers and equestrians should consider the pack trail in the Little Lime Creek drainage (see route 6.6). The roads in Lime Park are fine for all activities.

6.6

Peter Estin Hut to Harry Gates Hut via Lime Drainage Trail

DIFFICULTY: Advanced
TIME: 5 ½ hours
DISTANCE: 6 ¼ miles
ELEVATION GAIN: 630 feet; loss: 2,130 feet

TEXT MAP: pp. 76-77
10TH MTN MAP: Burnt Mountain
USGS MAP: Crooked Creek Pass

This alternate route hits some good downhill skiing and cuts ¾ mile off the Lime Ridge Trail (route 6.5). Because it is unmarked and has a a small amount of potential slide danger, only advanced skiers should use this route.

Since you are going cold turkey from "blue diamond dependency," you should be extra sure to carry—and know how to use—your map, compass, and altimeter.

ROUTE DESCRIPTION: The best way to begin is by making turns down the bowl that starts just a few feet south of the hut. There can be avalanche danger here, so determine the conditions before you jump in, and use proper procedure while skiing.

To get the best ski line, stay a bit west of the bowl proper and ski a small ridge S to an opening in the creek bottom (10,560 feet). From here you can contour SE to the large open slope east of the creek. Work this slope, then traverse S to another smaller bowl. At 10,000 feet cross the creek and descend the west side of the creek to 9,850 feet, then intersect route 6.5 at the crossing of Little Lime Creek. Follow route 6.5 to the Harry Gates Hut.

SAFETY NOTES: For this route you should be skilled in avalanche hazard guesswork, navigation, and downhill skiing. Slide danger can be avoided by skiing through the trees on either side of the open areas.

SUMMER: Hikers and horses can use the pack trail that follows Little Lime Creek. Cyclists will find better riding on the dirt roads in the area.

6.7

Peter Estin Hut to Polar Star Inn

DIFFICULTY: Intermediate   **TEXT MAP:** pp. 104-105
TIME: 9 hours (Ironedge Trail)   **10TH MTN MAP:** New York Mountain
DISTANCE: 8 ¼ miles (Ironedge)   **USGS MAP:** Crooked Creek Pass,
ELEVATION GAIN: 1,900 feet; loss: 2,060 feet   Fulford

Since the routes from the Peter Estin Hut to the Polar Star Inn pass through or close to the Yeoman Park Trailhead, they are detailed in other route descriptions and only referenced here.

ROUTE DESCRIPTION: To travel from the Peter Estin Hut to the Polar Star Inn you can pick from several routes down into the East Brush Creek drainage, and several that climb out of the drainage, then head N to the Inn. The most direct route down from the Peter Estin Hut is the Ironedge Trail (route 6.3). Skiers with minimal downhill skills should consider using Hat Creek (route 6.2). Hat Creek adds about 4 miles to the trip.

You have two choices for the climb up from East Brush Creek to the Polar Star Inn. If you're coming from Hat Creek, use the Fulford Road route (7.1). If you skied the Ironedge Trail, ascend the Newcomer Spring route (7.2). Remember that whatever your route, this is a long trip; start early. For safety and summer notes see the routes referenced above.

6.8

Charles Peak and Fools Peak from the Peter Estin Hut

DIFFICULTY: Intermediate/expert   **TEXT MAP:** pp. 76, 105
TIME: Several hours to a full day **10TH MTN MAP:** N. Y. Mt., Burnt Mt.
DISTANCE: Charles Peak, 1 ½ mi. **USGS MAP:** Crooked Creek Pass,
          Fools Peak, 6 ¼ miles   Mt. Jackson

ELEVATION GAIN: Charles Peak, 900 feet; Fools Peak, 2,750 feet

If you want a branch route that climbs to alpine terrain from the Peter Estin Hut, you only have one choice — the Charles Ridge. Beginning at Charles Peak east of the Estin Hut and extending 4 miles to Eagle Peak, this ridge probes the Holy Cross Mountains where 14,005-foot Mount of the Holy Cross lords over scores of 12,000- and 13,000-foot peaks. In winter conditions intermediate skiers should venture no farther than Charles Peak. Here you'll find good skiing from the summit back towards the hut, and a worthy view. Advanced skiers can climb Fools Peak, and expert mountaineers can attempt a long ridge-run to Eagle Peak.

Skiing Charles Peak; Lime Park in the background.

ROUTE DESCRIPTION: To reach the summit of Charles Peak climb NE from the Peter Estin Hut into a clearing where you'll usually find some exuberant ski tracks — and skiers. Climb the clearing to the ridge, then follow the ridge SE to the summit. For your descent you can stick to the ridge, then ski the clearing or ski the open area west of the summit down to treeline, then traverse to the aforementioned clearing.

The summit of Fools Peak is a worthy goal, but the trip requires advanced skill in all aspects of winter mountaineering. Parties on this climb should carry avalanche rescue beacons. The route follows the Charles Ridge to the 12,100-foot saddle just west of the Fools Peak summit. From the saddle you cut a short traverse, then climb the west face to the summit, sticking to the ridge to your left (as much as you can) to lessen avalanche exposure. Return via the same route.

SAFETY NOTES: There is a great deal of slide terrain on the sides of Charles Ridge. While on the ridge it may take a bit of extra effort to stay off these slopes, especially while negotiating point 11,905. Remember that you are traveling above timberline in alpine conditions different than those you deal with down in the woods. Carry full bivouac gear and ski conservatively.

SUMMER: Charles Ridge is a wonderful alpine hike. You should have mountaineering skills to wander beyond Fools Peak.

Chapter 7 • Polar Star Inn

The Polar Star Inn is a privately owned back-country lodge located on 10th Mountain suggested routes, just below timberline on the west side of New York Mountain. The Inn, which sleeps 17, is booked by 10th Mountain.

ELEVATION: 11,040 feet
COUNTY: Eagle
TEXT MAP: pp. 104-105
10TH MTN MAP: New York Mountain
USGS MAP: Fulford
TRAILHEADS: Yeoman Park, West Lake Creek

The Polar Star Inn is a tall-standing structure with a big deck that looks west over the Colorado Plateau — a sunset watcher's paradise. There are 5 private bedrooms and running water that makes kitchen work a snap. The Polar Star has no showers, but you can get clean in the wood-heated sauna. The toilet is the traditional outhouse. The Inn was built in 1987.

Open year round, the Polar Star Inn provides all-season access to a huge area of National Forest, including the Holy Cross Wilderness. Outside the wilderness you'll find superb mountain bike riding on jeep trails and unimproved roads. One popular bike trail is the old Fulford Road that descends from the west end of Fulford down to East Brush Creek. Other good rides follow the jeep trail from Dubach Meadows out into the Bumpity Park area. If you're fit you can ride from Bumpity Park to Eagle. Hikers and equestrians can also find options in all directions.

Skiers can take their pick of trails to and from the Inn, as well as several fine branch routes. For starters, you'll find superb tree skiing just out the

door of the hut. For advanced skiers, a short easterly climb leads above timberline to the west slopes of New York Mountain (route 7.5). From there take your choice of bowls and steep gullies. Intermediate backcountry skiers can also climb New York Mountain, then use a low-angled route for descent.

If you plan a ski-through to the north from the Polar Star, be aware that you'll have to use a car shuttle to get from the West Lake Creek Trailhead to the nearest 10th Mountain suggested routes.

7.1

Yeoman Park Trailhead — Polar Star Inn via Fulford Road

DIFFICULTY: Intermediate   **TEXT MAP:** pp. 104-105
TIME: 5 hours up, 3 1/4 hours down   **10TH MTN MAP:** New York Mountain
DISTANCE: 6 1/4 miles   **USGS MAP:** Fulford
ELEVATION GAIN: 2,080 feet; loss: 100 feet

This 10th Mountain suggested route follows distinct road-cuts and well-marked trails. It is heavily traveled by snowmobiles and skiers. Thus, the foot-travel-only Newcomer Spring route (7.2) might be a more attractive alternative for skiers.

ROUTE DESCRIPTION: From parking at Yeoman Park Trailhead (probably at Yeoman Park Campground) ski or walk (depending on snow cover) back N across the bridge and turn right onto the East Brush Creek Road. Follow the obvious road-cut up the valley for just under 1/2 mile and make a hard left turn onto the well-signed Fulford Road. Follow the Fulford Road as it climbs NW then N around a shoulder, then winds up through superb forest via several switchbacks to McGinley Gulch. Stay on the road from McGinley Gulch as it climbs NW 1/4 mile, then turns N around another shoulder, then drops 3/4 mile and 100 vertical feet to cross Nolan Creek (10,060 feet) just E of the small group of buildings known as Fulford.

Just after you cross the bridge over Nolan Creek, turn right on another snow-covered road leading towards Upper Town and ski 1/8 mile to a left (N) turn onto a marked 10th Mountain trail. If you had your nose to the grindstone on the roads to this point, look up. This section does not follow a snow-covered road, so it requires more attention. Climb 1 mile up 5 switchbacks to the New York Mountain jeep trail (10,520 feet). Take a right on the snow-covered jeep trail and follow it as it climbs 1/2 mile to 10,830 feet. Leave the jeep trail here and continue NE on a 10th Mountain marked trail 1/2 mile to the Polar Star Inn.

REVERSE ROUTE DESCRIPTION: From the front of the Polar Star Inn, carefully locate the 10th Mountain marked trail leading SW down the mountain in a dropping traverse. At 1/2 mile (10,830 feet) the trail intersects the New York Mountain jeep trail. Ski down the jeep trail 1/2 mile (to 10,520 feet) and turn S off the jeep trail. If you want the quickest downhill, take care not to miss this turn.

After you turn off the jeep trail, ski 5 fast switchbacks (experts can cut

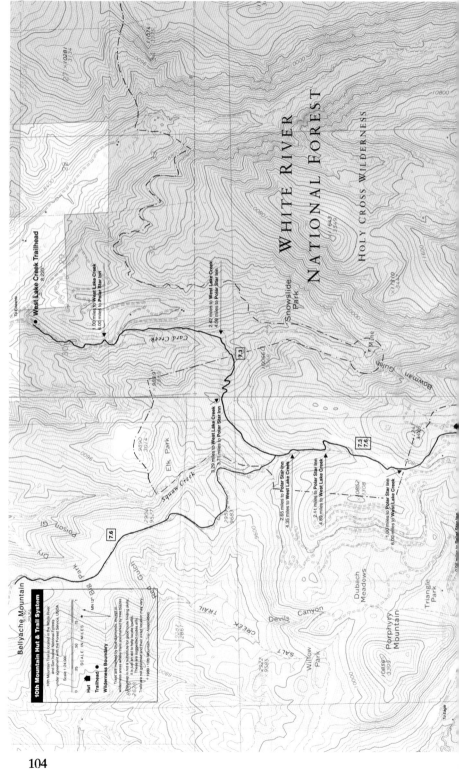

Bellyache Mountain

10th Mountain Hut & Trail System

10th Mountain Trails located in the White River
and San Isabel National Forests
"under agreement with the Forest Service, USDA"

Scale 1:24,000

SCALE IN MILES
0   .25   .50   .75   1

MN 12°

Hut ■
Trailhead ●
Wilderness Boundary

Trails are marked by blue diamonds, except in
wilderness areas where trails are marked by tree blazes.

This map is not a substitute for good route finding skills.
It is still an aid to help locate huts.
These maps suggest, but do not delineate, trails.
Trailhead not delineated and their exact location may vary.

© 1989 • 10th Mountain Trail Association

West Lake Creek Trailhead
8,220

1.00 miles to West Lake Creek
6.00 miles to Polar Star Inn

2.42 miles to West Lake Creek
4.58 miles to Polar Star Inn

3.29 miles to West Lake Creek
3.71 miles to Polar Star Inn

2.65 miles to Polar Star Inn
4.35 miles to West Lake Creek

2.11 miles to Polar Star Inn
4.89 miles to West Lake Creek

1.00 miles to Polar Star Inn
6.00 miles to West Lake Creek

WHITE RIVER
NATIONAL FOREST

HOLY CROSS WILDERNESS

Snowslide
Park

Elk Park

Squaw Creek

Card Creek

Dry Park

Poison Gr.

Big Park

Bowman Gulch

Dubach
Meadows

Devils Canyon

Willow
Park

Porphyry
Mountain

Triangle
Park

SALT CREEK TRAIL

7.3

7.6

7.3
7.6

To Edwards

To Eagle

104

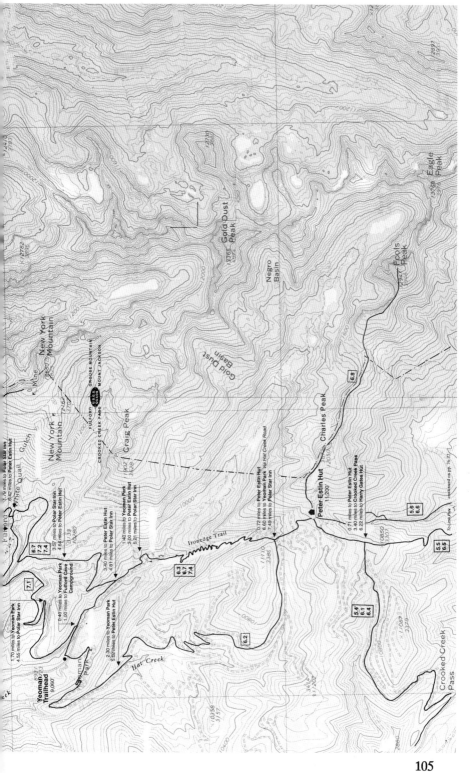

Eagle Peak

Gold Dust Peak

Fools Peak

Negro Basin

Gold Dust Basin

New York Mountain

New York Mountain

Mine

White Quail Gulch

Fulford

FULFORD
CRAIG PEAK

GROUSE MOUNTAIN

MOUNT JACKSON

CROOKED CREEK PASS

Craig Peak

Charles Peak

5.8

Peter-Estin Hut
11,200'

0.71 miles to Peter Estin Hut
3.40 miles to Crooked Creek Pass
6.22 miles to Harry Gates Hut

0.72 miles to Peter Estin Hut
6.60 miles to Yeoman Park via Fall Creek Road
7.49 miles to Polar Star Inn

5.6
6.6

5.5
6.5

5.4
6.1
6.4

Ironedge Trail

3.40 miles to Peter Estin Hut
4.81 miles to Polar Star Inn

1.40 miles to Yeoman Park
3.00 miles to Peter Estin Hut
5.31 miles to Polar Star Inn

6.3
6.7
7.4

6.2

3.57 miles to Polar Star Inn
4.64 miles to Peter Estin Hut

6.7
7.2
7.4

0.40 miles to Yeoman Park
1.00 miles to Fulford Cave
Campground

7.1

1.70 miles to Yeoman Park
4.55 miles to Polar Star Inn

3.70 miles to Polar Star Inn
6.62 miles to Peter Estin Hut

Yeoman Park
Trailhead
9,060'

2.30 miles to Yeoman Park
5.00 miles to Peter Estin Hut

Hat Creek

Crooked Creek Pass

continued on pp. 76-77

To Lime Park

105

some of these) down to Upper Town, then W ⅛ mile down a snow-covered road to intersect the Fulford Road. Turn left (SW) onto the Fulford Road and ski the distinct, snow-covered Fulford Road 4 ⅛ miles to the Yeoman Park Trailhead.

For an easier downhill stay on the jeep trail and follow it to the Fulford Road, which you then ski SE to intersect the 10th Mountain suggested route near Fulford.

SAFETY NOTES: There is no avalanche danger on this route. Take care while tree skiing down to Upper Town.

SUMMER: The roads on this route make for fine mountain biking. To reach the Polar Star Inn by bicycle or car, simply stay on the Fulford Road past Fulford. You can either stay on the Fulford Road as it traverses through Triangle Creek then swings around and climbs New York Mountain, or you can use the New York Mountain jeep trail. Both routes are well rendered on the USGS Fulford map. There may be no sign at the turnoff from the main road to the Polar Star Inn. The turnoff is usually closed with a cable gate.

7.2

Yeoman Park Trailhead — Polar Star Inn via Newcomer Spring

DIFFICULTY: Intermediate
TIME: 4 ¾ hours up, 3 hours down
DISTANCE: 6 miles
ELEVATION GAIN: 2,140 feet; loss: 160 feet

TEXT MAP: pp. 104-105
10TH MTN MAP: New York Mountain
USGS MAP: Crooked Creek Pass, Fulford

Pick this 10th Mountain suggested route for a more serene wilderness experience. It avoids snowmobile trails and climbs more efficiently than other routes which stick to the roads. This trail is slightly harder to find than route 7.1.

ROUTE DESCRIPTION: From the Yeoman Park Trailhead ski or walk (depending on snow cover) back N across the bridge from the campground and turn right onto the East Brush Creek Road on the north side of the valley. Ski the Brush Creek Road upvalley. At just under ½ mile, while still in Yeoman Park, you'll come to the distinct switchback left (NW) onto the Fulford Road. Do not make this turn. Instead, continue another ¾ mile to 9,280 feet. At this point look carefully to your left for a 10th Mountain marked trail which leaves the road. Turn left onto the trail (put your skins on) and follow it as it climbs a few hundred feet E (paralleling the road below), then switchbacks left (NW).

Stay on the trail as it makes a climbing traverse to 9,520 feet, switchbacks right, and climbs to 10,000 feet. The trail eases off here, gradually climbs N, makes a long contour around a shoulder, then drops about 80 vertical feet to Nolan Creek at 10,180 feet. Cross Nolan Creek, then follow the trail N as it winds ¾ mile to Upper Town (10,060 feet), where you take the right (N) turn onto the 10th Mountain marked route. See route 7.1 for the remainder of the route from Upper Town to the Polar Star Inn.

REVERSE ROUTE DESCRIPTION: To reverse the route, follow 7.1 to Upper Town. Take care in Upper Town to turn left (E) off 7.1 onto a well-marked 10th Mountain trail that leads several hundred feet, crosses White Quail Gulch, then turns south and leads you across Nolan Creek. From here stay on the trail as it winds through beautiful forest, then drops down several switchbacks into East Brush Creek. Here the main road leads right (W) down the valley to the Yeoman Park Trailhead, or up the valley to the Ironedge Trail (see route 6.3).

SAFETY NOTES: There is no slide danger on this route. Don't tangle with any aspens on the downhills and watch your feet at the stream crossings.

SUMMER: Hikers and horse people should check this one out. Cyclists should use the roads in route 7.1.

7.3

West Lake Creek Trailhead — Polar Star Inn

DIFFICULTY: Intermediate   **TEXT MAP:** p. 104
TIME: 8 ½ hours up, 6 hours down   **10TH MTN MAP:** New York Mountain
DISTANCE: 7 miles   **USGS MAP:** Grouse Mountain, Fulford
ELEVATION GAIN: 3,000 feet; loss: 180 feet

This fine wilderness ski tour is a 10th Mountain suggested route. Remember that a large chunk of the trail is in designated wilderness and thus marked with tree blazes instead of the ubiquitous blue diamonds.

ROUTE DESCRIPTION: The first portion of this trip makes several critical turns. From the West Lake Creek Trailhead ski a snow-covered road up the east side of Card Creek. Stay on the road as it crosses Card Creek at ¼ mile, then follows the west side of Card Creek another ¾ mile to another crossing (8,560 feet). Just past this crossing it is critical to swing back right (SW) to stay in the Card Creek drainage. From here the snow-covered jeep trail climbs the east side of the drainage for 1 ¼ miles to another critical junction at 9,370 feet.

Here you turn right (SW) off the jeep trail onto the Card Creek Springs foot trail. Follow this trail S then W past Card Creek Springs (not that obvious), then up 500 vertical feet via 4 switchbacks to Card Creek Saddle (9,980 feet). From the saddle follow the 10th Mountain marked trail as it drops along the New England Traverse W then NW into the Squaw Creek drainage to 9,800 feet. Stay on the trail as it takes a gradually climbing traverse ½ mile, crosses Squaw Creek, then follows the Squaw Creek drainage (crosses creek several more times) up to nondescript Squaw Creek Saddle (wilderness boundary) at the head of the drainage (10,620 feet). The trail passes slightly to the east of the low point in the saddle. From Squaw Creek Saddle follow the 10th Mountain marked trail one more mile SE to the Polar Star Inn. In stormy weather visibility may be poor above the saddle, so take the time for a compass and altimeter reading near the saddle.

REVERSE ROUTE DESCRIPTION: The reverse of this route is a little easier because once you're at Card Creek Saddle, Card Creek leads you down to the West Lake Creek Trailhead, even if you lose the trail markers. The main thing to remember is that this trip uses two drainages and that you must switch at the proper point. To do so, take care to reach Squaw Creek Saddle from the Polar Star Inn (use your compass). Drop N from Squaw

Creek Saddle down Squaw Creek to 9,840 feet. Turn NW then E here, drop a bit more, then take a climbing traverse to Card Creek Saddle.

SAFETY NOTES: This trip is basically a walk through the forest, so it has no slide danger. Since it does switch drainages, take care with route-finding to hedge against the dire consequences of trail marker addiction.

SUMMER: This route makes a fine hike and horseback ride. If you like mountain biking, you'll find some good riding up to the wilderness boundary from the West Lake Creek Trailhead, but remember that even possessing a bicycle in the wilderness is a heinous crime (unless your bike is disguised as a horse).

7.4

Polar Star Inn to Peter Estin Hut via Ironedge Trail

DIFFICULTY: Intermediate	**TEXT MAP:** pp. 104-105
TIME: 9 hours	**10TH MTN MAP:** New York Mountain
DISTANCE: 8 ¼ miles	**USGS MAP:** Crooked Creek Pass,
ELEVATION GAIN: 1,920 feet; loss: 1760 feet	Fulford

This is the only efficient ski route from the Polar Star Inn to the Peter Estin Hut. Even so, it is a long trail which requires many navigation decisions. The route is described in detail under the referenced routes.

ROUTE DESCRIPTION: First, pick a route from the Polar Star Inn down into the East Brush Creek drainage. The Newcomer Spring route (reverse route 7.2) is the most direct. Once on the snow-covered East Brush Creek Road, use the Ironedge Trail (route 6.3) to ascend to the Peter Estin Hut.

SAFETY NOTES: Get an early start for this long route. See referenced routes for other safety suggestions.

SUMMER: To descend from the Polar Star Inn to the East Brush Creek drainage, cyclists should use the dirt roads via Fulford. Hikers and equestrians can use any number of trails, including the Newcomer Spring route (7.2). The Ironedge Trail is a good uphill horse and hiking route, but too steep for bicycle travel. Cyclists should use the Hat Creek Road (route 6.2) to ascend to the Peter Estin Hut.

7.5

New York Mountain from Polar Star Inn

DIFFICULTY: Int./Advanced
TIME: Half day to full day
DISTANCE: 2 miles round trip
ELEVATION GAIN: 1,380 feet round trip

TEXT MAP: pp. 104-105
10TH MTN MAP: New York Mountain
USGS MAP: Fulford, Grouse Mountain

This popular summit climb gives you some honest mountain skiing and good views. Downhillers will like the turn options, but this terrain is above timberline, so be ready for dreaded trap crust.

ROUTE DESCRIPTION: The route is simple. Put your skins on at the Polar Star Inn, climb SE to timberline, then choose a route that intersects New York Mountain's north ridge. Follow the ridge to the summit. You'll want climbing skins for this route, and you'll probably end up walking up windscoured areas. Possible downhill skiing varies with snow cover. In general, try the west face (open areas drop down into the trees) or the upper part of White Quail Gulch.

SAFETY NOTES: Suddenly, this route takes you into alpine regions above timberline — a different environment than the forest below. Visibility can deteriorate rapidly and snow conditions can make downhill skiing all but impossible. There is steep avalanche terrain on the east side of the north and south summit ridges, as well as slide potential in upper White Quail Gulch. Also, given a load of extremely unstable snow, any of the slopes on New York Mountain could avalanche. Beware of cornices on all ridges.

SUMMER: This summit is a fine goal for a hike. The trail is too steep and rocky for bicycles and horses.

7.6

Bellyache Mountain from Polar Star Inn

DIFFICULTY: Advanced
TIME: 12 hours or overnight
DISTANCE: 14 miles round trip
ELEVATION GAIN: 1,500 feet round trip

TEXT MAP: p. 104
10TH MTN MAP: New York Mountain
USGS MAP: Fulford

If you have less interest in downhill turns and a strong desire to cover the country, consider this trip. It is seldom skied, long, and intricate, but covers some pleasing terrain. If it sounds too long, remember that the return uses the same route, so just plan a closer destination.

ROUTE DESCRIPTION: To begin, ski from the Polar Star on the marked 10th Mountain suggested route down Squaw Creek (reverse route 7.3). Use your map and altimeter; at 9,840 feet in Squaw Creek leave the 10th Mountain route and continue down the west side of Squaw Creek to a gulch at 9,700 feet. Follow a road-cut as it contours through the gulch, then gradually climbs and contours N then W around a shoulder, then drops 140 vertical feet into a saddle (9,590 feet) on Bellyache Ridge.

Bellyache Ridge is a broad, timbered, flat-topped ridge with lots of parks and good views. Using your map, compass, and altimeter, stick to the general route of the road marked on the USGS Fulford map. It gradually descends through timber and clearings to Big Park, then climbs 120 vertical feet back up into the large parks on top of Bellyache Mountain. This is a good final goal for the trip, as the trail past here loses altitude rapidly and would add too much time to your return. To reverse the route, follow your tracks back to the Polar Star Inn. Allow time for the climb back up Squaw Creek.

SAFETY NOTES: There is one critical consideration for success on this route — navigation. Be sure your party includes at least one expert orienteer. Since the route is so long, don't skimp on emergency bivouac gear.

SUMMER: The road on Bellyache Mountain provides terrific cycling, but getting there can be a formidable challenge. The problem is that the connecting route from the Polar Star — the Squaw Creek Trail — is in designated wilderness and thus closed to bicycles. Instead, you have to follow the roads on Logged Off Mountain as far north as you can, then staying just west of the wilderness boundary, shoulder your bike and bushwhack down to the Bellyache Mountain Road. Since the bushwhack would be an uphill grunt on your return, you should consider riding all the way to Eagle or Edwards (be sure to carry the Seven Hermits and Wolcott USGS maps if you take that option).

Chapter 8 • Shrine Mountain Inn

Whithe still located far enough from paved roads to keep a backcountry mood, the Shrine Mountain Inn is the easiest 10th Mountain "ski in" accommodation to access, being just 2 1/3 miles from Vail Pass Trailhead. The Inn consists of two privately

ELEVATION: 11,209 feet
COUNTY: Eagle
TEXT MAP: pp. 114-115
10TH MTN MAP: Resolution Mountain
USGS MAP: Vail Pass
TRAILHEADS: Vail Pass, Vail Trailhead for Commando Run, Red Cliff

owned cabins that sleep a total of 18 people. Most amenities are available: kitchen, hot and cold running water, showers, lights, and sauna. You bring your own sleeping bag or rent bedding and a towel. Catered meals are available if arranged in advance. The Inn is booked through 10th Mountain.

The Shrine Mountain Inn is open all year. During the summer the Inn is surrounded by fine cycling, horseback riding, and hiking. The Shrine Pass dirt road (see route 8.3) is a popular bicycle cruise and a nice auto tour as well. Cyclists, hikers, and equestrians who want less auto dust can follow the Commando Run (route 8.2) to Vail. This is also a popular ski route in either direction.

WARREN OHLRICH

For ski-throughs, use Shrine Mountain Ridge (route 8.4) for the fastest route to the Fowler/Hilliard Hut, or Shrine Pass (route 8.3) to get to Red Cliff. If you want to stay for a few nights and ski, cut some turns in the Black Lake Glades (route 8.7), or take a scenic tour up Shrine Mountain (route 8.4). For regional skiing you can connect with Copper Mountain Resort by using a ski trail that parallels I- 70, or ski to Janet's Cabin (route 8.6). You can book lodging in Red Cliff through 10th Mountain.

8.1

Vail Pass Trailhead — Shrine Mountain Inn

DIFFICULTY: Novice   **TEXT MAP:** p. 115
TIME: 2 hours up, 1 hour down   **10TH MTN MAP:** Resolution Mountain
DISTANCE: 2 ¾ miles   **USGS MAP:** Vail Pass
ELEVATION GAIN: 696 feet; loss: 67 feet

This is the shortest trailhead to hut route in the 10th Mountain system. Heavy use of the trail by snowmobiles and skiers is a mixed blessing, as the route is almost always packed out but there can be hundreds of trails leading in all directions. Even though it looks simple, make a few map checks just to be sure of your route. This is a 10th Mountain suggested route.

ROUTE DESCRIPTION: From the Vail Pass Trailhead ski SW on the snow-covered Shrine Pass Road. At ⅛ mile swing N on a switchback, ski ¼ mile to another switchback (10,720 feet), then ski SW and W as the road parallels West Tenmile Creek while climbing up the ridge that forms the north side of the drainage. After a long ⅞-mile climbing traverse, the road leads to an 11,156-foot saddle on the ridge. This has been mistaken by many to be Shrine Pass, as it is a pass of sorts. Enjoy the view at the saddle (you can see Shrine Mountain Inn from here if you look carefully), but take care to follow the snow-covered Shrine Pass Road as it stays on the south side of the ridge and gradually drops ¾ mile NW to the real Shrine Pass. Shrine Pass is named for its views of Mount of the Holy Cross which rises to the west. Holy Cross is famed for several snowfields on the north face that sometimes look like a Christian cross.

The pass looks more like a large park than the classic "pass summit." Nevertheless, it is the divide between the Turkey Creek and West Tenmile Creek drainages. On Shrine Pass take care not to ski too far NW. Look for a White River National Forest sign. Ski W from this sign several hundred yards across a clear area and enter a conifer forest at a red stock gate. Follow an obvious road-cut through the forest ¼ mile S to the Shrine Mountain Inn. Use your map, compass, and altimeter for insurance. The large inn is visible from several hundred feet down the road.

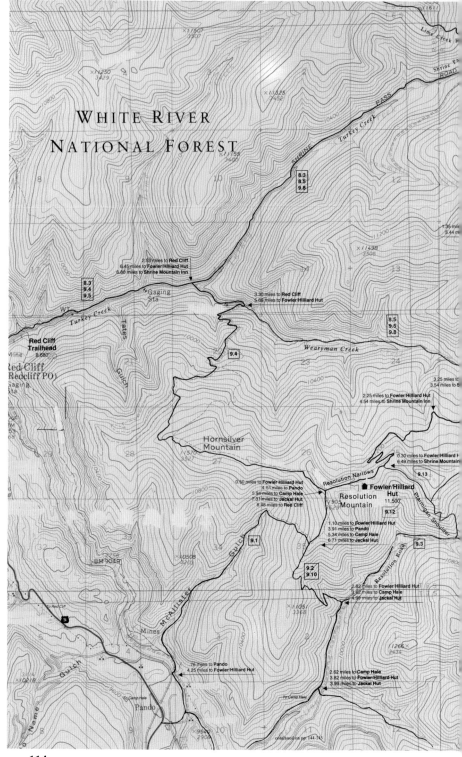

WHITE RIVER
NATIONAL FOREST

2.53 miles to **Red Cliff**
6.45 miles to **Fowler/Hilliard Hut**
6.60 miles to **Shrine Mountain Inn**

3.30 miles to **Red Cliff**
5.68 miles to **Fowler/Hilliard Hut**

8.3
9.4
9.5

Gaging
Sta

Turkey Creek

Wearyman Creek

**Red Cliff
Trailhead**
8,680'

8.5
9.5
9.8

Red Cliff
(Redcliff PO)
aging
Sta

9.4

3.25 miles to
3.54 miles to S

2.25 miles to **Fowler/Hilliard Hut**
4.54 miles to **Shrine Mountain Inn**

Hornsilver
Mountain

6.30 miles to **Fowler/Hilliard H**
6.49 miles to **Shrine Mountain**

9.13

Resolution Narrows

📷 **Fowler/
Hilliard
Hut**
11,500'

0.50 miles to **Fowler/Hilliard Hut**
4.51 miles to **Pando**
5.94 miles to **Camp Hale**
7.31 miles to **Jackal Hut**
8.48 miles to **Red Cliff**

**Resolution
Mountain**

9.12

1.10 miles to **Fowler/Hilliard Hut**
3.91 miles to **Pando**
5.34 miles to **Camp Hale**
6.71 miles to **Jackal Hut**

9.1

9.2
9.10

9.3

2.82 miles to **Fowler/Hilliard Hut**
3.62 miles to **Camp Hale**
4.98 miles to **Jackal Hut**

.76 miles to **Pando**
4.25 miles to **Fowler/Hilliard Hut**

2.62 miles to **Camp Hale**
3.82 miles to **Fowler/Hilliard Hut**
3.99 miles to **Jackal Hut**

To Camp Hale

Pando

continued on pp 144-145

114

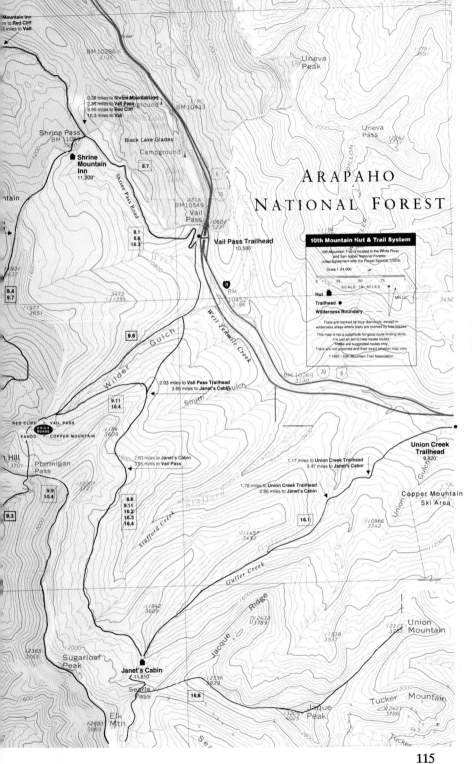

Mountain Inn
les to Red Cliff
3 miles to Vail

BM 10286
3735

Uneva
Peak

Uneva
Pass
3242

0.38 miles to Shrine Mountain Inn
2.35 miles to Vail Pass
8.95 miles to Red Cliff
16.3 miles to Vail

BM 10433

Shrine Pass
BM 10?
3?

Black Lake Glades

8.7

Campground

Shrine
Mountain
Inn
11,209'

Shrine Pass Road

ARAPAHO
NATIONAL FOREST

8.4
9.7

8.1
8.6
16.3

BM 10549
Vail
Pass

Vail Pass Trailhead
10,580'

10th Mountain Hut & Trail System

10th Mountain Trail is located in the White River
and San Isabel National Forests
under agreement with the Forest Service, USDA.
Scale 1:24,000

0   .25   .50   .75   1
SCALE IN MILES

Hut

Trailhead

Wilderness Boundary

Trails are marked by blue diamonds, except in
wilderness areas where trails are marked by tree blazes

This map is not a substitute for good route finding skills,
it is just an aid to help locate routes.
These are suggested routes only
Trails are not groomed and their exact location may vary

© 1991 - 10th Mountain Trail Association

BM
10452
3786

9.6

West Tenmile Creek

Wilder Gulch

BM 10269
3730

2.03 miles to Vail Pass Trailhead
3.65 miles to Janet's Cabin

9.11
16.4

Smith Gulch

RED CLIFF   VAIL PASS
U.S.G.S.
QUADS
PANDO   COPPER MOUNTAIN

Union Creek
Trailhead
9,820'

Hill

Ptarmigan
Pass

2.63 miles to Janet's Cabin
3.85 miles to Vail Pass

1.17 miles to Union Creek Trailhead
3.47 miles to Janet's Cabin

Copper Mountain
Ski Area

9.9
10.4

1.78 miles to Union Creek Trailhead
2.86 miles to Janet's Cabin

9.3

8.6
9.11
16.2
16.3
16.4

Stafford Creek

16.1

10966
3342

Guller Creek

Jacque Ridge

12434
3789

Union
Mountain

Sugarloaf
Peak

Janet's Cabin
11,610'

11538
3517

Searle
Pass

16.6

Jaque
Peak

Tucker Mountain

Elk
Mtn.

12693
3869

12242
3786

Tucker

115

REVERSE ROUTE DESCRIPTION: From the Shrine Mountain Inn ski the 10th Mountain marked trail downhill N through clearings, then NE to Shrine Pass. Pick up the Shrine Pass road here and follow it SE 2 ⅓ miles to the Vail Pass Trailhead.

SAFETY NOTES: This is certainly the easiest trailhead to hut trip on the 10th Mountain suggested routes. As a result, it is used by many novice ski tourers — as it should be. But every skier should remember that given poor visibility during a storm, even this simple trail could be dangerous.

SUMMER: The Shrine Pass Road is a good cycling route. Hikers can explore Shrine Mountain and the surrounding drainages. Horse people can ride the road, but heavy car traffic could be a problem.

8.2

Shrine Mountain Inn — Vail Trailhead via Commando Run

DIFFICULTY: Expert
TIME: 13 hours up, 8 hours down
DISTANCE: 16 ¼ miles
ELEVATION GAIN: 2,080 feet; loss: 5,069 feet

TEXT MAP: pp. 114-115
10TH MTN MAP: Resolution Mountain
USGS MAP: Vail Pass, Red Cliff, Vail East

This is a popular, traditional tour. It is named after the commandos of the 10th Mountain Division who used the route for informal training during the Camp Hale days in the 1940s (see Preface). For the first 8 miles the Commando Run follows a superb timbered ridge with several summits that poke up just above timberline, offering great views. This route is higher and longer than most 10th Mountain suggested routes and has more downhill skiing. Thus, you'll find it a nice alternative if you have the skills to enjoy it. The Commando Run is a section of the Colorado Trail, a "trans-state" route that connects Durango and Denver. The Colorado Trail is marked with small white triangles that say Colorado Trail. The traditional Commando Run starts at Vail Pass. To conform to the 10th Mountain suggested routes, however, this description starts at the Shrine Mountain Inn.

ROUTE DESCRIPTION: From the Shrine Mountain Inn ski back down the 10th Mountain suggested route (reverse route 8.1) to Shrine Pass. Ski the snow-covered Shrine Pass Road 1 ¼ miles down Turkey Creek (good downhill cruising) to 10,660 feet. Leave the Shrine Pass Road here (time for skins) and take a right (N) turn onto the Lime Creek Road. A sign here says Lime Creek Road No. 728, but the sign may be covered by snow.

Ski up the Lime Creek Road ½ mile to a low-angled area (10,990 feet). The road forks here, with a sign indicating Timber Creek to the right and Lime Creek to the left. Take a left (W) and ski several hundred feet up the

Lime Creek Road to a lightly timbered area. This is where the real back-country skiing begins.

Watch carefully for an indistinct signpost on the right that says Colorado Trail. Turn right (N) off the Lime Creek Road and follow the Colorado Trail to the upper left (W) of the light timber, then contour around the left (west) side of point 11,611 at about the 11,400- foot level. From the west side of point 11,611 follow the ridge to the summits of points 11,710 and 11,696. Enjoy the terrific views (strip your skins), then descend N to a heavily timbered saddle. Stay on the ridge from the saddle, climb a bit, then contour around the left (west) side of point 11,618. Take care with your route-finding here, as you can get too far west and end up in Two Elk Creek. Descend the ridge to Two Elk Pass and enjoy the open views. Dig out your map, spot the back bowls of Vail Ski Area (all the south-facing terrain west of Siberia Peak is part of the ski area), and identify your next goal – point 11,816 to the NW. This is Siberia Peak, the highest point on the Commando Run. Put on your skins and sweat it out.

At the summit of Siberia Peak you have two choices. For the classic ridge run, continue W from the summit of Siberia Peak along a narrow ridge crest, gradually deviate to the S until you are following the ski area boundary, which eventually takes you to a catwalk on the ridge. Follow the catwalk to the restaurant/lift terminus known as Far East, pick up a trail map, then ski N down the ski area to Vail. Take care not to ski down into the Vail bowls, as you need a lift ticket to get back up!

For a more woodsy escapade, drop N from the summit of Siberia Peak, then take the fall line, staying a bit east of center (skier's right). This area is called Mushroom Bowl and, if the snow is good, it will give some "fine turning." As you near the apex of Mushroom Bowl be sure you are on the north side of the drainage, then intersect the snow-covered Mill Creek Road. Follow the road down Mill Creek, where you'll enter the Vail Ski Area. Pick up a trail map and plan a route down to Vail Village (see Chapter 1, Vail Trailhead for the Commando Run).

REVERSE ROUTE DESCRIPTION: Skiing the Commando Run from Vail is an arduous trek that will take all but the strongest groups more than one day (without ski lifts). From the Vail Trailhead for the Commando Run, ski or ride to the lift 10 terminus. Head E and into Mill Creek, then follow the snow-covered Mill Creek Road as it climbs the valley on the north side of Mill Creek.

At 10,400 feet the road begins to wander up long switchbacks. Leave the road and climb a fairly direct line to the summit of Siberia Peak. Drop to Two Elk Pass (if the skiing is good strip your skins, then re-skin at the pass) and stay on the ridge south of Two Elk Pass for 1 ¾ miles to points 11,696 and 11,710. Take care in the timber past Two Elk Pass, it is all too

easy to drop into Two Elk Creek.

Still sticking to the ridge, swing E at point 11,710 and ridge run to point 11,611. Drop down the southeast side of point 11,611 to intersect the Lime Creek Road in a sparsely timbered area at 10,840 feet. Ski the Lime Creek Road downhill E to a low-angled area and continue downhill E to the Shrine Pass Road. Climb the Shrine Pass Road to Shrine Pass, then follow route 8.1 to the Shrine Mountain Inn or Vail Pass.

You can also get to Siberia Peak by riding Vail ski lifts 21 and 22. If you use ski lifts to access the backcountry, be sure to exit the ski area at the designated gates. You can get good weather and avalanche information by dialing 4652 on the red phones within the Vail Ski Area.

SAFETY NOTES: The east side of Siberia Peak is steep and often capped by a dangerous cornice. Other slopes on the peak are usually wind scoured into stability, but should be carefully examined for avalanche hazard. Good emergency egress can be made down Two Elk Creek to the bottom of the Vail Bowl ski lifts. Remember that the lifts may be closed, and that Two Elk Creek has some narrow sections with possible bank-sluff hazard and danger from avalanche control in the Vail bowls.

SUMMER: Hikers, equestrians, and mountain cyclists will find that, with the amount of use this trail is getting, the Commando Run section of the Colorado Trail is well maintained, easy to follow, and fun. Cyclists must occasionally shoulder their steeds.

8.3

Red Cliff Trailhead — Shrine Mountain Inn via Shrine Pass Road

DIFFICULTY: Light Intermediate
TIME: 7 hours up, 5 hours down
DISTANCE: 9 miles
ELEVATION GAIN: 2,529 feet

TEXT MAP: pp. 114-115
10TH MTN MAP: Resolution Mountain
USGS MAP: Red Cliff, Vail Pass

This 10th Mountain suggested route follows the well-used, snow-covered Shrine Pass Road. It is a long trip with comparatively easy navigation. Thus, this is a good "classroom tour" for the freshman backcountry skier.

ROUTE DESCRIPTION: In the town of Red Cliff find the Shrine Pass Road and reconnoiter your parking (see Chapter 1, Red Cliff Trailhead). In general, remember that you will follow the distinct, snow-covered Shrine Pass Road up the Turkey Creek drainage to Shrine Pass. At Shrine Pass you leave the main road and take a dedicated 10th Mountain suggested route to the Shrine Mountain Inn.

Start with waxed skis. At 2 ½ miles (9,000 feet) on the Shrine Pass Road you'll pass an obvious intersection at Wearyman Creek. Here route 9.4 takes off to the right (S). Take care to stay on the Shrine Pass Road and ski 4 miles up Turkey Creek to the only switchback on the road in a large clearing at 10,360 feet. In poor weather it is possible to lose the road here, especially with high winds. Just remember that the road leaves the gut of the drainage and climbs E through the clearing (staying on the north side of the drainage). The important thing is to find the road as it re-enters timber at the east end of the clearing, otherwise you'll have to beat some dense timber and brush.

Just ¼ mile into the timber (10,660 feet) you'll pass the left (north) turnoff of the Lime Creek Road (see route 8.2). Stay on the Shrine Pass Road and continue E then SE through light timber to Shrine Pass, a nondescript, flat clearing that forms the divide between Turkey Creek and West Tenmile Creek. Ski to the east end of the Shrine Pass clearing. Look for a White River National Forest sign facing east. Ski W from this sign several hundred yards across a clear area and enter a conifer forest at a red stock gate. Follow an obvious road-cut through the forest ¼ mile S to the Shrine Mountain Inn. Use your map, compass, and altimeter for insurance. The large inn is visible from several hundred feet down the road.

REVERSE ROUTE DESCRIPTION: Take care to identify Shrine Pass, then ski the snow-covered Shrine Pass Road to Red Cliff. Reverse the directions above.

SAFETY NOTES: Be sure to stay on the Shrine Pass Road, as there are several tempting turnoffs along the way. Don't let the ease of following this road lull you into complacent route-finding — use your skills. The Shrine Pass Road is heavily used by snowmobiles, so keep your eyes and ears open, and be courteous.

SUMMER: This is a fine horse, hike, or bike route. The Shrine Pass Road has heavy auto use in the summer.

8.4

Shrine Mountain Inn to Fowler/Hilliard Hut via Shrine Mountain Ridge

DIFFICULTY: Intermediate   **TEXT MAP:** pp. 114-115
TIME: 6 hours   **10TH MTN MAP:** Resolution Mountain
DISTANCE: 6 ¾ miles   **USGS MAP:** Vail Pass, Red Cliff,
ELEVATION GAIN: 1,221 feet; loss: 930 feet   Pando

This 10th Mountain suggested route begins with a terrific ridge run and some good downhill skiing, but ends with a long "treadmill" logging road through the forest. Before you start, be certain that the weather will be good enough for travel above timberline (see Appendix 2). Several groups have reported near disasters from trying the Shrine Mountain Ridge during wind storms. If you're looking for branch routes from the Shrine Mountain Inn, use this route to climb Shrine Mountain. Experts will find some skiing on the east face of Shrine Mountain, but intermediates should retrace their steps back to the Inn.

ROUTE DESCRIPTION: From the Shrine Mountain Inn climb SW 1 mile and 531 vertical feet to Shrine Mountain Saddle (11,740 feet). This is the first saddle southeast of Shrine Mountain. Enjoy the awesome view of the Holy Cross Mountains and take the time to evaluate your position. For the next 1 ¼ miles the trail stays above timberline, skirting and gradually dropping around the west side of Shrine Mountain Ridge. In poor or deteriorating weather you should consider turning back (see Chapter 9 for other routes to the Fowler/Hilliard Hut).

Continuing from Shrine Mountain Saddle, use your compass, map, and altimeter to make an accurate dropping traverse to timberline on the southwest face of the ridge, on the north side of the Wearyman Creek drainage. From here you can ski directly down to the apex of the drainage at 11,000 feet or take a more gradual dropping traverse SE into the drainage. With good snow you can make some fine turns with the former option. Novice downhillers should stick to the latter.

At 11,000 feet in the Wearyman Creek drainage you'll be in an elongated park. Near the lower (west) end of the park find the channel where Wearyman Creek leaves the park. Here you'll find the marked 10th Mountain suggested route. It crosses to the west side of Wearyman Creek for a short distance, enters the trees on a snowcat trail, and drops down a steep hill to a small clearing. From the clearing stay on the 10th Mountain suggested route as it climbs SW through forest for a short distance to a distinct logging road (10,880 feet). Follow this road SW; it is very low-angled and seems to go on forever. Persevere, perhaps using cross country wax, and ski 1 ¾ miles on the road to the 11,200-foot level, where it begins to climb SE via a series of low-angled, inefficient switchbacks. If you're using wax you might like these switchbacks. Many skiers, however, put their skins on and cut directly up the hill, use the switchbacks for reference, and regain the 10th Mountain suggested route at the last switchback.

Whatever your choice in routes, once you gain the ridge at the 11,400-foot level (Ptarmigan Ridge), follow it W then SW ⅓ mile to the Fowler/ Hilliard Hut. You cannot see the hut until you reach the small knob several hundred yards southeast of the site.

There is a good variation for this route that gives you a lot more high altitude ridge-running. Simply stay on Shrine Mountain Ridge all the way to the saddle that divides the Wearyman and Wilder drainages. From the saddle climb S to Ptarmigan Pass, then ascend the ridge W to the summit of Ptarmigan Hill. Drop down the west side of Ptarmigan Hill to a distinct road-cut. Ski the road W as it skirts the south side of Ptarmigan Ridge and then intersects the 10th Mountain marked route 8.4 leading W along the ridge to the Fowler/Hilliard Hut.

SAFETY NOTES: Take care with route-finding and weather on the alpine portion of this route. There is an active avalanche path on the south face of Ptarmigan Hill.

SUMMER: This route is a fine hike. A short section of trail, connecting Wearyman Creek with the logging road to the SW, is just a marked route through the forest with no real path. Cyclists will enjoy all the roads in the area. Shrine Mountain Ridge is too high and rough for equestrian traffic, but the roads and "real" trails in the area are fine horse routes.

Atop Shrine Pass headed west. This pass is a nondescript clearing.

8.5

Shrine Mountain Inn to Fowler/Hilliard Hut via Shrine Pass Road and Wearyman Creek Road

DIFFICULTY: Expert	**TEXT MAP:** pp. 114-115
TIME: 15 hours	**10TH MTN MAP:** Resolution Mountain
DISTANCE: 14 miles	**USGS MAP:** Vail Pass, Red Cliff,
ELEVATION GAIN: 2,670 feet; loss: 2,379 feet	Pando

This is the only low-altitude route connecting the Shrine Mountain Inn to the Fowler/Hilliard Hut. It is rated expert because of it's length.

ROUTE DESCRIPTION: To begin, ski the 10th Mountain marked trail from the Shrine Mountain Inn N then NE down to Shrine Pass, a nondescript, lightly timbered flat that forms the divide between Turkey Creek and West Tenmile Creek. Turn NW at the pass onto the Shrine Pass Road. This road will be indistinct at the pass, but easier to identify as you ski lower into the Turkey Creek drainage. Ski down the Shrine Pass Road 6 miles to 9,000 feet. Turn left (S) off the Shrine Pass Road onto the Wearyman Creek Road; this intersection is obvious. Follow route 9.5 for 7 ¾ miles to the Fowler/Hilliard Hut.

SAFETY NOTES: This is a very long route. If you reach the low point of the route (on Shrine Pass Road) very late, consider bailing out in Red Cliff.

SUMMER: All these roads make fine bicycle routes.

8.6

Shrine Mountain Inn to Janet's Cabin via Shrine Pass Road and Upper Stafford Creek

DIFFICULTY: Advanced	**TEXT MAP:** p. 115
TIME: 7 hours	**10TH MTN MAP:** Resolution Mountain
DISTANCE: 8 ½ miles	**USGS MAP:** Vail Pass, Copper Mtn.
ELEVATION GAIN: 1,197 feet; loss: 796 feet	

Use this for the most efficient backcountry route to Janet's Cabin. You can also reach Janet's by skiing down the Vail Pass bicycle path to Copper Mountain, then following the Guller Creek route (16.1) up to Janet's.

ROUTE DESCRIPTION: From the Shrine Mountain Inn follow route 8.1 (reverse route) down to Vail Pass. Follow route 16.2 from Vail Pass to Janet's Cabin.

SAFETY NOTES: See referenced routes.

SUMMER: See referenced routes. Cyclists should explore the Vail Pass bicycle path.

8.7

Black Lake Glades from Shrine Mountain Inn

DIFFICULTY: Intermediate
TIME: Half day or more
DISTANCE: 4 ¾ miles round trip
ELEVATION GAIN: 776 feet round trip

TEXT MAP: p. 115
10TH MTN MAP: Resolution Mountain
USGS MAP: Vail Pass

Within a day of the Shrine Mountain Inn, the best place to go downhill skiing is the Black Lake Glades. You can reach this area from the Inn or from Vail Pass. One run nets you about 700 vertical feet of skiing and you can push as many laps as your lungs allow.

ROUTE DESCRIPTION: The Black Lake Glades are easy to find. At Vail Pass just look NW and you'll see the gladed north-facing slopes dropping to the Black Lakes. To ascend, skin up through the glades or use the Shrine Pass Road (see route 8.1) as a route to saddle 11,156, and explore downhill from there. If you're skiing from the Shrine Mountain Inn, head back down to Shrine Pass (see route 8.1). Experts can head N from the pass to point 11,325, then ski to Black Lake No. 2; intermediates should follow the Shrine Pass Road SE to the aforementioned saddle at 11,156 feet and ski from there. In general, you'll find more mellow terrain the closer you are to the Vail Pass Trailhead.

SAFETY NOTES: Though the Black Lake Glades are not classic slide paths, there can be pocket slab avalanches on the steeper slopes. If you're staying at the Inn, give yourself enough time to return before dark.

SUMMER: This is trailless ski terrain unsuitable for bikes and horses. The sparsely timbered areas around Shrine Pass are good for alpine hikes.

Chapter 9 • Fowler/Hilliard Hut

Owned by 10th Mountain, the Fowler/Hilliard Hut sits at timberline about ½ mile northeast of the summit of Resolution Mountain. The south windows give you a marvelous view towards the Jackal Hut and some of the highest peaks in Colorado.

ELEVATION: 11,500 feet
COUNTY: Eagle
TEXT MAP: pp. 114-115, 144-145
10TH MTN MAP: Res. Mt., Chicago Rdg.
USGS MAP: Pando
TRAILHEADS: Pando, Red Cliff, Vail Pass

Up to 16 people can find bed space in the Fowler/Hilliard Hut. It has photo-electric lighting and a roomy kitchen replete with utensils and two gas cooktops. The sleeping area is all upstairs, with communal eating and lounging downstairs. This averts "party angst" for those bedding early. Loud noise still penetrates, however, so remember your earplugs.

The Fowler/Hilliard Hut was built in 1988 with funds from over 260 people and businesses. It is a a memorial to well-known Denver residents Ann Fowler and Ed Hilliard who were killed in a climbing accident on North Maroon Peak near Aspen.

More than 6 fine ski routes connect the Fowler/Hilliard Hut to other huts and trailheads. Intermediate level skiers will enjoy the Resolution Creek route (9.2), or they can take a slightly more direct climb on the McAllister Gulch route (9.1). The Wearyman Creek route (9.5) is long but avoids travel above timberline. Experts can enjoy a high route over Hornsilver Mountain (9.4) and a less direct alternate high route that climbs over Ptarmigan Hill (9.3).

For a northerly ski-through, you'll want to use the Shrine Mountain Ridge route (9.7) to go north to the Shrine Mountain Inn. For a ski south to the Jackal Hut, take the high route (9.9) or Pearl Creek (route 9.10). If the weather looks scary, consider low routes 9.8 and 9.10 for ski-throughs.

If you love "base skiing" you can't do much better than the Fowler/Hilliard Hut. From the southeast bowl of Resolution Mountain, to the low-angled glades north of the hut, to Ptarmigan Hill—there are turns for everyone. Many groups spend one night at the Fowler/Hilliard, get a ski run the next morning, then ski on to a trailhead or another hut. You can get a few turns this way, especially if you take a more direct line down to your chosen route. But consider staying for at least 2 nights at the Fowler/Hilliard so you can enjoy a day of "light pack cruising" around the hut.

9.1

Pando Trailhead — Fowler/Hilliard Hut via McAllister Gulch

DIFFICULTY: Intermediate
TIME: 5 hours up, 3 ½ hours down
DISTANCE: 5 ¼ miles
ELEVATION GAIN: 2,500 feet; loss: 200 feet

TEXT MAP: p. 144
10TH MTN MAP: Chicago Ridge
USGS MAP: Pando

This is the most direct 10th Mountain suggested route to the Fowler/Hilliard Hut. Since you pass over a high saddle, keep an eye on the weather.

ROUTE DESCRIPTION: Begin at the Pando Trailhead. Ski E across a bridge over the Eagle River, then ¼ mile E and NE across Camp Hale. You'll intersect a snow-covered north/south road at the base of the mountain. Turn left (N) and ski ½ mile to a right turn (NE) onto the McAllister Gulch jeep trail. This is where you leave the valley (put your skins on). Follow the road as it makes a climbing traverse N, then swings NE into McAllister Gulch. At about 9,400 feet you'll encounter some private property signs. These designate property on the northwest side of the road — skiers should stay on the road.

Put your head down and work the long 2-mile climb to the head of McAllister Gulch. At 10,440 feet take a right turn SE and continue slugging it out to 11,300 feet on the southwest ridge of Resolution Mountain (intersection with route 9.2).

Climb the ridge crest for a short distance to 11,400 feet. Next, take a ¾-mile climbing traverse NE then N across the west face of Resolution Mountain, ending at the 11,700-foot saddle (Resolution Saddle) on the northwest ridge. On a clear day you can see the hut from here — a welcome sight. Ski down E from the saddle and cut a short traverse that leads you to a distinct east/west cleft called the Resolution Narrows. Take care to not ski N downhill from the saddle. Continue E down Resolution Narrows to the Fowler/Hilliard Hut in a clearing at 11,500 feet. To get some "bonus turns," experts should consider ascending Resolution Mountain from the southwest ridge, then cutting turns down to the hut.

REVERSE ROUTE DESCRIPTION: Before you leave the hut, take time to read your map. Identify the distinct east/west cleft of the Resolution Narrows that climbs up the north side of Resolution Mountain. Put on your skins. Ski the Resolution Narrows to the 11,700-foot Resolution Saddle. Remove your skins at the saddle. Take a left (S) here and glide across the west face of Resolution Mountain to 11,400 feet on the southwest ridge. Drop down the southwest ridge 100 vertical feet, then turn right (NW), drop into McAllister Gulch, and follow the McAllister Gulch jeep trail to the Eagle River valley and Camp Hale. Ski ½ mile S in Camp Hale, then turn W, ski across the flats, and cross a bridge over the Eagle River to the Pando Trailhead at Highway 24.

If visibility is poor in Camp Hale you may have trouble finding the exact trailhead and bridge. In this case you can strike cross country to Highway 24, your only obstacles being the Eagle River and up to a mile of trail to break out. In midwinter you can usually find a snow bridge over the river.

SAFETY NOTES: There can be slide danger on the open slopes of Resolution Mountain. Beware of cornices on all the ridges. The trails out of Camp Hale are quite often used by snowmobiles, so keep your ears open.

SUMMER: The McAllister Gulch jeep trail is a fine hike, bike, and horse route. It connects to the Hornsilver Mountain jeep trail (see route 9.4), but does not connect to the Fowler/Hilliard Hut. To get to the hut with a bike you can portage from the 11,700-foot saddle, then down Resolution Narrows.

9.2

Pando Trailhead — Fowler/Hilliard Hut via Resolution Creek

DIFFICULTY: Intermediate
TEXT MAP: p. 144
TIME: 5 ½ hours up, 4 hours down
10TH MTN MAP: Chicago Ridge
DISTANCE: 6 ½ miles
USGS MAP: Pando
ELEVATION GAIN: 2,500 feet; loss: 200 feet

This longer trailhead to hut route has easier downhill skiing than route 9.1. The two routes join together for the climb around Resolution Mountain. You'd have to toss a coin to decide between the Pando or Camp Hale trailheads for "best trailhead" for this route. Base your choice on parking and bridges; the route below is described from the Pando Trailhead. This is a 10th Mountain suggested route.

ROUTE DESCRIPTION: From the Pando Trailhead ski E across the main north/south Camp Hale Road, across a bridge over the Eagle River, then E and NE to intersect a snow-covered road running north/south at the base of the mountain. You can ski this road S and intersect the Resolution Road, but to avoid "sled" traffic do the following. Ski the road at the base of the mountain N a short distance, then turn right and ski SE up through a gulch east of point 9,540 (again, this is not the main Camp Hale Road). One mile from Pando you intersect the distinct Resolution Road. Take a left (NE) and ski 2 ½ miles up the Resolution Road to 9,960 feet.

Leave the Resolution Road here and take a left (NW) onto a marked 10th Mountain trail. The blue diamonds take you up 980 vertical feet to a 10,940-foot saddle on the southwest ridge of Resolution Mountain. Most of this trail follows a distinct trail-cut through forest. In the occasional clearing take the time to really zero in on the route with your map. Remember: diamonds are for dummies.

Climb the southwest ridge of Resolution Mountain ¾ mile to 11,400 feet (you'll pass the intersection of route 9.1 at 11,300 feet). Next, take a ¾-mile climbing traverse NE then N across the west face of Resolution Mountain, ending at 11,700-foot Resolution Saddle on the northwest ridge of Resolution Mountain. Ski down E from the saddle and cut a short traverse that leads you to a distinct east/west cleft called the Resolution Narrows. Take care to not ski N downhill from the saddle. Continue E down Resolution Narrows to the Fowler/Hilliard Hut in a clearing at 11,500 feet. In clear weather the hut is visible from Resolution Saddle. To get some "bonus turns" experts should consider ascending Resolution Mountain, then cutting turns down to the hut.

REVERSE ROUTE DESCRIPTION: Before you leave the hut, take time to read your map. Identify the distinct east/west cleft of the Resolution Narrows that climbs up the north side of Resolution Mountain. Put on your skins. Ski the Resolution Narrows to 11,700-foot Resolution Saddle. Remove your skins at the saddle. Take a left (S) here and glide across the west face of Resolution Mountain to 11,400 feet on the southwest ridge. Drop down the southwest ridge 560 vertical feet (at 11,300 feet you'll pass the right turn onto route 9.1) to a saddle at 10,950 feet. Turn left (SE) and drop down switchbacks 980 vertical feet to the distinct Resolution Road. Ski the Resolution Road SW 2 miles to Camp Hale.

For the Pando Trailhead, take a right just before you make a final short drop into the flats of Camp Hale and ski N on a road tucked in behind point 9,540. Just N of point 9,540 you'll intersect a main north/south snow-covered road. Take a left (S) here, turn W, and ski across the flats to a bridge over the Eagle River. The Pando Trailhead is several hundred feet west of the bridge.

If visibility is poor in Camp Hale, you may have trouble finding the Pando Trailhead and bridge. In this event you can strike cross country to Highway 24, your only obstacles being the Eagle River and up to a mile of trail to break out. In midwinter you can usually find a snow bridge over the Eagle River.

SAFETY NOTES: There can be slide danger on the open slopes of Resolution Mountain. Be aware of cornices on all the ridges. The trails out of Camp Hale are used by snowmobiles quite often.

SUMMER: This route is fine for hiking. The section of trail from Resolution Creek climbing to Resolution Mountain is a marked ski route with no path for horse or bike travel. The Resolution Road is a good bicycle route.

9.3

Pando Trailhead — Fowler/Hilliard Hut via Ptarmigan Hill Traverse

DIFFICULTY: Advanced	**TEXT MAP:** p. 144
TIME: 8 hours up, 6 hours down	**10TH MTN MAP:** Chicago Ridge
DISTANCE: 9 miles	**USGS MAP:** Pando
ELEVATION GAIN: 2,983 feet; loss: 683 feet	

This alternate route is long but quite rewarding. It includes a grand 2-mile alpine traverse with a 12,143-foot summit.

ROUTE DESCRIPTION: From the Pando Trailhead follow route 9.2 to 9,960 feet on the Resolution Road, where route 9.2 climbs NW. Do not take route 9.2. Instead, stay on the distinct Resolution Road for 3 miles to Ptarmigan Pass, a broad saddle at 11,765 feet. Leave the road here and ascend the east ridge of Ptarmigan Hill. At the summit of Ptarmigan Hill you'll find a good view and several wooden shacks. Descend the west face of Ptarmigan Hill to a distinct saddle at 11,580 feet. This can be a fun little ski run, but it may have some difficult snow. Remember, "there is no such thing as bad snow — just poor skiers."

From the saddle follow a road-cut that contours through sparse timber around the south side of point 11,683, then leads to the 11,480-foot saddle where you converge with route 9.5/8.4. Continue ⅓ mile W and SW along the ridge to the Fowler/Hilliard Hut. The hut is not visible until you top a small 40-foot high mound several hundred feet east of the hut.

One worthy variation to this trail is called the Ptarmigan Shoulder route. Instead of skiing all the way to Ptarmigan Pass, turn off the Resolution Road at 10,704 feet and ski N up the east side of an intermittent stream in

a gulch. At 11,000 feet take a climbing traverse W to the ridge leading up
to point 11,683. Ascend the ridge to the road that contours the southwest
side of 11,683. This road is the last leg of the Ptarmigan Hill Traverse
described above. The Ptarmigan Shoulder is also a fine descent route.

REVERSE ROUTE DESCRIPTION: The Ptarmigan Hill Traverse is a nice
way to ski from the Fowler/Hilliard Hut back to the Pando Trailhead (or
see Wilder Gulch in route 9.6). From the hut follow the 10th Mountain suggested route ⅓ mile E and NE to the 11,480-foot saddle. Leave the 10th
Mountain suggested route and continue on a distinct road-cut that traverses the southwest face of point 11,683, leading to the 11,580-foot saddle
below the west face of Ptarmigan Hill. Ascend the west face to the summit
of Ptarmigan Hill, then descend the east ridge to Ptarmigan Pass. From
Ptarmigan Pass ski the Resolution Road 6 ½ miles down Resolution Creek
to Camp Hale.

For the Pando Trailhead, take a right just before you make a final short
drop into the flats of Camp Hale and ski N on a road tucked in behind
point 9,540. Just north of point 9,540 you'll intersect a main north/south

snow-covered road. Take a left (S) here, turn W, and ski across the flats to a bridge over the Eagle River. The Pando Trailhead is several hundred feet west of the bridge.

If visibility is poor in Camp Hale you may have trouble finding the Pando Trailhead and bridge. In this case you can strike cross country to Highway 24, your only obstacles being the Eagle River and up to a mile of trail to break out. In midwinter you can usually find a snow bridge over the Eagle River.

SAFETY NOTES: The road that traverses around the south ridge of Ptarmigan Hill (as shown on the USGS map) is tempting, but it crosses several slide paths on the south face of Ptarmigan Hill. Indeed, these paths sometimes run over the road lower down. Use proper precautions. Beware of cornices on the Ptarmigan Hill summit. Get an early start for this route.

SUMMER: This is a good hike or horse ride. Superfit cyclists might enjoy it as well, but the climb to Ptarmigan Hill from Ptarmigan Pass would be a portage.

9.4

Red Cliff Trailhead — Fowler/Hilliard Hut via Hornsilver Mountain

DIFFICULTY: Intermediate   **TEXT MAP:** p. 114
TIME: 10 hours up, 7 hours down   **10TH MTN MAP:** Resolution Mountain
DISTANCE: 9 miles   **USGS MAP:** Pando, Red Cliff
ELEVATION GAIN: 3,180 feet; loss: 360 feet

This 10th Mountain suggested route includes a scenic alpine ridge run. It is long and arduous, but rewarding.

ROUTE DESCRIPTION: Begin at the Red Cliff Trailhead. Ski up the distinct snow-covered Shrine Pass Road 2 ½ miles to 9,000 feet. You can wax to here, but put on your skins for the climb ahead. Leave the Shrine Pass Road and turn right (S) on the well-marked and heavily traveled Wearyman Creek Road. Ski up the Wearyman Creek Road ¾ mile to 9,280 feet. Leave the Wearyman Creek drainage here and take a hard right on a westerly climbing traverse on the Hornsilver Mountain jeep trail. This turn is fairly obvious, but take care with your map reading.

Now the real push begins. Stay on the marked 10th Mountain suggested route as it winds through timber, climbing 2 ½ miles SW to where you intersect the west ridge of Hornsilver Mountain at 11,200 feet near timberline. From here climb the ridge E to the summit of Hornsilver Mountain, then stick to the crest of Hornsilver Ridge as you ski 1 mile SE over one small bump to a major saddle at 11,450 feet. Stay on the ridge and continue climbing SE towards the summit of Resolution Mountain. After ½ mile and 242 feet of climbing, you'll reach another smaller saddle at 11,700 feet (Resolution Saddle), a short distance below the summit of Resolution Mountain.

Leave the ridge here by skiing from the north side of the saddle on a short traverse E that leads you to a distinct east/west cleft (Resolution Narrows) that leads downhill E to the hut. Take care to not ski N downhill from the saddle – if you do this you'll miss Resolution Narrows and have to camp in Wearyman Creek. Ski E down Resolution Narrows to the Fowler/Hilliard Hut in a clearing at 11,500 feet. The hut is visible from Resolution Saddle and from the east slopes of Resolution Mountain. To get some "bonus turns" experts should consider ascending Resolution Mountain from the southwest ridge, then cutting turns down to the hut.

REVERSE ROUTE DESCRIPTION: To ski this route from the hut, use your map to identify the distinct east/west cleft (Resolution Narrows) that climbs up the north side of Resolution Mountain. Ski Resolution Narrows to the 11,700-foot saddle on the northwest ridge of Resolution Mountain. From the saddle descend the ridge 250 vertical to another more defined saddle at 11,450 feet. Stay on the ridge and ski to the summit of Hornsilver Mountain. Drop down the west ridge of Hornsilver Mountain to 11,200 feet, then turn N and descend through forest into the Wearyman Creek drainage.

At Wearyman Creek you intersect the distinct, well-used Wearyman Creek jeep trail. Ski this road downvalley ¾ mile to the snow-covered Shrine Pass Road, which you than ski downvalley 2 ½ miles to the Red Cliff Trailhead.

SAFETY NOTES: Take care with cornices on the Hornsilver and Resolution ridges. This is a long route with several miles of skiing near or above timberline. Thus, get an early start and be prepared for wind chill.

SUMMER: This route is a good hike or horse ride. Most cyclists will find good riding on the roads in the Wearyman Creek drainage. If you are a fit expert cyclist, explore the Hornsilver Mountain section of the route.

9.5

Red Cliff Trailhead — Fowler/Hilliard Hut via Wearyman Creek Road

DIFFICULTY: Intermediate   **TEXT MAP:** pp. 114-115
TIME: 12 hours up, 9 hours down   **10TH MTN MAP:** Resolution Mountain
DISTANCE: 10 miles   **USGS MAP:** Red Cliff, Pando
ELEVATION GAIN: 3,000 feet; loss: 180 feet

As a route to or from the Red Cliff Trailhead, this alternate route lacks the spectacular ridge run of route 9.4, but it could be a better choice in terrible weather. Since it's not a 10th Mountain suggested route, the Wearyman Creek Road section is not marked with the ubiquitous blue diamonds. However, it is often packed by snowmobile and follows distinct logging roads cut through the forest.

ROUTE DESCRIPTION: Start at the Red Cliff Trailhead and ski up the Shrine Pass Road 2 ½ miles to 9,000 feet. Here take the obvious right turn of the Wearyman Creek Road into the Wearyman Creek drainage. To be doubly sure about this spot, count the drainages on your right as you ski from Red Cliff, then correlate these with your map.

Follow the Wearyman Creek Road ¾ mile up the Wearyman Creek drainage to 9,280 feet. Here, route 9.4 leaves the road and heads W up the side of the drainage (with good weather consider route 9.4).

To stick with the 9.5 alternate route, just continue up the Wearyman Creek Road. Though unmarked by 10th Mountain, it is distinct and heavily used. After a long 4-mile pull you'll arrive at an elongated park (11,000 feet). About ⅛ mile up from the lower (west) end of the park find the channel where Wearyman Creek leaves the park. Here you'll find the marked 10th Mountain suggested route. It follows the west side of Wearyman Creek for a short distance and crosses to the southeast side of the creek. Here you leave the creek and drop down a steep hill (a strong snowplow is useful) about 150 vertical feet to a small clearing. From the clearing stay on the 10th Mountain suggested route as it climbs SW through forest for a short distance to a distinct logging road.

Climb SW on this road. It is very low-angled and seems to go on forever. Persevere, perhaps using cross country wax, and ski 1 ¾ miles on the road to the 11,200-foot level, where it begins to climb SE via a series of low-angled, inefficient switchbacks. If you're using wax you might like these switchbacks. Many skiers, however, put their skins on and cut directly up the hill, using the switchbacks for reference, and regaining the 10th Mountain suggested route at the last switchback.

Whatever your choice in routes, once you gain the ridge (Ptarmigan Ridge) at the 11,400-foot level, follow it W then SW ⅓ mile through sparse timber to the Fowler/Hilliard Hut. You cannot see the hut until you reach the top of a small 40-foot high mound several hundred feet east of the site.

REVERSE ROUTE DESCRIPTION: This route is simple to reverse. Follow route 9.7 to the elongated park at 11,000 feet in the Wearyman Creek drainage. Ski to the west end of the park and find the distinct cut of the Wearyman Creek Road. Follow the Wearyman Creek Road 4 miles to the snow-covered Shrine Pass Road. Take a left (W) on the Shrine Pass Road and ski the road 2 ½ miles to the Red Cliff Trailhead.

SAFETY NOTES: This route is long, so get an early start. Beware of bank sluffs and larger slides on the mountainside above the Wearyman Creek Road. Also, be aware that helicopter skiers occasionally use these slopes, and they could trigger slides.

SUMMER: Horses and hikers will enjoy this whole route. Cyclists will have to portage the section between the elongated park and the logging road.

9.6

Vail Pass Trailhead — Fowler/Hilliard Hut via Wilder Gulch and Ptarmigan Hill

DIFFICULTY: Advanced
TIME: 7 hours up, 4 ½ hours down
DISTANCE: 7 miles
ELEVATION GAIN: 1,603 feet; loss: 683 feet

TEXT MAP: pp. 114-115
10TH MTN MAP: Resolution Mountain
USGS MAP: Vail Pass, Red Cliff, Pando

This alternate route could be considered the most direct line to the Fowler/Hilliard Hut, given weather good enough for 2 miles of ridge-running. During poor weather you can use a variation into Wearyman Creek to avoid the high ridge.

ROUTE DESCRIPTION: Start from the Vail Pass Trailhead. Put your skins on and, instead of skiing the Shrine Pass Road, ski S across West Tenmile Creek, then take a climbing traverse S then SW into Wilder Gulch. Ski about 3 miles and 1,165 vertical feet up Wilder Gulch to Ptarmigan Pass (11,765 feet). In general, the ski route follows the timber on the left side of the valley to about 11,200 feet. Here you swing W, then back S to Ptarmigan Pass. The USGS map shows the trail passing through a clearing at the saddle between the Wearyman and Wilder drainages. You need not ski the exact trail as long as you're careful about reaching Ptarmigan Pass, a broad saddle at 11,765 feet.

From Ptarmigan Pass ascend the east ridge of Ptarmigan Hill. At the summit of Ptarmigan Hill (12,143 feet) you'll find a good view and several wooden shacks. Descend the west face of Ptarmigan Hill to the saddle at 11,580 feet. This can be a fun little ski run, but may have some difficult snow. Remember, "there is no such thing as bad snow—just poor skiers."

From the saddle follow a road-cut that contours through sparse timber around the south side of point 11,683, then leads to the 11,480-foot saddle where you converge with route 9.5/8.4. Continue ⅓ mile W and SW along the ridge to the Fowler/Hilliard Hut. The hut is not visible until you top a small 40-foot high hill several hundred feet east of the hut.

Packed in a pulk,
this toddler is headed to the huts
with mom and dad.

REVERSE ROUTE DESCRIPTION: Follow reverse route 9.3 from the Fowler/Hilliard Hut to Ptarmigan Pass. From Ptarmigan Pass descend Wilder Gulch NE to about 10,600 feet, traverse N out of Wilder Gulch, cross West Tenmile Creek, and continue N to the Vail Pass Trailhead.

To reverse the alternate Wilder/Wearyman saddle route, take the reverse route 9.5 to 11,000 feet in the Wearyman drainage. From there ski up the Wearyman Creek ¾ mile and 300 vertical feet to the saddle. Descend Wilder Gulch to Vail Pass as described above.

SAFETY NOTES: If you're dependent on blue diamond trail markers, this route is not for you. In Wilder Gulch make any deviations you need to avoid potential bank sluffs. Be careful with the cornices on Ptarmigan Hill. With poor weather follow reverse route 9.5 into Wearyman Creek, then climb E over Wearyman Saddle and descend Wilder Gulch to Vail Pass.

SUMMER: This is a fine hike or horse ride. Cyclists will have to shoulder their bikes to get up Wilder Gulch.

9.7

Fowler/Hilliard Hut to Shrine Mountain Inn via Shrine Mountain Ridge

DIFFICULTY: Intermediate
TIME: 5 1/2 hours
DISTANCE: 6 3/4 miles
ELEVATION GAIN: 930 feet; loss: 1,221 feet

TEXT MAP: pp. 114-115
10TH MTN MAP: Resolution Mountain
USGS MAP: Vail Pass, Red Cliff, Pando

This is the shortest 10th Mountain suggested route from the Fowler/Hilliard Hut to the Shrine Mountain Inn. It is scenic and a challenge to those who have just reached "intermediate status" with wilderness skiing.

ROUTE DESCRIPTION: From the front steps of the Fowler/Hilliard Hut ski several hundred feet NE through sparse timber, then drop a short distance to a timbered saddle at 11,480 feet. From here follow a distinct snow-covered logging road down into the Wearyman Creek drainage. Novice downhillers can relax on the low-angled switchbacks of this road. Experts can ski the glades between the switchbacks. In either case, be sure you are on the road when it makes a last switchback at 11,240 feet, then heads E and NE on a low-angled traverse 1 1/2 miles to road's end at 10,880 feet. Leave the road here and continue NE on a marked 10th Mountain trail that descends through dense timber to a small clearing in the creek bottom at 10,830 feet. Continue NE through the clearing, then climb a steep 150 vertical foot hill up into the elongated park at 11,000 feet.

Cross to the north side of the park, put your skins on, and climb E then NW to 11,700 feet (timberline) on the west face of Shrine Mountain Ridge. Next, take a strict traverse 1 1/2 miles across the west face to Shrine Mountain Saddle (11,740 feet, the saddle just southeast of Shrine Mountain). This traverse passes through sparse timber and clearings at timberline. At the north end of Shrine Mountain Saddle, use your map and compass to get your exact travel direction. Next, you should look at the cornices and develop a safe strategy for egress from the saddle. Drop down the northeast side of the saddle, and immediately you'll find an obvious trough. On the east side of this trough you'll find the marked 10th Mountain suggested route. The blue diamonds take you along the east side of the trough for several hundred yards, then 1 mile NE to the Shrine Mountain Inn.

SAFETY NOTES: This route includes almost 2 miles of timberline travel, where wind chill can make you wish for the sauna at the Inn, and poor visibility can break the best navigator. On the northeast side of Shrine Mountain Saddle take care to avoid any threatening wind-loaded slopes under the cornices. This is done by remaining on the small ridge east of the aforementioned trough.

SUMMER: This route is a fine hike. A short section of trail connecting Wearyman Creek with the logging road to the SW is just a marked route through the forest with no real path. Cyclists will enjoy all the roads in the area. Shrine Mountain Ridge is too high and rough for equestrian traffic, but the roads and "real" trails in the area are fine horse routes.

9.8

Fowler/Hilliard Hut to Shrine Mountain Inn via Wearyman Creek Road and Shrine Pass Road

DIFFICULTY: Advanced
TIME: 13 hours
DISTANCE: 14 miles
ELEVATION GAIN: 2,379 feet; loss: 2,670 feet

TEXT MAP: pp. 114-115
10TH MTN MAP: Resolution Mountain
USGS MAP: Vail Pass, Red Cliff, Pando

A storm howls at the Fowler/Hilliard Hut – you need to ski to the Shrine Mountain Inn. The bleak option of timberline travel on route 9.6 is pushing you into a grand funk. What do you do? Use this alternate route. It's long and indirect, but safe in a storm. The route is rated advanced because of it's length.

ROUTE DESCRIPTION: Take 10th Mountain suggested route 9.7 to the 11,000-foot elongated park at Wearyman Creek. Leave route 9.7 here and ski to the far west end of the elongated park, where you'll find the distinct cut of the Wearyman Creek Road. Ski this road 4 miles down the valley to the Shrine Pass Road (9,000 feet).

In general, you turn E on the Shrine Pass Road and ski the road 5 miles up-valley to Shrine Pass. In detail: At 4 miles (from 9,000 feet) in a large clear area (10,320 feet) you hit the only switchback on the road. In poor weather it is possible to lose the road here, especially with high winds. Just remember that the road leaves the gut of the drainage and climbs E through the clearing (staying on the north side of the drainage). The important thing is to find the road as it re-enters timber at the east end of the clearing, otherwise you'll have to beat dense timber and brush.

Just 1/4 mile into the timber (10,660 feet) you'll pass the left turnoff of the Lime Creek Road (see route 8.2). Stay on the Shrine Pass Road and continue E then SE through light timber to Shrine Pass, a nondescript flat clearing that forms the divide between Turkey Creek and West Tenmile Creek. Ski to the east end of the Shrine Pass clearing. Look for a White River National Forest sign facing east. Ski W from this sign several hundred yards across a clear area and enter a conifer forest at a red stock gate. Follow an obvious road-cut through the forest 1/4 mile S to the Shrine Mountain Inn. Use your map, compass, and altimeter for insurance. The large inn is visible from several hundred feet down the road. You cannot see it from Shrine Pass.

SAFETY NOTES: Be sure to stay on the Shrine Pass Road, as there are several tempting turnoffs along the way. Don't let the ease of following this road lull you into complacent route-finding—use your skills. The Shrine Pass Road is heavily used by snowmobiles, so keep your eyes and ears open, and be courteous.

SUMMER: This route is a fine horse ride or hike. Cyclists will enjoy the Wearyman Creek Road. To do the whole route on a bike, you'd have to portage the short section of 10th Mountain marked trail that connects SW from the elongated park to the upper road.

9.9
Fowler/Hilliard Hut to Jackal Hut via Elk Ridge High Route

DIFFICULTY: Advanced   **TEXT MAP:** p. 144
TIME: 7 hours   **10TH MTN MAP:** Chicago Ridge
DISTANCE: 7 miles   **USGS MAP:** Pando
ELEVATION GAIN: 2,000 feet; loss: 1,840 feet

This alternate route to the Jackal Hut will give you more challenge and better views than the Pearl Creek route (9.10). It is unmarked and includes several miles above timberline. Thus, you should put plenty of time into studying your map, compass, and altimeter.

ROUTE DESCRIPTION: Start with cross country wax. From the Fowler/Hilliard Hut ski the 10th Mountain marked trail ¼ mile E and NE to the 11,480-foot saddle. Leave the 10th Mountain suggested route and continue SE on a distinct road-cut that traverses ¾ mile through timber along the southwest side of point 11,683 to a saddle. Leave the road at the saddle and climb E to the summit of Ptarmigan Hill. You might need skins for this climb. Descend E off Ptarmigan Hill down to Ptarmigan Pass (11,765 feet).

From Ptarmigan Pass climb E to 12,200 feet on Elk Ridge. Walk or ski Elk Ridge (depending on snow cover) 3 ½ miles S to intersect Tim's Traverse (route 16.5) at the 12,600-foot saddle above Searle Basin. Ski Tim's traverse 2 ½ miles W to Jackal Hut.

SAFETY NOTES: This is an unmarked, high altitude route.

SUMMER: Use this route for a fine high altitude hike.

9.10

Fowler/Hilliard Hut to Jackal Hut via Pearl Creek

DIFFICULTY: Intermediate
TIME: 8 hours
DISTANCE: 8 miles
ELEVATION GAIN: 2,238 feet; loss: 2,078 feet

TEXT MAP: p. 144
10TH MTN MAP: Chicago Ridge
USGS MAP: Pando

This roundabout 10th Mountain suggested route includes a scenic traverse of Resolution Mountain. For a more direct line with more downhill skiing, experts should consider skiing down Resolution Bowl from the front porch of the hut. This option puts you at about 10,400 feet on the Resolution Road, which you ski a mile downvalley to intersect the 10th Mountain suggested route described below. Only experts should make the complete descent of Resolution Bowl, as it necks down to steep, dense timber near the bottom. Lower down, the east side of the bowl is better than the west.

ROUTE DESCRIPTION: To take the 10th Mountain suggested route, follow route 9.2 from the Fowler/Hilliard Hut over the northwest shoulder of Resolution Mountain and down to Resolution Road. Ski 1 mile down Resolution Road to 9,678 feet (the Pearl Creek/Resolution Creek confluence). From here you leave Resolution Road and climb the Pearl Creek drainage.

In detail: Turn left (SE) off Resolution Road onto another distinct road-cut that takes a bridge across Resolution Creek. Once on the south side of the creek, look for a 10th Mountain marked trail that leaves the road-cut and heads directly into the Pearl Creek drainage. Follow this trail for 1 ¾ miles on the southwest side of the creek to 10,320 feet, where you cross to the northeast side of the drainage and climb another ½ mile to 10,560 feet.

At 10,560 feet you're still deep in the Pearl Creek drainage, with the Jackal Hut high above you. To get there, make a 90-degree turn right (S) and climb the south side of the Pearl Creek drainage to the 11,420-foot saddle on the ridge between Pearl Creek and the East Fork of the Eagle River. This section of trail passes through intermittent clearings.

From the saddle, stick to the ridge and ski W for ¾ mile to the open clearing at the highest point on the ridge (11,716 feet), then drop SW to the Jackal Hut (11,660 feet) which sits just below and to the south of the highest part of the ridge. The building is visible from several hundred feet away, but you can miss it if you are skiing on the north side of the wide ridge crest, especially in a whiteout. If you know how long it takes you to ski ¾ mile, and you use your altimeter, you'll be sure to find it. Lazy mountaineers should look sharp!

SAFETY NOTES: Take care on the downhill into Resolution Creek. There can be slide danger in Resolution Bowl, both from large slab releases and small bank sluffs. Use proper precautions; stay on top of your orienteering.

SUMMER: You can hike down Resolution Bowl, but it'll make your knees hurt. The 10th Mountain recommended route is best for hiking, but the downhill into Resolution Creek is too rough for horses and bikes. Cyclists can get to the Jackal from the Fowler/Hilliard by riding around Ptarmigan Hill to Resolution Road (see route 9.3). Descend Resolution Road to Camp Hale, then take Ranch Creek (see route 10.2) to the Jackal Hut.

9.11

Fowler/Hilliard Hut to Janet's Cabin via Wilder Gulch

DIFFICULTY: Intermediate
TIME: 9 hours
DISTANCE: 8 miles
ELEVATION GAIN: 968 feet; loss: 858 feet

TEXT MAP: pp. 114-115
10TH MTN MAP: Resolution Mountain
USGS MAP: Copper Mountain, Pando, Red Cliff, Vail Pass

Use this route for the most direct trip to Janet's Cabin from the Fowler/ Hilliard. It's a long trail that passes through several drainages. Get an early start. As an alternative, drop to Vail Pass from Wilder Gulch, car shuttle to Copper Mountain Resort, then follow Guller Creek (route 16.1) to Janet's.

ROUTE DESCRIPTION: Take reverse route 9.6 and ski down to the 11,080-foot level in upper Wilder Gulch. Traverse E for 1 mile to 11,280 feet on the ridge between Wilder Gulch and Smith Gulch. Move S off the ridge here and take a traversing climb another mile to timberline at a small saddle and knob in the Stafford Creek drainage (11,640 feet).

Traverse the head of Stafford Creek by following an 11,600-foot contour, and gain an open saddle on the south ridge of the drainage at 11,680 feet. Take a slightly dropping contour SE from the saddle ¼ mile down to Janet's Cabin at the head of Guller Creek. If you find yourself above timberline you have gone too high.

SAFETY NOTES: Because much of this trail passes through open areas, do not depend on trail markers. Much of the terrain above timberline is exposed to avalanches. The correct trail avoids avalanche hazard by dipping in and out of the trees. But since the exact trail can be hard to find, skiers on this route should know how to identify avalanche hazard. Be prepared for extreme weather and know your escape routes.

SUMMER: This is a good alpine hike. Lack of trail tread makes the route unsuitable for bicycles and horses.

9.12

Resolution Mountain from Fowler/Hilliard Hut

DIFFICULTY: Intermediate/Expert
TIME: Several hours or more
DISTANCE: ¾ mile
ELEVATION GAIN: 405 feet

TEXT MAP: pp. 114, 144
10TH MTN MAP: Resol. Mt., Chi. Ridge
USGS MAP: Pando

Rising to the southwest of the Fowler/Hilliard Hut, Resolution Mountain is the only alpine terrain close to the hut. Skiing from the summit, you can find runs at almost all points of the compass. Beware of cornices, especially to the north and east of the summit. The wind can make poor snow conditions in the summit area, so explore lower down if you have trouble making turns.

ROUTE DESCRIPTION: To climb to the summit of Resolution Mountain, simply follow the northeast ridge from the Fowler/Hilliard Hut. Be careful with the cornices. One of the finest expert runs is a 1,000 vertical foot drop into Resolution Bowl (the bowl below the hut). The bottom portion of this bowl has quite a bit of brush, and the snow can be poor. You're better off skiing the bowl part way down, then skinning back up to the hut. If the southeast slopes have breakable crust, move around to the west or north.

All abilities will find good powder skiing in the glades down the hill northeast of the hut. Ski in such a way as to intersect the lower switchback of the logging road which ascends to the hut from the Wearyman Creek drainage (see routes 9.5 and 8.4), then follow the logging road back up to the hut. You can also find good glade skiing between the switchbacks on the logging road. If you have skins, it is most efficient to cut the switchbacks on the climb back up. Another good bet for intermediate and advanced skiers are the slopes of Ptarmigan Hill (see route 9.3). Again, be careful of avalanche slopes and use the exposure with the best snow.

SAFETY NOTES: Any of the open slopes on Resolution Mountain are potential slide areas. If you lack avalanche safety skills, stick to the glade skiing north of the hut.

SUMMER: The short walk to the summit of Resolution Mountain is a fine hike. It's a bit steep for all but the "extreme equestrian." Cyclists should leave their rigs at the hut.

9.13

Ptarmigan Hill from the Fowler/Hilliard Hut

DIFFICULTY: Intermediate
TIME: 3 ½ hours round trip
DISTANCE: 4 miles round trip
ELEVATION GAIN: 683 feet round trip

TEXT MAP: pp. 114, 144
10TH MTN MAP: Resol. Mt., Chi. Ridge
USGS MAP: Pando

Many skiers would rather explore the peaks than practice their turns. If you feel that way, do this tour.

ROUTE DESCRIPTION: The route is simple — it follows the ridge leading E from the hut 2 miles to the summit of Ptarmigan Hill. For details see route 9.3

SAFETY NOTES: Remember that this route is mostly at or above timberline. See route 9.3.

SUMMER: This is a fine hike. Horses and cyclists should stick to the road that traverses along the south side of the ridge and intersects the Resolution Road at 11,360 feet.

Chapter 10 • Jackal Hut

Located near timberline, the Jackal Hut has good local skiing and terrific views of several 14,000-foot peaks. The hut is owned by 10th Mountain and conforms to 10th Mountain's basic hut specifications. It is almost identical to the Fowler/Hilliard Hut.

ELEVATION: 11,660 feet
COUNTY: Eagle
TEXT MAP: pp. 144-145
10TH MTN MAP: Chicago Ridge
USGS MAP: Pando
TRAILHEADS: Pando, S. Camp Hale

As is the case with several other eastern 10th Mountain huts, the Jackal Hut is very close to a trailhead. While this can make trailhead to hut skiing less appealing for experienced skiers, it is a boon for those in the learning stage. Fortunately, you can do plenty of base skiing from the Jackal Hut, so consider carrying a few days supplies in from the trailhead and spending several nights at the hut.

The Jackal Hut was built with money donated by Jack Schuss and Al Zesiger, two strong supporters of 10th Mountain. Their example should serve to remind us all that the 10th Mountain huts exist only because of countless monetary donations and volunteer work hours.

The quickest trailhead to hut route to the Jackal Hut is the Ranch Creek route (10.2). For ski-throughs north to the Fowler/Hilliard Hut, you can choose between an alternate high route (10.4) or a 10th Mountain sug-gested route (10.5) that sticks more to the valleys but still hits timberline. For a ski-through south to Vance's Cabin, use route 10.6. You won't find much alpine ski mountaineering near the Jackal Hut, but nearby glades provide excellent powder skiing.

10.1

Pando Trailhead – Jackal Hut via Pearl Creek

DIFFICULTY: Intermediate   **TEXT MAP:** p. 144
TIME: 8 hours up, 6 hours down   **10TH MTN MAP:** Chicago Ridge
DISTANCE: 7 1/4 miles   **USGS MAP:** Pando
ELEVATION GAIN: 2,516 feet; loss 56 feet

This 10th Mountain suggested route is the longest trail to the Jackal Hut. Most often, the Pearl Creek section is used as part of the ski-through between the Jackal and Fowler/Hilliard huts.

ROUTE DESCRIPTION: From the Pando Trailhead ski E across the main north/south Camp Hale Road, across a bridge over the Eagle River, then E and NE to intersect a snow-covered road running north/south at the base of the mountain. Ski this road N a short distance, then turn right and ski SE up through a gulch east of point 9,540 (this is not the main Camp Hale Road). One mile from Pando you intersect the distinct Resolution Road. Take a left (NE) and ski 1 1/2 miles up the Resolution Road to 9,678 feet.

Turn right (SE) off the Resolution Road onto another distinct road-cut that crosses a bridge over Resolution Creek. Once on the south side of the creek, look for a 10th Mountain marked trail that leaves the road-cut and heads directly into the Pearl Creek drainage. Follow this trail for 1 3/4 miles on the southwest side of the creek to 10,320 feet where you cross to the northeast side of the drainage and climb another 1/2 mile to 10,560 feet.

At 10,560 feet you're still deep in the Pearl Creek drainage, with the Jackal Hut high above you. To get there make a 90-degree turn and climb through willows and clearings to 11,000 feet, then out of Pearl Creek to an 11,420-foot saddle on the ridge between Pearl Creek and the East Fork of the Eagle River.

From the saddle, stick to the ridge and ski 3/4 mile to the open clearing at the highest point on the ridge (11,716 feet), then drop 56 vertical feet SW to the Jackal Hut (11,660 feet) which sits just below and to the south of the highest part of the ridge. The building is visible from several hundred feet away, but you can miss it if you are skiing on the north side of the wide ridge crest, especially in a whiteout. If you know how long it takes you to ski 3/4 mile and you use your altimeter, you'll be sure to find it.

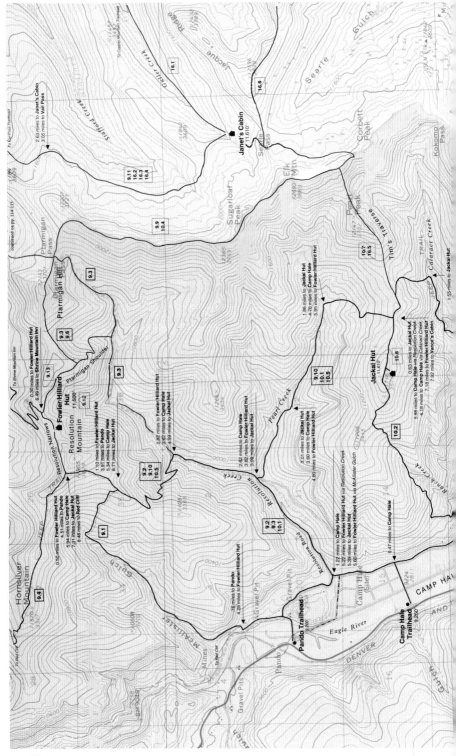

Janet's Cabin
11,610'

16.8

16.1

Corbett Peak

Searle Pass

Elk Mtn

Sugarloaf Peak

9.11
16.2
16.3
16.4

continued on pp. 114–115

9.9
10.4

Ptarmigan Hill

9.3

Kokomo Pass

2.63 miles to Janet's Cabin
3.05 miles to Vail Pass
To Vail Pass Trailhead

Gilfer Creek

Jacque Creek

Searle Gulch

Stafford Creek

Ptarmigan Pass

To Shrine Mountain Inn

9.3
9.6

0.30 miles to Fowler/Hilliard Hut
6.49 miles to Shrine Mountain Inn

9.13

Ptarmigan Shoulder

9.3

Resolution Narrows

Fowler/Hilliard Hut
11,500'

9.12

Resolution Mountain

1.10 miles to Fowler/Hilliard Hut
3.91 miles to Pando
5.34 miles to Camp Hale
6.71 miles to Jackal Hut

2.82 miles to Fowler/Hilliard Hut
3.82 miles to Camp Hale
4.99 miles to Jackal Hut

Pearl Creek

1.86 miles to Jackal Hut
4.76 miles to Camp Hale
5.95 miles to Fowler/Hilliard Hut

10.7
16.5

Tim's Traverse

To Jackal Hut

Cataract Creek

1.55 miles to Jackal Hut

9.2
9.10
10.5

9.10
10.1
10.5

2.62 miles to Jackal Hut
3.82 miles to Fowler/Hilliard Hut
3.99 miles to Fowler/Hilliard Hut

Jackal Hut
11,810'

10.8

0.63 miles to Jackal Hut
5.98 miles to Camp Hale via Resolution Creek
6.18 miles to Camp Hale via Cataract Creek
7.18 miles to Fowler/Hilliard Hut
7.92 miles to Vance's Cabin

9.1

0.50 miles to Fowler/Hilliard Hut
1.51 miles to Pando
4.31 miles to Camp Hale
7.31 miles to Jackal Hut
8.48 miles to Red Cliff

9.2
9.3
10.1

1.22 miles to Camp Hale
5.22 miles to Fowler/Hilliard Hut
5.39 miles to Jackal Hut
5.80 miles to Fowler/Hilliard Hut

10.2

To Red Cliff

Horsesilver Mountain

9.4

Resolution Road

Gravel Pit

Resolution Creek

McAllister Gulch

Ranch Creek

2.76 miles to Pando
4.25 miles to Fowler/Hilliard Hut

Gravel Pit

0.47 miles to Camp Hale

Pando Trailhead

Eagle River

Camp Hale Site

Camp Hale Trailhead
9,260'

CAMP HALE

DENVER AND

Gravel Pits

144

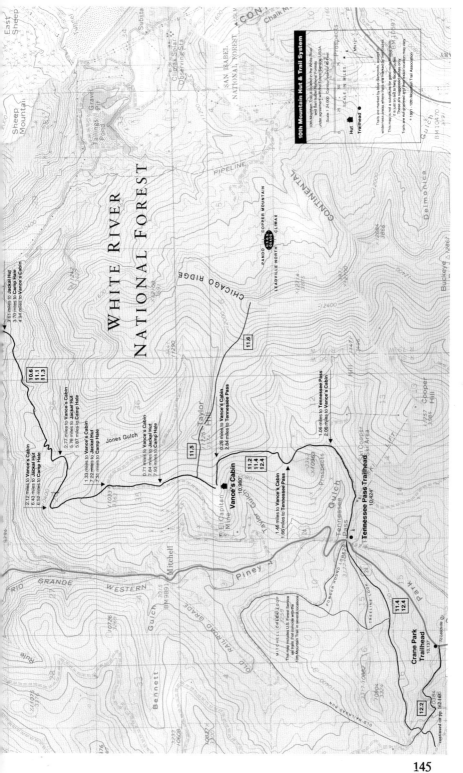

WHITE RIVER
NATIONAL FOREST

SAN ISABEL
NATIONAL FOREST

10th Mountain Hut & Trail System

10th Mountain Trail is located in the White River
and San Isabel National Forests
under agreement with the Forest Service, USDA.

SCALE IN MILES

Scale 1:24,000 Contour Interval 40 feet

Trails are marked by blue diamonds. In some
wilderness areas, where trails are marked by the Forest Service,
it is just an aid to help locate routes.

This map is not a substitute for good route-finding skills.

Trails are suggested and some
Trails are not groomed and their exact location may vary.

© 1991 - 10th Mountain Trail Association

Hut   Trailhead

CONTINENTAL

PANDO
COPPER MOUNTAIN
CLIMAX

U.S.S. QUAD

CHICAGO RIDGE

Jones Gulch

11.6

3.61 miles to Jackal Hut
3.70 miles to Camp Hale
4.34 miles to Vance's Cabin

10.6
11.1
11.3

2.12 miles to Vance's Cabin
6.43 miles to Jackal Hut
6.52 miles to Camp Hale

2.77 miles to Vance's Cabin
5.78 miles to Jackal Hut
5.87 miles to Camp Hale

1.33 miles to Vance's Cabin
2.84 miles to Jackal Hut
7.31 miles to Camp Hale

0.71 miles to Vance's Cabin
7.84 miles to Jackal Hut
7.93 miles to Camp Hale

0.28 miles to Vance's Cabin
2.84 miles to Tennessee Pass

1.06 miles to Tennessee Pass
2.06 miles to Vance's Cabin

11.5

Taylor Hill

11.2
11.4
12.4

Vance's Cabin
10,980'

El Capitan Mine

Taylor Gulch

1.45 miles to Vance's Cabin
1.66 miles to Tennessee Pass

Prospects

Tennessee Pass Ski Area

Tennessee Pass Trailhead
10,424'

Cooper Hill

Tennessee Pass Gulch

Piney

RIO GRANDE WESTERN

Mitchell

BM 9981

Old RAILROAD GRADE

POWDER HOUND LOOP

TREELINE LOOP

MITCHELL CREEK LOOP

This map includes U.S. Forest Service
ski trails that coincide with the
10th Mountain Trail in several locations.

11.4
12.4

Crane Park
Trailhead
10,137'

To Leadville

OLD RAILROAD RUN

12.2

Bennett

Delmonica Gulch

Buckeye

BM 10470

Cooper Hill

continued on pp. 162-165

145

REVERSE ROUTE DESCRIPTION: From the front steps of the Jackal Hut, traverse NE several hundred feet to the ridge crest. Descend the ridge E for ¾ mile to the distinct 11,420-foot saddle. Drop down the north side of the saddle into Pearl Creek. You can make turns for a few hundred vertical feet, but make sure you're on the 10th Mountain marked trail when the willows begin at 11,000 feet, otherwise you'll "wander in the willows."

Intersect Pearl Creek at 10,560 feet and cross to the north side of the creek. Descend the Pearl Creek drainage to Resolution Road in the Resolution Creek drainage. Ski Resolution Road SW 2 miles downvalley to Camp Hale. For the Pando Trailhead, take a right just before you make a final short drop into the flats of Camp Hale and ski N on a road tucked in behind point 9,540. Just north of point 9,540 you'll intersect a main north/south snow-covered road. Take a left (S) here, turn W, and ski across the flats to a bridge over the Eagle River. The Pando Trailhead is several hundred feet west of the bridge.

If visibility is poor in Camp Hale you might have trouble finding the Pando Trailhead and bridge. In this case you can strike cross country to Highway 24, your only obstacles being the Eagle River and up to a mile of trail to break out. In midwinter you can usually find a snow bridge over the Eagle River.

SAFETY NOTES: Use your survival ski skills on the descent from the 11,420-foot saddle.

SUMMER: Hikers and equestrians will enjoy this route.

10.2

South Camp Hale Trailhead — Jackal Hut via Ranch Creek

DIFFICULTY: Intermediate
TIME: 4 ¾ hours up, 3 hours down
DISTANCE: 4 miles
ELEVATION GAIN: 2,436 feet; loss: 56 feet

TEXT MAP: p. 144
10TH MTN MAP: Chicago Ridge
USGS MAP: Pando

This trailhead to hut route is short and to the point. It is a 10th Mountain suggested route and uses a portion of the popular snowmobile trail in Camp Hale; so keep an open ear and nimble feet.

ROUTE DESCRIPTION: From the South Camp Hale Trailhead, ski NE across the flats of Camp Hale (use a snow bridge to cross the Eagle River). Intersect the road at the base of the mountain, turn right (SE), and ski the snow-covered road ¼ mile to the well-signed intersection with the Ranch Creek Road.

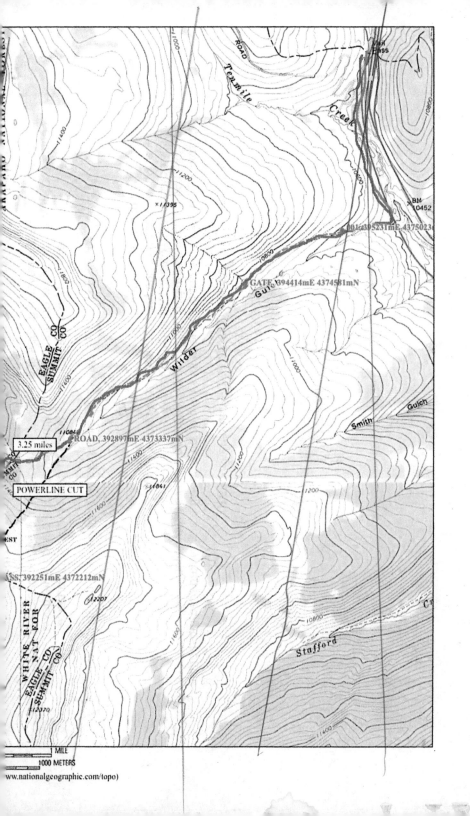

Ten mile

ROAD

Vail
Pass

Creek

×11395

BM
10452

01 395231mE 4375023

GATE 394414mE 4374581mN

Gulch

Wilder

Smith   Gulch

3.25 miles

11084

ROAD 392897mE 4373337mN

POWERLINE CUT

×11041

10800

1200

EAGLE CO
SUMMIT CO

WHITE RIVER NAT FOR
EAGLE CO
SUMMIT CO

SS 392251mE 4372212mN

2207

Stafford

Cr

MILE
1000 METERS

www.nationalgeographic.com/topo)

6—Safety info: Please travel in groups of 3 or more. Use radios if dropping back to group behind you. If injury or illness occurs, identify the emergency. One person write down details. Make a rescue plan. Safety of all is of utmost importance.

SKIERS should have avalanche beepers and know how to use them.

General Trail description: (see map)
Park at Shrine pass (parking fee is included in our hut permit)
Mostly downhill for .9 mile to Wilder Gulch trailhead
Approx. 3.54 mi up to Ptarmigan Pass …well-groomed/used by snowmobiles
Approx. 2.74 miles to the hut from the pass…we'll be on a snowmobile tracked road most of the way
Estimated time: 5.5—8 hours   DOOR LOCK combination: 8920

Bivvy Sack - thin me + 2 garbage bags
Radio - 7.29 + batteries
Map / Compass
7:30 AM of El Rio

Fowler-Hilliard hut trip emergency info.

1—Medical knowledge:
   Names of those who have basic first aid/CPR
   Who is carrying a first aid kit (more than band-aids/moleskin)

2—CORSAR cards—please! (helps local rescue group get financial reimbursement for your emergency) can be purchased at Walmart (fishing license area) or Eddie Bear in S-thorne. $3/year, $12/5 yr

3—All should know the route and all potential road heads. Look at maps at home, have a map and compass with you. Be knowledgeable…Don't rely on others who might make a mistake!!!

4—Emergency contact #'s:
   Summit Co: 970-453-2232 (will need this # from start of trip up to Ptarmigan Pass)
   Eagle Co: 970-328-8500 (will need this # from Ptarmigan Pass to Fowler-Hilliard and anything we are doing around the hut)

   OR: 911
   Other #'s: Holy Cross Ranger Dist: 970-827-5715
               Dillon Ranger Dist: 970- 468- 5400
               NOVA Guides : 719-486-2623 (snowmobile pack support…Camp Hale/Pando)

   Pat Soats 486-5315 *cell-970-390-0809*
                        Dave or Greg

5—Communication devices: Generally, do not rely on *cell phones*. However, take them…it may just work when we need it.
   Hand-held radios. EVERYONE should have one—turn on when on the trail. Have extra

Feb 27 — MARCH 2, 2006

13

Wearyman   Creek   JEEP TRAIL

24

25

26

WearymanConnect NO NO

look for gate/

stay on ridge from gate to hut

Ptarmigan Hill 12,143

probable terrain course

HUT 389089mE 4372294mN   11683

Ptarmi

1.48 mi

cornice

Resolution Mountain

LAST LEG, 2.74 miles

snowmobile trail inter

10382   10600   10704

36

N ✱ MN
10½°

1000 FEET

Map created with TOPO!® ©2003 National Geog

Put on your skins here. Take a left (N) on the Ranch Creek Road and follow a distinct road-cut that climbs Ranch Creek 2 miles to 10,700 feet. Here you'll break into a clearing with several beautiful old cabins. Climb NE through the clearing and re-enter the timber at about 10,900 feet. Follow the trail up several switchbacks. Strong skiers will certainly want to cut some of these switchbacks. If you do so, take care to relocate the 10th Mountain marked trail.

At 11,220 feet the trail takes an important right turn (E), then climbs 1/4 mile (around 2 more switchbacks) to a large open area on the ridge. Follow the ridge E for 1/2 mile to the ridge top at 11,716 feet. As you are skiing along the flat, sparsely timbered ridge top, you'll see the stove pipes of the hut down to your right. In poor visibility take care not to overshoot the hut. Your altimeter can help prevent this, since the main goal is the high point of the ridge. Ski a few hundred feet E along the ridge top, then double back W to the hut.

REVERSE ROUTE DESCRIPTION: From the front steps of the hut take a climbing traverse NE to the ridge crest, then head W over the ridge top. Stick to the broad ridge crest for 1/2 mile, then drop W into the Ranch Creek drainage on a marked 10th Mountain suggested route. Experts can cut most of the switchbacks on the marked trail and enjoy turns down the fall line in the clearing beginning at about 10,900 feet. Be careful to intersect the road-cut at the lower edge of a clearing. The road down the Ranch Creek drainage is easy to follow. At the flats of Camp Hale use your map to reach the South Camp Hale Trailhead. If a whiteout cuts the view, just strike out across the flats on a compass bearing and you'll hit Highway 24. If you're really good, you should be able to follow a bearing to within a few feet of the trailhead.

SAFETY NOTES: This trail begins as one of those "nose to the grindstone" climbs. However, the last part of the route (on the ridge) requires attention to navigation.

SUMMER: The Ranch Creek Road is a good bike, horse, and hiking route. It does not connect to the hut, but cyclists can easily manage the short portage.

10.3

South Camp Hale Trailhead — Jackal Hut via Cataract Creek

DIFFICULTY: Intermediate
TIME: 5 1/2 hours up, 4 hours down
DISTANCE: 5 1/3 miles
ELEVATION GAIN: 2,436 feet; loss: 56 feet

TEXT MAP: pp. 144-145
10TH MTN MAP: Chicago Ridge
USGS MAP: Pando

This is the "medium length" trailhead to hut route for the Jackal Hut. It is more useful as a descent on the route to Vance's Cabin (see route 10.6).

ROUTE DESCRIPTION: Start at the South Camp Hale Trailhead with waxed skis. Ski NE across the flats of Camp Hale (find a snow bridge to cross the Eagle River). Intersect the road at the base of the mountain, turn right (SE), and ski the snow-covered road 2 1/4 miles up the flat drainage of the East Fork of the Eagle River. Put your skins on here and take a left (9,560 feet) onto the welll-signed Cataract Creek jeep trail. From here climb the jeep trail. The Colorado Trail uses the Cataract Creek jeep trail, so you'll find the little triangular Colorado Trail markers along with standard 10th Mountain markers. Cataract Creek is nestled in a steep-sided gulch, so the road winds as it works its way through the gulch. At 10,720 feet in the Cataract Creek drainage you leave the jeep trail and climb N 1/2 mile and 700 vertical feet to a wide saddle (11,420 feet) atop the north ridge of the drainage.

Ski W from the saddle over a bump to another 11,420-foot saddle (intersection with route 10.1). From here stick to the ridge and ski 3/4 mile W to the open clearing at the highest point on the ridge (11,716 feet), then drop S to the Jackal Hut (11,660 feet) which sits just below and to the south of the highest part of the ridge. The hut is visible from several hundred feet away, but you can miss it if you are skiing on the north side of the wide ridge crest, especially in a whiteout.

REVERSE ROUTE DESCRIPTION: From the front steps of the Jackal Hut traverse NE several hundred feet to the ridge crest. Descend the ridge E 3/4 mile to the distinct 11,420-foot saddle dividing the Catarack Creek and Pearl Creek drainages. Continue SE from the saddle, traversing around the south side of point 11,475 to another 11,420-foot saddle. Drop S from here into the Cataract Creek drainage and intersect the Cataract Creek jeep trail at 10,720 feet. Descend the jeep trail to the valley floor of the Eagle River drainage, then follow the main snow-covered road W downvalley to the Camp Hale trailheads.

SAFETY NOTES: For the most part the Cataract Creek jeep trail keeps you out of a steep-sided gulch. One section of the road, however, from 10,360 feet down to the creek crossing at 10,160 feet, would take you under a dangerous steep bank. Bypass this to the east on a short route with standard 10th Mountain markings.

SUMMER: The Cataract Creek jeep trail is a fine bicycle route, but you have to portage along the ridge to the hut. Hikers and horse people will enjoy this whole route.

10.4

Jackal Hut to Fowler/Hilliard Hut via Elk Ridge High Route

DIFFICULTY: Advanced   **TEXT MAP:** p. 144
TIME: 8 hours   **10TH MTN MAP:** Chicago Ridge
DISTANCE: 7 miles   **USGS MAP:** Pando
ELEVATION GAIN: 1,840 feet; loss: 2,000 feet

This alternate route to the Fowler/Hilliard Hut will provide more downhill skiing and better views than the Pearl Creek route (10.5). It is unmarked and includes several miles above timberline. Thus, you should put plenty of time into using your map, compass, and altimeter.

ROUTE DESCRIPTION: From the Jackal Hut climb Tim's Traverse (see route 10.7) to Elk Ridge. Follow Elk Ridge N for 3 ½ miles, then leave the ridge and drop W to Ptarmigan Pass. Elk Ridge includes numerous summits and may be devoid of snow. Be ready to walk.

From Ptarmigan Pass climb W to the summit of Ptarmigan Hill. Drop down the west side of Ptarmigan Hill to the road-cut that contours through sparse timber around the southwest side of 11,683. Follow this road SW and W one mile to the 11,480-foot saddle where you converge with route 9.5/8.4. From here continue ⅓ mile W and SW along the ridge to the Fowler/Hilliard Hut. The hut is not visible until you top a small 40-foot high hill several hundred feet east of the hut.

SAFETY NOTES: This route follows ridges to avoid avalanche slopes. Even so, you could encounter slide danger while contouring around summits. Cornices can also be a hazard. With snow cover, the north and south sides of Ptarmigan Hill are avalanche slopes.

SUMMER: Enjoy this route as an "off-trail" hike. Equestrians and cyclists should stick to the roads and maintained trails.

10.5

Jackal Hut to Fowler/Hilliard Hut via Pearl Creek

DIFFICULTY: Intermediate   **TEXT MAP:** p. 144
TIME: 7 1/2 hours   **10TH MTN MAP:** Chicago Ridge
DISTANCE: 8 miles   **USGS MAP:** Pando
ELEVATION GAIN: 2,078 feet; loss: 2,238 feet

This is a basic ski-through route. It uses marked 10th Mountain suggested routes and includes some scenic timberline travel.

ROUTE DESCRIPTION: From the front steps of the Jackal Hut traverse NE several hundred feet to the ridge crest. Descend the ridge E for ¾ mile to a distinct 11,420-foot saddle. Drop down the north side of the saddle into Pearl Creek. You can get in some turns for a few hundred vertical feet, but make sure you're on the 10th Mountain marked trail when the willows begin at 11,000 feet, otherwise you'll have to "beat the rushes."

Intersect Pearl Creek at 10,560 feet and cross to the north side of the creek (route 9.9/10.4 intersects here). Descend the Pearl Creek drainage 2 ⅛ miles to the Resolution Creek drainage. Cross a bridge over Resolution Creek and gain the distinct cut of the Resolution Road.

Ski the Resolution Road 1 mile upvalley to 9,960 feet. Leave the Resolution Road here and take a left (NW) onto a marked 10th Mountain trail. The blue diamonds take you up to a 10,940-foot saddle on the southwest ridge of Resolution Mountain. Most of this trail follows a distinct trail-cut through forest. In the occasional clearing, take time to zero in on the route with your map. Remember: diamonds are for dummies.

Climb the southwest ridge of Resolution Mountain for ¾ mile to 11,400 feet (you'll pass the intersection of route 9.1 at 11,300 feet). Next, take a ¾-mile climbing traverse NE then N across the west face of Resolution Mountain, ending at 11,700-foot Resolution Saddle on the northwest ridge of Resolution Mountain. Ski down E from the saddle and make a short traverse that leads to a distinct east/west cleft called the Resolution Narrows. Take care not to ski N downhill from the saddle. Continue E down the Resolution Narrows to the Fowler/Hilliard Hut in a clearing at 11,500 feet. In clear weather the hut is visible from Resolution Saddle. To get some "bonus turns" experts should consider ascending Resolution Mountain, then cutting turns down to the hut.

SAFETY NOTES: There can be slide danger on the open slopes of Resolution Mountain. Be aware of cornices on all the ridges. The trails out of Camp Hale are used by snowmobiles quite often.

SUMMER: This route is not recommended for hiking. The section of trail from Resolution Creek climbing to Resolution Mountain is a marked ski route with no path for horse or bike travel. The Resolution Road is a good bicycle route.

10.6

Jackal Hut to Vance's Cabin via Cataract Creek

DIFFICULTY: Intermediate
TIME: 7 hours
DISTANCE: 8 ½ miles
ELEVATION GAIN: 1,420 feet; loss: 2,100 feet

TEXT MAP: pp. 144-145
10TH MTN MAP: Chicago Ridge
USGS MAP: Pando

This 10th Mountain suggested route is the standard ski-through route from the Jackal Hut to Vance's Cabin.

ROUTE DESCRIPTION: From the front steps of the Jackal Hut traverse NE several hundred feet to the ridge crest. Descend the ridge E for ¾ mile to the distinct 11,420-foot saddle dividing the Cataract Creek and Pearl Creek drainages. Continue SE from the saddle over point 11,475 to another 11,420-foot saddle. Drop S from here into the Cataract Creek

On the ridge from the Jackal Hut to the Cataract Creek trail.

drainage and intersect the Cataract Creek jeep trail at 10,720 feet. Descend the jeep trail to the valley floor of the Eagle River drainage.

Follow a snow-covered main road for ¼ mile upvalley. Just after the snow-covered road crosses the East Fork of the Eagle River (no bridge), leave the main road and ski right (S) several hundred feet across a flat area. Swing SW and begin a climbing traverse that leads up a marked trail-cut for 2 miles through timber to Jones Gulch. Stay on the northeast side of Jones Creek and parallel the creek to a marshy clearing at the 10,400-foot level.

Follow the marked trail W along the north side of the clearing, then continue on a climbing traverse NW (on sections of road and trail) to 10,600 feet on a shoulder. Swing S and climb the shoulder to 11,033 feet. From here the trail leaves the crest of the shoulder and follows a long 1 ½-mile climbing traverse through medium density timber to the lower edge of a burn area at 11,000 feet on the west shoulder of Taylor Hill.

The hut sits at the lower southwest end of the burn on the side of a rise and is hard to see when you enter the burn. However, there are structures near the hut that you can see from a little farther away.

SAFETY NOTES: For the most part, the Cataract Creek jeep trail keeps you out of a steep-sided gulch. One section of the road, however, from 10,360 feet down to the creek crossing at 10,160 feet, would take you under a dangerous steep bank. You bypass this to the east on a short route with standard 10th Mountain markings.

SUMMER: This is not a suitable summer route (see Chapter 11 for Vance's Cabin summer ideas).

10.7
Jackal Hut to Janet's Cabin via Tim's Traverse

DIFFICULTY: Expert	**TEXT MAP:** p. 144
TIME: 6 hours	**10TH MTN MAP:** Chicago Ridge
DISTANCE: 4 ½ miles	**USGS MAP:** Copper Mountain, Pando
ELEVATION GAIN: 1,180 feet; loss: 1,230	

This alternate route is a fine connection between two terrific huts.

ROUTE DESCRIPTION: From the front steps of the Jackal Hut traverse NE for several hundred feet to the ridge crest. Descend the ridge E for ¾ mile to the distinct 11,420-foot saddle dividing the Cataract Creek and Pearl Creek drainages. Leave the marked trail here by continuing E and NE up the ridge for 1 mile and 580 vertical feet to Pearl Peak. Summit Pearl Peak or contour the south side (depending on avalanche conditions) and continue climbing E up the ridge to 12,600 feet on Elk Ridge.

Descend S for ¼ mile down Elk Ridge to a saddle (12,460 feet). Read your map here and identify Searle Pass to the north across the basin, then drop into the basin and traverse to Searle Pass. From the pass descend 430 vertical feet NW and W to Janet's Cabin. The hut is located at 11,610 feet, just below timberline a few hundred feet northwest of Guller Creek.

SAFETY NOTES: Much of this route passes through avalanche terrain. You should carry avalanche rescue equipment and be expert with hazard avoidance. Ski this route during a period of stable snow, such as a cold day during the spring corn-snow season.

SUMMER: You can enjoy a nice alpine hike via this route.

10.8
Ski Tours from Jackal Hut

DIFFICULTY: Intermediate to Advanced
TEXT MAP: p. 144
10TH MTN MAP: Chicago Ridge
USGS MAP: Pando

The Jackal Hut is located in the midst of some fine glade skiing. You'll find slopes on all exposures, so move around to get good snow.

ROUTE DESCRIPTION: One good run takes the open areas at the head of Pearl Creek just west of the 10th Mountain suggested route. Cut over to the trail as soon as the trees tighten and use the trail for your climb back up. Be careful of small cliffs farther to the west.

You can also ski S from the front porch. Head down the open area, then into trees that soon thicken into an unskiable forest. Enjoy a few laps.

You can get another good run by simply following the Ranch Creek route (10.2). Cut the switchbacks down to 11,000 feet, then make figure-eights in the open area down to the forest. Do laps here until dinnertime.

SAFETY NOTES: By exploring you can find dozens of hidden powder caches. If you go wild, make sure you have time to climb back to the hut before dark. Beware of sudden drop-offs and cliff areas.

Chapter 11 • Vance's Cabin

Vance's Cabin is a privately owned hut located on
a timbered mountainside near
Tennessee Pass. Through compact, it sleeps 16. It has a gas
stove, gas lights, refrigerator,
and sauna. Reservations are
taken by 10th Mountain. Con-
struction of the cabin began in 1980 and was completed in 1988.

ELEVATION: 10,980 feet
COUNTY: Eagle
TEXT MAP: pp. 144-145
10TH MTN MAP: Chicago Ridge
USGS MAP: Pando
TRAILHEADS: South Camp Hale,
Tennessee Pass

The quick trail to Vance's Cabin is the Piney Gulch route (11.2). For ski-
throughs use route 11.3 to head north, and route 11.4 to head south.
Novice mountaineers will find enjoyable day trips on Taylor Hill to the east
of the cabin. Experts can explore Chicago Ridge farther to the east.

In the past, Vance's Cabin has been open in late summer and fall (as well
as in winter). The best hiking, bike, and horse route to the hut takes Piney
Gulch (route 11.2). For cyclists, a short road route uses the road shown on
the USGS map climbing from Highway 24 up past the El Capitan Mine,

then up to the cabin. There is no parking at the start of this road. All the dirt roads and trails in the area are worth exploring. You'll find good alpine hiking on Taylor Hill and farther east on Chicago Ridge.

11.1

South Camp Hale Trailhead — Vance's Cabin via East Fork Eagle River

DIFFICULTY: Intermediate
TIME: 7 hours up, 5 hours down
DISTANCE: 8 miles
ELEVATION GAIN: 1,700 feet

TEXT MAP: pp. 144-145
10TH MTN MAP: Chicago Ridge
USGS MAP: Pando

This 10th Mountain suggested route is the longer trailhead to hut route for Vance's Cabin. It serves most often as part of the ski-through route from the Jackal Hut, but it also makes a fine tour in it's own right.

ROUTE DESCRIPTION: From the South Camp Hale Trailhead ski E across the flats of Camp Hale (no bridge across Eagle River). Intersect the snow-covered road at the base of the mountain (usually packed by snowmobile) and ski this road for 2 1/4 miles up the East Fork of the Eagle River to 9,560 feet, just past a flat marshy area with a small pond. In winter this pond will be obscured by snow. Turn right (S) off the road just after you cross the East Fork of the Eagle River (no bridge). Continue S for several hundred feet across the flat area. Swing SW and begin a climbing traverse that leads up a marked trail-cut for 2 miles through timber to Jones Gulch. Stay on the northeast side of Jones Creek and parallel the creek to a marshy clearing at the 10,400-foot level.

Follow the marked trail W along the north side of the clearing, then continue on a climbing traverse NW (on sections of road and trail) to 10,600 feet on a shoulder. Swing S and climb the shoulder to 11,033 feet. From here the trail leaves the crest of the shoulder and follows a long 1 1/2-mile climbing traverse through medium density timber to the lower edge of a burn area at 11,000 feet on the west shoulder of Taylor Hill.

The hut sits at the lower southwest end of the burn on the side of a rise and is not too visible from where you enter the burn. However, several structures around the hut are easier to spot.

REVERSE ROUTE DESCRIPTION: From the front door of Vance's Cabin ski N across a clearing. In the timber at the north end of the clearing take care to find the marked 10th Mountain trail that leads N from the clearing on a 1 1/4-mile traverse (on roads and trails) to 11,033 feet. From here continue N down the ridge for 3/4 mile to 10,600 feet.

Turn right (E) and follow another dropping traverse to a flat marshy clearing at 10,400 feet in Jones Gulch. Stick to the north edge of the clearing, cross Jones Creek, then descend N down the east side of Jones Gulch (can be a scary downhill). When the angle eases off at 10,220 feet, turn right (E) again and drop through several curves to a long easterly trail-cut that takes you to the East Fork of the Eagle River.

Cross the Eagle River and ski the snow-covered road for 2 ¾ miles downvalley to the South Camp Hale Trailhead. Take care not to overshoot the trailhead. Basically, when the road you skied NW (down the East Fork) turns N, take a hard left and ski SW across the flats of former Camp Hale for ½ mile to the trailhead at Highway 24.

Experts can save a great deal of distance — and get more turns — by continuing down the fall line from the turn at 11,600 feet. There is some dense timber on this route, so only experts should attempt it.

SAFETY NOTES: During storms, visibility in the flats of Camp Hale can be limited. Careful use of compass bearings can keep you on the correct path.

SUMMER: This trail is unsuitable for summer travel. Vance's Cabin may be open in the summer; check with 10th Mountain for the latest information. The dirt roads and trails in the area, however, are fine horse, bike, and hiking routes.

11.2
Tennessee Pass Trailhead — Vance's Cabin via Piney Gulch

DIFFICULTY: Intermediate	**TEXT MAP:** p. 145
TIME: 4 hours up, 3 hours down	**10TH MTN MAP:** Chicago Ridge
DISTANCE: 3 ⅛ miles	**USGS MAP:** Leadville North, Pando
ELEVATION GAIN: 556 feet	

This is one of the shortest, easiest trailhead to hut routes in the whole 10th Mountain system. As such, it's a good "first hut" tour. But it still follows a backcountry trail, so be realistic. It is a 10th Mountain suggested route, but the standard 10th Mountain trail markings can be confused with the cross country trail markings at the beginning of the route.

ROUTE DESCRIPTION: Begin at the Tennessee Pass Trailhead. Park on the west side of Highway 24, cross the highway and walk up the obvious road east for ½ mile to the parking lot of the Ski Cooper ski area. You can ski on the north side of the road if walking is not to your taste.

Once in the parking lot, find the start of the Nordic trail system at the

Kids can enjoy the huts, but families should be considerate of others.

northeast corner of the lot next to the Nordic Center building. Follow the maintained Nordic trail NE along a water ditch that traverses into Piney Gulch. At ¾ mile from the Nordic Center the gulch splits (10,520 feet). Leave the Nordic trail system here and ski up the left fork of the gulch for ¼ mile to a large clearing (10,660 feet).

Climb NW up through the clearing to the north end of the saddle north of point 10,963. At the saddle use your map and compass to identify the slopes of Taylor Hill. Climb E for a short distance, then swing back N and make a long ½-mile traverse along the west face of Taylor Hill. At 11,160 feet, just to the east of the hut, you enter an open area. Turn left here and descend ¼ mile to Vance's Cabin. Some structures around the cabin are visible from several hundred yards.

REVERSE ROUTE DESCRIPTION: From the front door of Vance's Cabin ski N for ¼ mile, then turn right (E) and climb to 11,160 feet on the west face of Taylor Hill. Turn right (S) and ski a level traverse for ½ mile through timber, then drop S and W to the saddle north of point 10,963. You don't quite ski to the apex of the saddle. Instead, from the north end of the saddle, turn SE and drop through clearings to 10,660 feet in the north fork of Piney Gulch. Ski down the gulch a short distance, cross the creek and follow the east side of the creek to the confluence of the north and south forks of Piney Gulch. From here follow the Ski Cooper Nordic trail system to the Ski Cooper parking area. Take the Ski Cooper access road to the Tennessee Pass Trailhead. You can walk this road or ski next to it on the north side.

SAFETY NOTES: Don't let the short length of this route make you lazy.

SUMMER: This is the preferred summer route to Vance's Cabin.

11.3

Vance's Cabin to Jackal Hut via Cataract Creek

DIFFICULTY: Intermediate
TIME: 8 hours
DISTANCE: 8 ½ miles
ELEVATION GAIN: 2,156 feet; loss: 1,476 feet

TEXT MAP: pp. 144-145
10TH MTN MAP: Chicago Ridge
USGS MAP: Pando

This 10th Mountain suggested route is the standard ski-through route from Vance's Cabin to the Jackal Hut. It includes a nice ridge crest and a fairly direct climb.

ROUTE DESCRIPTION: From Vance's Cabin take reverse route 11.1 down to the crossing of the East Fork of the Eagle River. Follow the snow-covered road (north side of valley) for ¼ mile downvalley to the Cataract Creek jeep trail. Turn right (N) and follow route 10.3 up the Cataract

Creek jeep trail and on to the Jackal Hut. The Colorado Trail uses the Cataract Creek jeep trail, so you'll find the little triangular Colorado Trail markers along with standard 10th Mountain markers.

SAFETY NOTES: See notes on routes 10.3 and 11.1.

SUMMER: See notes on routes 10.3 and 11.1.

11.4

Vance's Cabin to 10th Mountain Division Hut via Tennessee Pass

DIFFICULTY: Intermediate	**TEXT MAP:** pp. 145, 162
TIME: 9 hours	**10TH MTN MAP:** Ch. Ridge, Galena Mt.
DISTANCE: 9 miles	**USGS MAP:** Pando, Leadville North,
ELEVATION GAIN: 1,150 feet; loss: 760 feet	Homestake Reservoir

This 10th Mountain suggested route is the standard ski-through from Vance's Cabin to the 10th Mountain Division Hut. It passes Ski Cooper ski area and crosses a major highway. Plan a resupply for the highway if you're on a long ski-through.

ROUTE DESCRIPTION: Take reverse route 11.2 to Tennessee Pass, then follow route 12.1 to the 10th Mountain Division Hut.

SAFETY NOTES: This is a long route, so start early. See notes for routes 11.2 and 12.1.

SUMMER: See notes for routes 11.2 and 12.1.

11.5

Taylor Hill from Vance's Cabin

DIFFICULTY: Intermediate	**TEXT MAP:** p. 145
TIME: Several hours to half day	**10TH MTN MAP:** Chicago Ridge
DISTANCE: 1 ½ miles round trip	**USGS MAP:** Pando
ELEVATION GAIN: 745 feet round trip	

This branch route is a fine climb with plenty of ski options.

ROUTE DESCRIPTION: Put on your skins at the cabin. From the front door of Vance's Cabin ski N about ¼ mile, then turn right (E) and climb to 11,160 feet on the west face of Taylor Hill. At 11,160 feet, where the marked trail turns right (S), leave the trail and continue to climb E for ½ mile to the summit of Taylor Hill (11,725 feet). For good skiing stay north of the ascent route and enjoy open slopes back down to the clearing just north of the cabin.

You can also find some glade skiing by dropping from the Taylor Hill summit S into Piney Gulch, then picking up route 11.2 back to the cabin. This is a more advanced option. If you want shorter runs, play on the open slope behind the cabin.

SAFETY NOTES: Stay away from the steep north face of Taylor Hill and beware of cornices on the summit.

SUMMER: This is a fine alpine hike.

11.6

Chicago Ridge from Vance's Cabin

DIFFICULTY: Advanced   **TEXT MAP:** p. 145
TIME: Full day round trip   **10TH MTN MAP:** Chicago Ridge
DISTANCE: 4 ½ miles round trip   **USGS MAP:** Pando
ELEVATION GAIN: 1,562 feet round trip

If you thought Taylor Hill was a mountain, wait until you see Chicago Ridge! This majestic crest winds for 5 miles along a north/south axis to the east of Vance's Cabin. If you were ambitious enough, you could gain the high point via this route, then ski the ridge S all the way to the outskirts of Leadville.

ROUTE DESCRIPTION: To climb from Vance's Cabin to the high point of the ridge, follow route 11.5 to the summit of Taylor Hill. As you'll see, Taylor Hill is really just a west shoulder of Chicago Ridge. From Taylor Hill simply drop E into saddle 11,635, then continue climbing E. Stick with the ridge until you gain point 12,542 on Chicago Ridge. Ascend the ridge S from here for ½ mile to the summit. Return via the same route

SAFETY NOTES: Carefully judge slide hazard on the broad ridge leading to point 12,542 on Chicago Ridge. Watch for cornices on the ridge and don't let the excitement of a ski descent win over good judgment. With Colorado's midwinter snowpack, sticking to the ridges is how you survive years of mountaineering.

SUMMER: This is a fine alpine hike. It is not suitable for horses or bicycles.

Chapter 12 •10th Mountain Division Hut

H igh on a gladed hillside near timberline, the 10th Mountain Division Hut is nestled in the arms of the Continental Divide. The log structure sleeps 16 and provides the standard 10th Mountain amenities, as well as a private upstairs bedroom.

ELEVATION: 11,370 feet
COUNTY: Lake
TEXT MAP: pp. 162-163
10TH MTN MAP: Galena Mountain
USGS MAP: Homestake Reservoir
TRAILHEADS: Tennessee Pass,
Crane Park

Completed during the summer of 1989, the hut was built with funds given by a group of 10th Mountain Division veterans: Bill Boddington (10th Mountain board), Col. Pete Peterson, Maury Kuper, and Bill Bowerman.

Approaching the 10th Mountain Division Hut from the south.

For travel between the hut and the Tennessee Pass Trailhead, consider the 10th Mountain suggested route (12.1) that heads up the North Fork of West Tennessee Creek. While other routes are possible, they have not been used enough for inclusion here. The route from the 10th Mountain Division Hut to Uncle Bud's Hut (12.3) dips through more than 6 main and subsidiary drainages as it parallels the Continental Divide far above. You'll get good use out of your map on this route!

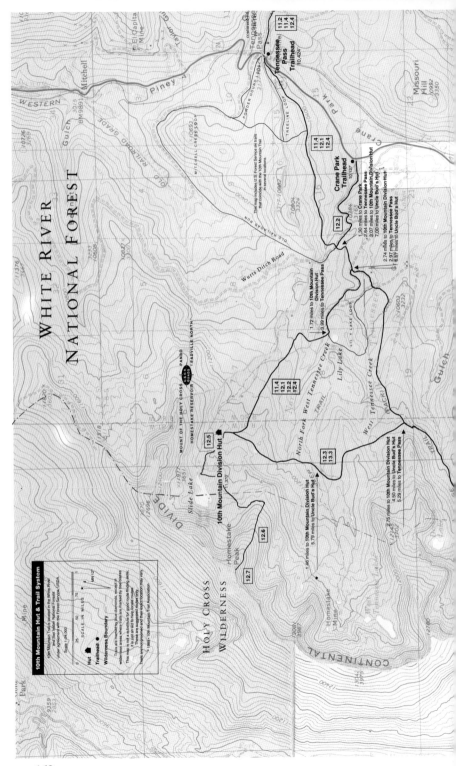

WHITE RIVER

NATIONAL FOREST

HOLY CROSS
WILDERNESS

10th Mountain Hut & Trail System

10th Mountain Trails located in the White River
and San Isabel National Forests
under agreement with the Forest Service, USDA.
Scale 1:24,000

SCALE IN MILES

Hut
Trailhead
Wilderness Boundary

Trails are marked by blue diamonds, except in
wilderness areas, where trails are marked by tree blazes.
This map is not a substitute for good route finding skills.
There are suggested routes.
These are not groomed and their exact location may vary.
© 1991 10th Mountain Trail Association

Tennessee
Pass
Trailhead
10,424'

11.2
11.4
12.4

continued on p. 160

Crane Park
Trailhead
10,130'

11.4
12.1
12.4

This map includes US Forest Service ski trails
that coincide with the 10th Mountain Trail
in several locations.

12.2

1.30 miles to Crane Pass
2.64 miles to Tennessee Pass
2.07 miles to 10th Mountain Division Hut
7.00 miles to Uncle Bud's Hut

2.74 miles to 10th Mountain Division Hut
2.97 miles to Tennessee Pass
6.67 miles to Uncle Bud's Hut

1.72 miles to 10th Mountain
Division Hut
3.99 miles to Tennessee Pass

Lily Lake

11.4
12.1
12.2
12.4

12.3
13.3

10th Mountain Division Hut

12.5

1.46 miles to 10th Mountain Division Hut
5.79 miles to Uncle Bud's Hut

2.75 miles to 10th Mountain Division Hut
4.50 miles to Uncle Bud's Hut
5.29 miles to Tennessee Pass

12.6

12.7

CONTINENTAL

162

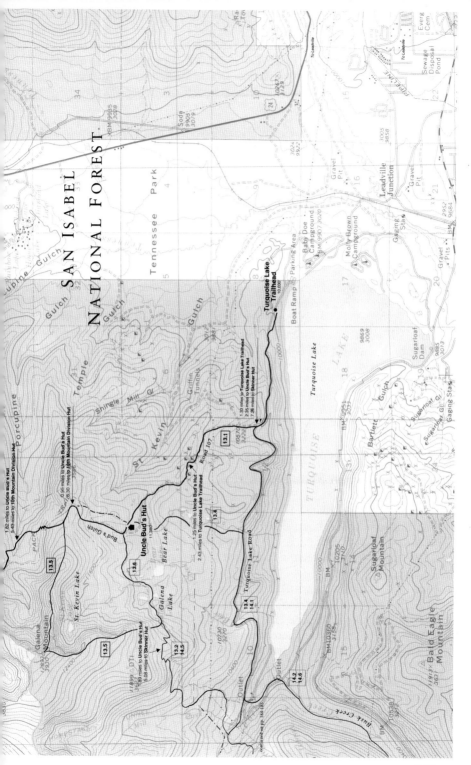

SAN ISABEL NATIONAL FOREST

Porcupine Gulch

Temple Gulch

Shingle Mill Gl

St. Kevin Gulch

Griffin Gulch

Tennessee Park

1.80 miles to Uncle Bud's Hut
5.45 miles to 10th Mountain Division Hut

0.95 miles to Uncle Bud's Hut
6.30 miles to 10th Mountain Division Hut

Tunnels

Road 107

13.1

1.93 miles to Turquoise Lake Trailhead
2.35 miles to Uncle Bud's Hut
7.26 miles to Skinner Hut

Turquoise Lake Trailhead

Boat Ramp Parking Area

Baby Doe Campground

Molly Brown Campground

Leadville Junction

Gravel Pit

Gravel Pit

Gravel Pits

Sewage Disposal Pond

Evergreen Cem

To Leadville

To Leadville

SPUR LINE

Gaging Sta.

Turquoise Lake

TURQUOISE LAKE

Sugarloaf Dam

Bartlett Gulch

Sugarloaf Gulch

Gaging Sta.

Sugarloaf Mountain

Bald Eagle Mountain

Bust Creek

PACK

Galena Mountain

St. Kevin Lake

Bud's Gulch

Uncle Bud's Hut

13.6

Bear Lake

Galena Lake

Turquoise Lake Road

13.5

13.2
14.5

1.25 miles to Uncle Bud's Hut
2.43 miles to Turquoise Lake Trailhead

13.4

13.4
14.1

14.2
14.6

2.80 miles to Uncle Bud's Hut
5.08 miles to Skinner Hut

Outlet

Outlet

continued on pp. 164-165

163

Plenty of mellow ski terrain surrounds the 10th Mountain Division Hut. You can make short scenic timberline probes or enjoy glade skiing at lower elevations. For experts, the Continental Divide looms above with plenty of peak climbs, bowl skiing, and ridge runs. In particular, cone-shaped Homestake Peak just begs to be skied.

Several befuddling aspects, mostly arising from trail marking, add spice to ski touring in this area, . First of all, portions of the Main Range Trail shown on the USGS are not accurate. This is due to rerouting of the trail over the years. Secondly, the Main Range Trail is used for part of the Colorado Trail, which extends from Durango to Denver. As a result, the names Main Range Trail and Colorado Trail are often synonymous. To reduce confusion, these sections are called Main Range/Colorado Trail herein. The Colorado Trail is marked with small white triangles with the words Colorado Trail. Thirdly, a system of Forest Service managed ski trails (the Tennessee Pass ski touring trails) are used as portions of the Colorado Trail, and in turn used as 10th Mountain trails. The problem is that these are marked with blue diamonds similar to 10th Mountain blue diamonds. Finally, a network of marked snowmobile trails (marked with orange diamonds) pass through the area. The 10th Mountain suggested routes both intersect and follow all these trails, hence the possibility of confusion. The best way to deal with this situation is by extra careful map, compass, and altimeter use. Wherever possible, the route descriptions below attempt to clarify points of confusion. Forewarned is forearmed.

12.1

Tennessee Pass Trailhead — 10th Mountain Division Hut via North Fork West Tennessee Creek

DIFFICULTY: Intermediate
TIME: 5 hours up, 3 ½ hours down
DISTANCE: 5 ¾ miles
ELEVATION GAIN: 1,150 feet; loss: 204 feet

TEXT MAP: p. 162
10TH MTN MAP: Galena Mountain
USGS MAP: Homestake Reservoir, Leadville North

This 10th Mountain suggested route avoids several popular snowmobile trails, but still uses some "sled" play areas. Its primary purpose is to connect 10th Mountain Division Hut with Vance's Cabin as described in route 11.4. For the most efficient access to the 10th Mountain Division Hut, use the Crane Park Trailhead (route 12.2).

ROUTE DESCRIPTION: Start at the Tennessee Pass Trailhead parking lot with cross country wax. At the south edge of the lot, about 100 feet from Highway 24, you'll find a Forest Service "double post" trailhead sign. One trail leads SW and soon branches into the trails of the Forest Service managed Tennessee Pass ski touring area.

Take the trail starting at the "double post" trailhead, then stay left to follow the marked Colorado Trail (small white triangles). Basically, this section of the Colorado Trail parallels the Continental Divide by traversing several miles of hillside above Highway 24. At 2 ¼ miles the trail crosses through a small gulch at 10,380 feet, then climbs a short distance to cross the obvious Wurts Ditch Road at 10,480 feet. Look out for snowmobiles here!

Drop S then SW from the Wurts Ditch Road to intersect another road at 10,320 feet in the West Tennessee Creek drainage. Put your skins on here if your wax has a light grip. Take care here not to drop onto a lower road into West Tennessee Creek. Instead, stay right and follow the road that leads up the North Fork of West Tennessee Creek 1 mile to pass just north of Lily Lake (10,589 feet).

Swing right (N) as you pass Lily Lake, cross the creek and a marshy area, then climb N for ½ mile to a low-angled clearing. From here the route climbs NW for 1 ¼ miles along the south side of the south fork of Slide Creek through a series of clearings until it reaches the south end of a large flat marshy area just below and to the south of the hut. The trail to this point can be confusing because of myriad snowmobile and ski tracks. In general, it follows the south Slide Creek drainage, but winds around enough to make "drainage tracking" hard. Your best insurance is to take great care near Lily Lake to identify the distinct cone of Homestake Peak. Using this as a landmark, pay attention to your map, compass, and altimeter to stick to the trail. The route is marked by 10th Mountain, but don't depend on trail markers for navigation.

You can see the hut from the south side of the last low-angled marshy clearing—it's perched on a low-angled hillside on the north side of the clearing. With poor visibility this could be a confusing area, so take care.

REVERSE ROUTE DESCRIPTION: If you're skiing from hut to trailhead, you're in for a treat. First, ski the 10th Mountain suggested route across the flat clearing southwest of the hut, then take the fall line and enjoy a ski run through clearings down to the area just north of Lily Lake. From there intersect the North Fork Road and follow it down to a road fork at 10,340 feet. Turn left (N) off the road at the fork onto the Colorado Trail (also a marked 10th Mountain trail) and climb through a burn area, then through timber ⅓ mile NE and N to the obvious Wurts Ditch Road (10,480 feet). Cross the Wurts Ditch Road, drop into a small gulch, then ski a long 2 ¼-mile traverse E and NE through timber to the Tennessee Pass Trailhead.

SAFETY NOTES: This is a relatively mellow route. It does take some confusing permutations to avoid the snowmobile trails, so put energy into your navigation.

SUMMER: The roads and trails marked on the USGS maps make fine horse, bike, and hiking routes for this hut. For regional routes, the Wurts Ditch Road is a fabulous bike ride in its own right, as is the Slide Lake jeep trail. Cyclists should be aware of the wilderness boundaries (see text maps). The 10th Mountain trail that traverses from Tennessee Pass into the West Tennessee Creek drainage is only suitable for skiing.

12.2

Crane Park Trailhead — 10th Mountain Division Hut via West Tennessee Creek

DIFFICULTY: Intermediate   **TEXT MAP:** p. 162
TIME: 4 ½ hours up, 3 hours down   **10TH MTN MAP:** Galena Mountain
DISTANCE: 4 ½ miles   **USGS MAP:** Homestake Reservoir,
ELEVATION GAIN: 1,353 feet; loss: 120 feet   Leadville North

This route follows most of route 12.1, but has a more direct access from the Crane Park Trailhead. The actual Crane Park Trailhead varies with snow closure (see Chapter 1, Crane Park Trailhead).

ROUTE DESCRIPTION: To begin, either drive or ski up the gravel pit road from Crane Park to the obvious intersection of the Wurts Ditch Road. If you end up at the gravel pit, you have gone too far. The Wurts Ditch Road is usually well signed, but signs have a way of changing. Ski up the well-traveled, snow-covered Wurts Ditch Road just over ¼ mile to 10,480 feet. Here you turn left (S) off the road onto the Colorado Trail and follow route 12.1 to the hut.

REVERSE ROUTE DESCRIPTION: Follow route 12.1 to the Wurts Ditch Road. Turn right (SE) on the Wurts Ditch Road and follow it just over ¼ mile downhill to the aforementioned gravel pit road. This is the trailhead if the gravel pit road is plowed. If it is not plowed, turn left (N) and follow the gravel pit road to snow closure near Crane Park.

SAFETY NOTES: This route is very short, but stay alert and leave the trailhead before noon!

SUMMER: The 2 ¾-mile Slide Lake jeep trail from Wurts Ditch Road is a fine mountain bike route. See route 12.1 for other summer information.

12.3

10th Mountain Division Hut to Uncle Bud's Hut via Main Range/Colorado Trail

DIFFICULTY: Intermediate
TIME: 8 hours
DISTANCE: 7 1/4 miles
ELEVATION GAIN: 1,460 feet; loss: 1,450 feet

TEXT MAP: pp. 162-163
10TH MTN MAP: Galena Mountain
USGS MAP: Homestake Reservoir

For all practical purposes this 10th Mountain suggested route is the only intermediate trail from the 10th Mountain Division Hut to Uncle Bud's Hut. Lower routes would follow devious tracks through dark forest and force you to share trails with snowmobiles. Higher routes are all advanced and expert, mainly because of avalanche terrain. This route is longer than it looks on the map, and traverses through many subsidiary drainages. This is a change for skiers used to chugging up and down valleys, and requires attentive map work. The route is scenic, with changing views of the Mosquito Range to the east and the Continental Divide to the west and south. Various trails in this area can create confusion (see chapter introduction).

ROUTE DESCRIPTION: Start without skins, perhaps with a bit of cross country wax. From the front deck of the 10th Mountain Division Hut, ski S into the large marshy clearing, then S across the clearing to intersect a stream in a shallow gulch. The trail splits at this point, with the left (E) fork following routes 12.1/12.2 to trailheads. For your route, take the right (W) fork and follow the standard marked 10th Mountain trail as it traverses SW to a small pond, then drops through a clearing S to the North Fork West Tennessee Creek (11,100 feet), your second drainage crossing from the hut (count them as you go).

Continue S as you climb a small ridge (11,130 feet) that separates the North Fork West Tennessee Creek from the west fork of West Tennessee Creek. Next, drop S through timber to 10,980 feet in the beautiful open valley of West Tennessee Creek. Navigation in West Tennessee Creek can be difficult when visibility isn't the best. Cross the middle fork of West Tennessee Creek, then climb 1/4 mile SW to a flat marshy area at West Tennessee Creek (11,080 feet).

Swing E for 1/4 mile through the marshy area, then enter a trail cut in dark timber. Follow this trail E, then turn right (S) and climb to a small lake. From this lake climb to a small saddle (11,140 feet), then drop S through a clearing into a marshy area in a subsidiary drainage. Cross S through the marshy area and continue descending SE to intersect the Colorado Trail at 10,880 feet. (At this point the Colorado Trail is marked on the USGS map as the Main Range Trail. To add to the confusion, it is also the Longs Gulch Trail in the USFS Tennessee Pass ski touring trail system.)

Turn right and follow the trail as it leads SW for 1 ¼ miles up Longs Gulch to 10,900 feet. Here you'll see some possible avalanche slopes on the north side of the drainage. Avoid these by staying in the timber to the south of the trail. Regain the trail in the timber and follow it as it climbs SW to a flat saddle with several small lakes.

Drop S into Porcupine Gulch from the saddle and cross Porcupine Creek at 11,240 feet. Still counting drainages? Climb S out of Porcupine Gulch, pass timberline, and continue climbing to 11,800 feet on an alpine shoulder. This is the high point of your route. The climb out of Porcupine Gulch switchbacks up through a slice of timber to avoid avalanche slopes to the right, then stays high to pass above other avalanche prone slopes. Take extra care to choose a safe route here, as you could easily deviate into avalanche terrain. The trail as marked on the text map is accurate, while the trail on the USGS map is inaccurate. If you have time, take a scenic detour at the shoulder and climb point 12,313.

At any rate, it's all downhill from the shoulder to Uncle Bud's Hut, so strip your skins. From your position on the shoulder, ski E down to to timberline at a sparsely timbered saddle (11,680 feet). At this point it is very important to swing W and stay in Bud's Gulch (unnamed on the USGS map, marked on the text map), since it's all too easy to ski the tempting glades down into St. Kevin Creek and end up far from the hut. A compass check can help you here.

Skiing down Bud's Gulch takes you through timber for 400 vertical feet to 11,360 feet where you broach an elongated low-angled clearing. The 10th Mountain marked route follows the Colorado Trail down the left side of the clearing to 11,260 feet. You then swing E and climb through sparse timber ⅛ mile and 120 vertical feet back up to the hut.

This last little climb can be bothersome after all the drainages you've trudged through. On the map it looks like you can contour to the hut from the upper end of Bud's Gulch, but this route is blocked by some fairly dense forest. The alternate that works — if you are good with navigation — is to ski the wide rib dividing St. Kevin Gulch from Bud's Gulch. You may encounter a few snowmobiles here, but you'll get to the hut quicker. Stay to the east side of the rib in light timber and traverse the east side of several bumps. Again, don't drop down into St. Kevin Gulch. The hut is only visible from several hundred feet away on either route.

SAFETY NOTES: Refer to your map often on this route, as cutting all the drainages can be confusing. An altimeter can help a great deal with this sort of skiing. You drop into a drainage, read your elevation, and you know exactly where you are (provided you have counted drainages).

SUMMER: The Colorado Trail is a fine hike or horse route. Most of the route is within designated wilderness, so cyclists should look for other routes. Portions of the 10th Mountain route described above (those that leave the established trails) are marked ski trails with no summer tread.

12.4

10th Mountain Division Hut to Vance's Cabin via Tennessee Pass

DIFFICULTY: Intermediate	**TEXT MAP:** pp. 162, 145
TIME: 8 hours	**10TH MTN MAP:** Galena Mt., Ch. Ridge
DISTANCE: 9 miles	**USGS MAP:** Leadville North, Pando,
ELEVATION GAIN: 760 feet; loss: 1,150 feet	Homestake Reservoir

This 10th Mountain suggested route is the standard ski-through between the 10th Mountain Division Hut and Vance's Cabin. It crosses a major highway (U.S. 24) at Tennessee Pass, then passes by the Ski Cooper ski area. If you're on a long ski-through, plan a resupply at the highway.

ROUTE DESCRIPTION: From the 10th Mountain Division Hut follow reverse route 12.1 to the parking area at Tennessee Pass. From there, take route 11.2 to Vance's Cabin.

SAFETY NOTES: See notes on routes 11.2 and 12.1.

SUMMER: See notes on routes 11.2 and 12.1.

12.5

Slide Lake from 10th Mountain Division Hut

DIFFICULTY: Intermediate
TIME: Several hours round trip
DISTANCE: 1 ¼ miles round trip
ELEVATION GAIN: 330 feet round trip

TEXT MAP: p. 162
10TH MTN MAP: Galena Mountain
USGS MAP: Homestake Reservoir

If you itch for a timberline tour but lack the skills to climb the Divide or ski the couloirs, take a scenic cruise to Slide Lake.

ROUTE DESCRIPTION: The route is simple. Put your skins on at the hut, then simply climb the hill northwest of the hut, bearing right (N) as the hill gets steeper. At timberline, around 11,500 feet, keep Homestake Peak on your front left as you continue to Slide Lake (11,700 feet) in a superb high basin. On the return, ski the glades that tempted you as you climbed.

SAFETY NOTES: Avoid avalanche slopes on all sides of the Homestake Peak basin.

SUMMER: This is a fine horse ride or hike. Cyclists can ride the Slide Lake jeep trail to the marked wilderness boundary just below the lake.

12.6

Homestake Peak from 10th Mountain Division Hut

DIFFICULTY: Advanced
TIME: 5 hours round trip
DISTANCE: 4 ½ miles round trip
ELEVATION GAIN: 1,839 feet round trip

TEXT MAP: p. 162
10TH MTN MAP: Galena Mountain
USGS MAP: Homestake Reservoir

In Colorado, about 736 peaks top the 13,000-foot mark. One of these is Homestake Peak (13,209 feet) which rises west of the 10th Mountain Division Hut. A classic glacier-made cone, Homestake has a relatively avalanche safe climbing route, and makes a good branch route from the hut. Most of the ski lines are too avalanche prone for safe winter descents, but the ascent route (east ridge) can yield some fine lines, provided the snow has not been wind-scoured. Consider a trip to Homestake Peak during the spring corn-snow season.

ROUTE DESCRIPTION: To climb Homestake Peak, follow route 12.5 to Slide Lake. From the south side of the lake, climb SE about ¼ mile and 200 vertical feet to a vegetated hillock at the 11,900-foot level. From here

170

avoid the avalanche runouts from Homestake's east ridge by contouring and gently climbing low-angled terrain to the broad ridge crest. Simply follow the ridge to the summit. The ascent route is the safest descent. During the spring corn season you can enjoy some fabulous ski lines down the north face of the east ridge from about the 12,400-foot level. For a real corn extravaganza, ski the bowls from the Continental Divide south of the peak, then traverse back to the hut. You'll find other corn-snow lines around Slide Lake.

SAFETY NOTES: While ascending the east ridge, evaluate avalanche danger to either side. Don't let temptation lead you into skiing down dangerous slopes.

SUMMER: This is a fine summit hike that adds a "Thirteener" to your list.

12.7
Continental Divide Ridge from 10th Mountain Division Hut

DIFFICULTY: Expert
TIME: Full day round trip
DISTANCE: 5 + miles round trip
ELEVATION GAIN: 2,000 feet round trip

TEXT MAP: p. 162
10TH MTN MAP: Galena Mountain
USGS MAP: Homestake Reservoir

One of the safest ways for advanced mountaineers to enjoy the winter high country is by doing ridge runs. The Continental Divide south from Homestake Peak is a fine candidate for such an endeavor. At the least, you can make a short probe to several small bumps close to the summit of Homestake Peak, enjoy the view, then get back to the hut by tea time. At the most, you can take the Divide to Galena Mountain, then descend to Turquoise Lake or Uncle Bud's Hut.

ROUTE DESCRIPTION: To do this route, take route 12.6 to the summit of Homestake Peak, then simply stick to the Divide ridge as it leads south. Where logic dictates, make small traverses below the high points of the ridge, usually on the west side.

SAFETY NOTES: You're very exposed to storms on a ridge such as this. In midwinter, most escape routes will be cut off by avalanche danger. Thus, you must plan this ridge run with care. Also, if you plan on traversing the entire ridge, a good weather prediction is mandatory (see Appendix 2). Consider corn-snow season for this route, as avalanche danger will be more predictable and the weather will be milder.

SUMMER: This is a fine hike. Beware of afternoon lightning.

Chapter 13 • Uncle Bud's Hut

U ncle Bud's Hut, owned by 10th Mountain, is similar in aspect and construction to the 10th Mountain Division Hut. Views from the south window-wall include a panorama of 14,421-foot

ELEVATION: 11,380 feet
COUNTY: Lake
TEXT MAP: pp. 162-163, 184-185
10TH MTN MAP: Galena Mountain
USGS MAP: Homestake Reservoir
TRAILHEADS: Turquoise Lake

Mount Massive and the logged pate of Bald Eagle Mountain. During the mining boom in the late 1800s, the land around Leadville was logged like Bald Eagle. That any forests still exist is a testament to the hearty species of conifer that grace the Rockies.

The hut was built as a memorial to 10th Mountain Division veteran Bud Winter (1925-1945), who died in Italy during World War II. Bud was a "born skier and mountaineer" and dearly remembered. Funds for the hut were given by Bud's brother, Dr. Fred Winter. His sister Laura contributed the proceeds from her poetry book *Laura's Lines*.

This hut, combined with the Skinner Hut and Betty Bear Hut, allows travel over Hagerman Pass to the Fryingpan drainage, thus forming a huge loop that strong skiers can enjoy.

Uncle Bud's Hut is very accessible from Leadville via a short trailhead to hut route from Turquoise Lake (route 13.1). Using this trail, experts can

get to the hut quickly, then spend a few days base skiing. Freshman skiers can use this route as a step on the learning ladder. For ski-throughs to the north and south from Uncle Bud's Hut, routes 13.2 and 13.3 use sections of the Main Range/Colorado Trail (marked on older USGS maps as the Main Range Trail). Branch routes from the hut range from mellow glade skiing to euro-style couloirs on Galena Mountain.

13.1

Turquoise Lake Trailhead — Uncle Bud's Hut

DIFFICULTY: Intermediate
TIME: 4 hours up, 3 hours down
DISTANCE: 3 ¾ miles
ELEVATION GAIN: 1,370 feet; loss: 20 feet

TEXT MAP: pp. 163, 185
10TH MTN MAP: Galena Mt., Con. Div.
USGS MAP: Homestake Reservoir,
    Leadville North

This 10th Mountain suggested route follows snow-covered roads through a beautiful lodgepole pine forest. It is a short route, with relatively easy navigation.

ROUTE DESCRIPTION: Begin with cross country wax at the Turquoise Lake Trailhead. Ski, drive, or walk N then W on the main road (if you had to start before the official trailhead because of snow cover). This road gradually climbs while paralleling the north shore of the lake. It is very distinct and easy to follow, the only possible false turns being several well-signed spurs to boat ramps and campgrounds. At 10,410 feet leave the main road by turning right (N) onto a well-defined road-cut. There is a stake here with the road number 107, but this may be covered by snow. There are also the standard 10th Mountain trail markers. All the following mileages are measured from this turn.

Put your skins on and follow Road 107 as it climbs N through conifer. If you notice, just ¼ mile after turning from the main road you'll pass an intersection at 10,570 feet. Be sure to stay north on 107 here. It can be all too easy, especially on an overcast day, to lose your bearings. Use your compass and altimeter.

At ½ mile from the main road you'll pass under a power line at 10,730 feet. This is a good landmark and altimeter calibration point. After the power line the road climbs N a short distance, swings W for about ⅓ mile, then makes a short steep climb N several hundred feet to a mining area in some flats (11,000 feet). Stay on the road in this area, as several dangerous open shafts can be hidden by snow. Though most mine evidence will be obscured by snow, you'll see lots of unnatural looking mounds and some wood ruins.

A skier looks west over Bud's Gulch; Galena Mountain is on the horizon.

Ski W on Road 107 through the mining area, then begin a climb NW for ½ mile (still on the road) to a clearing at 11,280 feet. The road to this point follows the ridge between St. Kevin Creek and Turquoise Lake, so as long as you're climbing you're on the route.

At the 11,280-foot clearing the 10th Mountain suggested route leaves Road 107 and takes a climbing traverse another ¼ mile NW to Uncle Bud's Hut (11,380 feet) at the top end of the clearing. The hut is visible from several hundred yards below. The possible mistake here would be to stay on Road 107 and traverse below the hut. You can see the hut from 107, so keep looking uphill for it. Also, use your altimeter as you get close.

REVERSE ROUTE DESCRIPTION: Descending Road 107 can be slightly hairy, as some tree-lined "toboggan chutes" test your ski skills. From the front of Uncle Bud's Hut take a descending traverse SE through a clearing. Intersect Road 107 at 11,280 feet. Stay on the road as it takes you downhill along the crest of the ridge between St. Kevin Gulch and Turquoise Lake. Swing N then SE through a flat area at the 11,000-foot level, then climb a small hill to a mining area.

Take care to find the road-cut at the east end of the mining area, where it makes a right turn (S) down a steep hill. From here the road-cut is easy to follow down to the main Turquoise Lake Road. Turn left (E) on the Turquoise Lake Road and follow it to the Turquoise Lake Trailhead (or to the snow closure).

SAFETY NOTES: This short route could lull you into false security. The problem is that many snowmobiles and backcountry skiers use the area, so trails can lead everywhere – and nowhere.

SUMMER: Road 107 is a fine horse, hiking, or bike route.

13.2

Uncle Bud's Hut to Skinner Hut via Main Range/Colorado Trail and Glacier Creek

DIFFICULTY: Advanced
TIME: 9 hours
DISTANCE: 7 miles
ELEVATION GAIN: 1,930; loss: 1,690 feet

TEXT MAP: pp. 184-185
10TH MTN MAP: Continental Divide
USGS MAP: Homestake Reservoir

The first leg of this route follows the Main Range/Colorado Trail. With new snow you can avoid trailbreaking on the Main Range/Colorado Trail by using the Turquoise Lake Road. See route 13.4 for details on this alternate route.

ROUTE DESCRIPTION: Wax your skis with cross country wax. Ski SW and W from Uncle Bud's Hut 140 vertical feet down into the clearing in the drainage (Bud's Gulch) west of the hut. Do not ski up Bud's Gulch, simply cross to the west side of the clearing and locate the obvious Forest Service "double post" trailhead sign (11,240 feet); this marks the Main Range/Colorado Trail.

Ski W out of Bud's Gulch on the Main Range/Colorado Trail. It takes a short climb up over a timbered rib, then traverses ¼ mile to the top of a clearing at 11,240 feet. Ski downhill a short distance, then ski between north and south Galena Lakes. Continue W then SW to pass the south edge of a small lake and climb via several switchbacks to timberline (11,400 feet) on the south ridge of Galena Mountain.

From timberline descend an open slope W and SW and take care to find the trail as it enters the trees. Descend this trail 2 miles through forest to 10,040 feet in the Lake Fork drainage. Here you join the trail that climbs to the Skinner Hut from the Turquoise Lake Road. It's very important to find this trail, since it follows the only feasible route to the hut. Take care not to mistake the trail to Timberline Lake for the 10th Mountain route up Glacier Creek. The Glacier Creek route is marked with the ubiquitous blue diamonds. See route 14.1 for the route up Glacier Creek to the Skinner Hut.

SAFETY NOTES: This route is long and requires expert orienteering. The climb up Glacier Creek is one of the steepest trails in the 10th Mountain system. Skins are mandatory. Take care when passing below avalanche slopes in Glacier Creek. Groups on this route should carry avalanche beepers and shovels. Remember that trail in wilderness is marked with tree blazes instead of blue diamonds.

SUMMER: All maintained trails on this route are good hiking and equestrian routes. Most of the Glacier Creek trail to the Skinner Hut is only a marked winter route. For a summer hike to the Skinner Hut, follow the Glacier Creek valley up high to its intersection with the Hagerman Pass Road, then take the road back to the hut.

13.3

Uncle Bud's Hut to 10th Mountain Division Hut via Main Range/Colorado Trail

DIFFICULTY: Intermediate　　**TEXT MAP:** pp. 162-163
TIME: 8 hours　　**10TH MTN MAP:** Galena Mountain
DISTANCE: 7 ¼ miles　　**USGS MAP:** Homestake Reservoir
ELEVATION GAIN: 1,450 feet; loss: 1,460 feet

This 10th Mountain suggested route is the only practical intermediate route between Uncle Bud's Hut and the 10th Mountain Division Hut. The route is long and, unlike most "valley" 10th Mountain routes, cuts through many drainages. You'll enjoy plenty of good views on this trail. The 14,000-foot peaks of the Mosquito Range loom to the east and the majestic Continental Divide rises to the west and south. As you can see on the USGS map, this route uses sections of the Main Range/Colorado Trail (marked on older maps as the Main Range Trail). The 10th Mountain route deviates in places from this trail for more efficient skiing and to avoid avalanche slopes.

ROUTE DESCRIPTION: To begin, leave your skins off and glide W from the hut for several hundred yards down into an elongated clearing (Bud's Gulch). At the bottom of the hill put your skins on at the wilderness boundary sign, ski N up the east side of the clearing, then enter the trees at the north end of the clearing (11,360 feet). Continue climbing NE to a sparsely timbered saddle at 11,680 feet. From the saddle climb W for ¼ mile up the ridge to 11,800 feet. This is the high point of the route and a good place for a long session with map and compass. Remember that these wilderness trails are marked with tree blazes.

Strip your skins on the ridge, then take a dropping traverse NW into Porcupine Gulch. To avoid avalanche terrain, this traverse starts above the marked route of the Main Range/Colorado Trail, then drops down short switchbacks through a strip of timber into Porcupine Gulch. Sticking to this timber avoids avalanche terrain to either side. Experts may wish to ski a good run west of the timber, but use careful avalanche safety procedures with this option. Cross Porcupine Creek at 11,240 feet. Next, climb up the north side of Porcupine Creek to a broad flat saddle at 11,480 feet (with several small lakes). This short climb is hardly worth reskinning for; try a bit of cross country wax under the middle of your ski, or just herringbone.

From the broad saddle, drop N via two switchbacks into Longs Gulch. Cross Longs Creek at 10,900 feet, then follow the Main Range/Colorado Trail down through intermittent clearings on the north side of Longs Creek to 10,740 feet. At this point your route (still on the Main Range/Colorado Trail) climbs NE out of Longs Gulch, then around the shoulder that separates Longs Gulch from the West Tennessee Creek drainages. The Main Range/Colorado Trail continues E here but your route travels N, so leave the Main Range/Colorado Trail when it starts to drop E (10,880 feet), and take a climbing traverse N to cross the south fork of West Tennessee Creek at 10,990 feet.

Climb up another shoulder N out of the south fork of West Tennessee Creek, then descend N past a small lake (11,140 feet). After the lake continue N a few hundred yards, then traverse W through dark timber and across a marshy clearing. Swing NE and drop 1/4 mile into the clearings of the main West Tennessee Creek drainage. From 10,980 feet in West Tennessee Creek climb NE then N over a small shoulder into the North Fork of West Tennessee Creek (11,100 feet), then N onto a sparsely treed hillside. Climb the west side of this clear area to a small lake at 11,340 feet.

You will now be in another relatively flat area. From the east side of the lake, ski E several hundred yards through timber, then swing NE and ski through 1/4 mile of intermittent clearings to a large flat clearing just south of the hut. You can see the hut from here; the trail crosses the clearing.

SAFETY NOTES: The 10th Mountain suggested route is safe from avalanches. Slight deviations from this route, however, will expose you to slide danger. There are many avalanche slopes above timberline. As you can see from the above description, this is a complex route. Allow plenty of time for orienteering.

SUMMER: The Main Range/Colorado Trail is a fine hike or horse ride. Most of the trail is in designated wilderness, where possession of a bicycle is a crime. The sections of the 10th Mountain route that deviate from the Main Range/Colorado Trail have no summer tread.

13.4

Uncle Bud's Hut to Skinner Hut via Turquoise Lake Road and Glacier Creek

DIFFICULTY: Advanced
TIME: 8 hours
DISTANCE: 7 1/4 miles
ELEVATION GAIN: 1,660; loss: 1,420 feet

TEXT MAP: pp. 184-185
10TH MTN MAP: Continental Divide
USGS MAP: Homestake Reservoir

The section of Main Range/Colorado Trail that connects Glacier Creek and Uncle Bud's Hut can add much time and effort to reaching the Skinner Hut from Uncle Bud's Hut, especially if new snow requires breaking trail. This alternate route uses the Turquoise Lake Road (usually packed by snow machine) to reach Glacier Creek.

ROUTE DESCRIPTION: To begin, you can follow the marked 10th Mountain trail back on Road 107 to the Turquoise Lake Road. But a possibly better route is to simply ski down the drainage south of Uncle Bud's Hut. Doing so allows you to intersect the Turquoise Lake Road at its high point of 10,680 feet, and eliminates some distance. To ski the drainage, simply head S downhill from Uncle Bud's Hut. Stick with the drainage down to the last lake at 10,800 feet. Ski W from the lake several hundred yards, then drop S down a headwall. You'll pass under the power lines here. Continue down the drainage keeping west of the stream. Several hundred yards above the Turquoise Lake Road you'll intersect a road-cut through the forest. Follow this to the Turquoise Lake Road.

Once you're on the Turquoise Lake Road, ski the road 2 1/2 miles W to the start of the Glacier Creek trail. Put on your skins here. The point where this trail leaves the Turquoise Lake Road is not obvious, and many parties have skied past it. For sure identification remember that the trail leaves the road at the upper north end of a curve that starts out heading W and turns S. Thus, if you find yourself skiing S you have missed the trail. Also, the Glacier Creek trail is marked with blue diamonds, and by a sign you can see from the road that says bridge (but don't go to the bridge). You'll see a Forest Service trailhead marker (for the Timberline Lake Trail) after you start up the trail, but the marker can't be seen from the road.

See route 14.1 for a description of the Glacier Creek climb to Skinner Hut.

SAFETY NOTES: Due to avalanche terrain and steep climbing, the Glacier Creek leg of this route is one of the few 10th Mountain suggested routes with an advanced rating. Intermediate backcountry skiers can manage this trail, provided they are accompanied by more experienced skiers. Skins are a necessity.

SUMMER: The trail up Glacier Creek is a bit of a bushwhack, and the route down the drainage from Uncle Bud's Hut has no summer tread.

13.5

Galena Mountain from Uncle Bud's Hut

DIFFICULTY: Advanced/Expert   **TEXT MAP:** pp. 163, 184-185
TIME: Full day   **10TH MTN MAP:** Galena Mt., Con. Div.
DISTANCE: 4 ½ miles round trip   **USGS MAP:** Homestake Reservoir
ELEVATION GAIN: 2,000 feet round trip

Rising to the west of Uncle Bud's Hut, Galena Mountain (12,893 feet) is sure to tempt mountaineers. While lower than the 13,000- and 14,000-foot peaks that stud the Continental Divide in the Leadville area, Galena offers good variety and is very accessible from the hut.

ROUTE DESCRIPTION: Two good routes work for this climb. One option, rated expert, ascends the prominent east ridge from 11,680 feet on the Main Range/Colorado Trail. The first part of the east ridge is a simple ridge run. After a deep notch (12,600 feet), rope-work is necessary to climb a vertical step. In the winter you must ascend this step to avoid avalanche danger on the northeast face. But in the spring, provided the snow is frozen spring corn, you can avoid the technical climbing by traversing onto the northeast face. This option requires expert snow climbing skills.

The longer winter route is rated advanced. Follow route 13.2 to timberline on Galena Mountain's broad south ridge. Leave the trail here and follow this ridge to the summit, either sticking to the right hand ridge crest or following the broad ridge. Your choice would be dictated by avalanche conditions. Whatever your ascent route, this ridge is a good way down.

Finally, expert mountaineers will enjoy the beautiful couloir that ascends to the summit of Galena Mountain from St. Kevin Lake. At 48 degrees maximum angle, this couloir makes both a good crampon climb or "extreme ski" during the spring season on a frozen spring snowpack. The most straightforward route to St. Kevin Lake follows the Bear Lake drainage from the Main Range/Colorado Trail.

SAFETY NOTES: All these routes pass through avalanche terrain and thus are safer on a spring "melt-freeze" snowpack while the snow is frozen in the morning.

SUMMER: The east ridge of Galena Mountain is a fine summer climb and the south ridge makes a good alpine hike.

Traversing into the north face of Galena Mountain to avoid the rock climbing on the east ridge.

13.6

Galena Lake from Uncle Bud's Hut

DIFFICULTY: Intermediate
TIME: 3 hours round trip
DISTANCE: 2 ½ miles round trip
ELEVATION GAIN: 310 feet round trip

TEXT MAP: p. 163
10TH MTN MAP: Galena Mountain
USGS MAP: Homestake Reservoir

This short branch route takes the Main Range/Colorado Trail to Galena Lake. Use it as a scenic tour, or get some turns in the glades west of the lake.

ROUTE DESCRIPTION: From Uncle Bud's Hut, ski W down into the clearing in the drainage west of the hut (Bud's Gulch). Do not ski up Bud's Gulch, simply cross to the west side of the clearing and locate the obvious Forest Service "double post" trailhead sign (11,240 feet); this marks the Main Range/Colorado Trail.

Ski W out of Bud's Gulch on the Main Range/Colorado Trail. It takes a short climb up through timber, then traverses ¼ mile to the top of a clearing at 11,240 feet. The Main Range/Colorado Trail takes a dropping traverse from here, then passes between north and south Galena Lakes. For a better ski route, take the fall line down to the flat marshy area where the clearing widens, then ski fairly flat terrain SW a short distance to Galena Lake. Take some time to explore the area; include Bear Lake in your quest. For the best downhill skiing, stay on the Main Range/Colorado Trail W then SW past the south edge of a small lake, then climb to timberline via several switchbacks. Pick your glade. Return via the same route.

SAFETY NOTES: This is a mellow excursion with no real safety problems. Remember that the Main Range/Colorado Trail is marked with tree blazes because it's in wilderness. Pay attention to your map, since it's likely you will deviate from the summer trail. Ski in control.

SUMMER: Enjoy this route as a hike.

13.7

Ski Tours from Uncle Bud's Hut

DIFFICULTY: Intermediate
TEXT MAP: pp. 163, 184-185
10TH MTN MAP: Galena Mountain, Continental Divide
USGS MAP: Homestake Reservoir

Several popular ski runs are accessible from Uncle Bud's Hut. Close by, the glades of St. Kevin Gulch can be reached by climbing N up the ridge behind the hut, then dropping E for the skiing. You can get back to the hut without skins by taking a short climbing traverse at the 11,300-foot level. For your first trip use your altimeter to find the traverse.

Another fun ski is point 12,313 on the east ridge of Galena Mountain. Access this via route 13.3. Enjoy the terrific view and the superb downhill skiing. Point 12,313 is worth several trips up and down. On the last trip try cutting over to St. Kevin Gulch for the final ski to the hut.

SAFETY NOTES: Ski downhill with care. Stay clear of the drop-off on the left (north) as you're descending from the top of point 12,313, and watch for rocks on the upper section

Chapter 14 • Skinner Hut

Perched at timberline on the east side of Hagerman Pass, the Skinner Hut is the second highest of the 10th Mountain huts. Owned by 10th Mountain, the hut sleeps 19 and breaks from the usual hut design by having only one story. The Continental Divide

ELEVATION: 11,620 feet
COUNTY: Lake
TEXT MAP: pp. 184-185, 196-197
10TH MTN MAP: Con. Div., U. Fryingpan
USGS MAP: Homestake Reservoir
TRAILHEADS: Turquoise Lake, Elk Wallow Campground, Hagerman Pass Road

is close by, as are plenty of options for high routes and ski descents. A superb view from the hut's east windows includes the 14,036-foot summit of Mount Sherman in the Mosquito Mountains east of Leadville. The Skinner Hut is named in honor of William Wood Skinner, 10th Mountain Division veteran. Funding was donated by Skinner's sister Elizabeth Guenzel. Construction was completed in 1990.

Because of steep terrain and possible avalanche danger, no route to the Skinner Hut is rated less than advanced. In this the Skinner Hut differs from the other 10th Mountain huts, most of which can be reached via snow-covered roads and low-angle trails. Indeed, more than one party has realized that the hut's name comes close to that of an essential piece of equipment for every route to the hut — skins. The Glacier Creek route

(14.1) is the most popular ascent to the Skinner Hut, but involves an extremely steep climb and descent. Busk Creek (route 14.2) will give you easier skiing, but involves more route-finding and distance. Skiing from the Skinner Hut to Betty Bear Hut via Hagerman Pass (route 14.4) is relatively benign, but does involve plenty of travel above treeline where wind and whiteouts can foil the best mountaineers.

14.1

Turquoise Lake Trailhead — Skinner Hut via Turquoise Lake Road and Glacier Creek

DIFFICULTY: Advanced   **TEXT MAP:** pp. 184-185
TIME: 8 hours up, 6 hours down   **10TH MTN MAP:** Continental Divide
DISTANCE: 8 ¾ miles   **USGS MAP:** Homestake Reservoir
ELEVATION GAIN: 2,280 feet; loss: 690 feet

This 10th Mountain suggested route is one of contrasts. You begin on a wide, flat snowmobile-packed road. Then a skin climb takes you 1,500 vertical feet in just 3 miles. It's a strenuous climb, but one that experienced skiers will appreciate for its efficiency, especially after the flat road.

ROUTE DESCRIPTION: Park at the Turquoise Lake Trailhead. Ski the snow-covered Turquoise Lake Road W about 2 miles (depending on starting point) to the road's high point (10,680 feet), then stay on the road for another 2 ½ miles of level sections and gradual downhills past the west end of Turquoise Lake. Here you must find the start of the Glacier Creek trail (which begins at the same point as the trail to Timberline Lake). Many parties ski the road past this point and have to double back — so take care.

For positive identification of the Glacier Creek trail, remember that the trail leaves the road at the upper north end of a curve that turns from heading W to heading S. Thus, if you find yourself skiing S on the road you have missed the trail, so pay attention to your direction of travel by using your map and compass. Also, the Glacier Creek trail is marked with blue diamonds and by a sign you can see from the road that says bridge (but don't go to this bridge). You'll see a Forest Service trailhead marker (for the Timberline Lake Trail) after you start up the trail, but the marker can't be seen from the road.

After leaving the Turquoise Lake Road, follow the Glacier Creek trail as it stays in the valley for a short distance, then bears left and follows a distinct cut through the forest. Soon you'll be on a steep climb through small clearings and timber, then break into a large clearing at 10,760 feet. This is called the Lunch Spot. Take a rest so you're ready for the next section of trail — you have some steep climbing ahead!

183

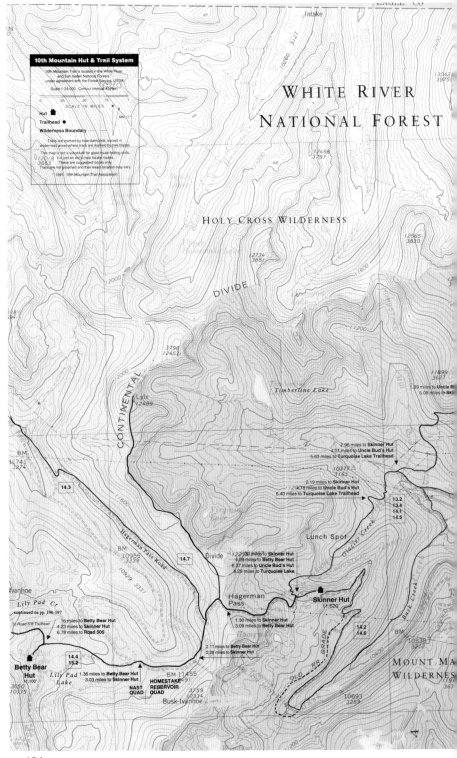

WHITE RIVER
NATIONAL FOREST

HOLY CROSS WILDERNESS

DIVIDE

10th Mountain Hut & Trail System

10th Mountain Trail is located in the White River
and San Isabel National Forests
under agreement with the Forest Service, USDA.

Scale 1:24,000   Contour Interval 40 feet

SCALE IN MILES

🏠 Hut

● Trailhead

Wilderness Boundary

Trails are marked by blue diamonds, except in
wilderness areas where trails are marked by tree blazes.

This map is not a substitute for good route finding skills.
It is just an aid to help locate routes.
These are suggested routes only.
Trails are not groomed and their exact location may vary.

©1991, 10th Mountain Trail Association

CONTINENTAL

Lyle
12499

Timberline Lake

2.96 miles to **Skinner Hut**
4.01 miles to **Uncle Bud's Hut**
5.63 miles to **Turquoise Lake Trailhead**

1.89 miles to **Uncle Bud's**
5.08 miles to **Ski**

2.19 miles to **Skinner Hut**
3.78 miles to **Uncle Bud's Hut**
6.40 miles to **Turquoise Lake Trailhead**

13.2
13.4
14.1
14.5

14.3

Hagerman Pass Road

BM
10955
3339

14.7

Divide

Virginia Lake

Lunch Spot

Glacier Creek

2.25 miles to **Skinner Hut**
4.09 miles to **Betty Bear Hut**
6.37 miles to **Uncle Bud's Hut**
8.29 miles to **Turquoise Lake**

Hagerman
Pass

Skinner Hut
11,620'

Busk Creek

Ivanhoe

Lily Pad Cr.

continued on pp. 196-197

to Road 505 Trailhead

.16 miles to **Betty Bear Hut**
4.23 miles to **Skinner Hut**
6.78 miles to **Road 505**

1.30 miles to **Skinner Hut**
3.09 miles to **Betty Bear Hut**

14.2
14.6

OLD RR GRADE

BM
10538
3212

MOUNT MA
WILDERNES

2.11 miles to **Betty Bear Hut**
2.28 miles to **Skinner Hut**

14.4
15.2

**Betty Bear
Hut**
11,100'

Lily Pad
Lake

1.36 miles to **Betty Bear Hut**
3.03 miles to **Skinner Hut**

NAST
QUAD

BM 11455

HOMESTAKE
RESERVOIR
QUAD

Busk-Ivanhoe

10693
3289

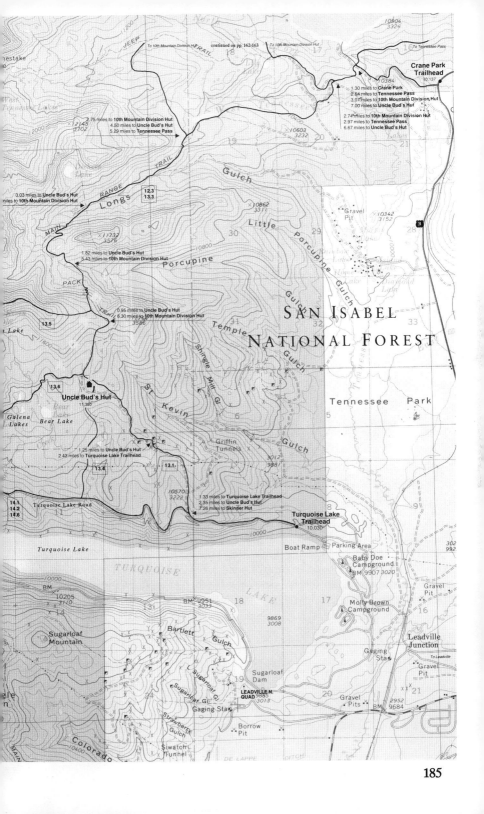

Continue upvalley from the Lunch Spot across open flats. With avalanche danger you can stay in the trees to your left, but the skiing is easier on the flats. Enter the woods again at the upper end of the last clearing. From here the trail climbs steeply up the apex of the drainage. Persevere for ½ mile to another open area at 11,200 feet.

Ski across the southern tip of a marshy area, enter the trees again, then test your skins as you climb to another small clearing at 11,400 feet. This is where the real challenge begins.

Cross the bottom end of the clearing (one at a time for possible avalanche danger), then follow a series of steep sidehill switchbacks that climb through forest to the Hagerman Pass Road at 11,600 feet. Turn left (E), ski the road a short distance, then follow a well-marked blue diamond trail uphill a bit, then slightly downhill to the hut. If you miss the blue diamonds the road-cut is obvious, but skiing the road will take you past the hut if you're not careful. The Skinner Hut is located a few hundred feet north of Hagerman Pass Road at 11,620 feet. You cannot see the hut from the road.

REVERSE ROUTE DESCRIPTION: The first steep section of this trail (that drops you into Glacier Creek) is a difficult downhill. Consider descending Busk Creek instead (route 14.2).

If you do opt for a return via Glacier Creek, ski W from the hut outhouse up a short hill (trail marked with blue diamonds), then down a short hill to intersect the Hagerman Pass Road. Look to your right for ski tracks and blue diamonds indicating the point where the Glacier Creek trail leaves the road and descends into the Glacier Creek drainage. Reverse the route above, perhaps deviating from the trail a bit as you make a series of switchbacks to get down the steep sections of trail.

Whatever you do, be sure to intersect the flat section of trail through the clearings at the 10,760-foot level. Carefully follow the trail downvalley from here as it descends steeply through small clearings and timber. The suggested route makes a boring descent into the gut of Glacier Creek to intersect the Turquoise Lake Road (the road is obvious). For better downhill fun, ski the marked trail down to about 10,200 feet, swing right (E) off the marked trail, then ski clearings and a line-cut down to the Turquoise Lake Road. With this option you'll intersect the Turquoise Lake Road a few hundred yards south of the official trail/road intersection.

SAFETY NOTES: Climbing skins are essential for the latter portion of this route. Be sure your skins are properly attached to your skis, since the crux of the climb is a steep sidehill. Take care identifying the intersection of the Glacier Creek trail with the Turquoise Lake Road. Many avalanche slopes run into the Glacier Creek valley. The most obvious paths are those that run down the northwest side of the valley into the flats at 10,760 feet. The official trail avoids exposure to these slides by staying close to the trees on the side of the valley, but most parties ski across the middle of the flats as this is a more obvious line. Doing so is an acceptable risk during low avalanche hazard, but with any doubt about stability you should stay to the side of the valley — or even in the trees. Also, spread your party out if conditions indicate high hazard. The marked trail passes below another smaller slide path at 11,400 feet. This path slides infrequently, but should be treated with caution. Parties using the Glacier Creek trail should carry avalanche beepers and shovels, and have at least one party member with knowledge of avalanche hazard avoidance.

SUMMER: The trail up Glacier Creek makes a fine hike (with some bushwhacking), and the Turquoise Lake Road is a scenic drive. For more civilized hiking take the trail to Timberline Lake.

14.2

Turquoise Lake Trailhead — Skinner Hut via Turquoise Lake Road and Busk Creek

DIFFICULTY: Advanced
TIME: 12 hours up, 8 hours down
DISTANCE: 11 ¾ miles
ELEVATION GAIN: 2,310 feet; loss: 720 feet

TEXT MAP: pp. 184-185, 197
10TH MTN MAP: Con. Div., U. Frypan.
USGS MAP: Homestake Reservoir, Mt. Massive

This alternate route avoids the steep climb up Glacier Creek. It's long and unmarked, but could be a good option for skiers with sleds or light touring gear. It is an easier descent for people without strong downhill skiing skills.

ROUTE DESCRIPTION: Follow the Turquoise Lake Road (see route 14.1) to the west end of Turquoise Lake and the Glacier Creek trailhead. Stay on the Turquoise Lake Road as it turns S then SE for 1 mile to cross over Busk Creek (a nondescript culvert) at 9,950 feet. Continue a few hundred feet past the culvert, then take a hard right (SW) off the road into the forest. A well-used snowmobile and ski route leads up through the forest for ¾ mile to the open flats in Busk Creek at the 10,200-foot level. Cross to the northwest side of Busk Creek and ski upvalley through open trees and clearings. Above 10,400 feet the valley narrows and you'll eventually be forced left (S) into denser timber. Cross back over to the southeast side of Busk Creek at approximately 10,500 feet and continue climbing through timber to the Hagerman Pass Road at 10,760 feet.

Here you have two choices:

A) Simply climb the Hagerman Pass Road 3 miles to the Skinner Hut. Most of the road is easy to follow via hillside cuts and obvious cuts through timber. One section at 11,000 feet can be obscured during heavy snow years, but a bit of map work will keep you on track. A power line makes a good landmark.

B) With high avalanche danger, several steep banks threaten the Hagerman Pass Road. You can avoid most of these by following an old rail grade above the road. To do so, leave the road a few hundred feet east of the obvious Carlton Tunnel portal and climb up through the trees to intersect the rail grade in an open area at 11,080 feet. The rail-grade route is not obvious here, but it soon follows a distinct cut NE, paralleling the Hagerman Pass Road and intersecting the road at the power lines (11,060 feet). Follow the Hagerman Pass Road from here to the Skinner Hut.

With either option remember that you cannot see the hut from the road. To be sure you find the hut, begin intense map and altimeter use at the sharp curve at 11,300 feet. When the road levels out at 11,600 feet, consider skiing to the right and following the ridge up to the hut. At times you'll find ski tracks leading from the road to the hut, but don't bet on this.

REVERSE ROUTE DESCRIPTION: Ski S from the Skinner Hut several hundred feet to the obvious cut of the Hagerman Pass Road. Ski the road 1 1/4 miles to the power line at the 11,060-foot level. With high avalanche danger leave the road at the power line and traverse on the old rail grade for 1 3/4 miles, then drop though light timber to intersect the Hagerman Pass Road near the Carlton Tunnel portal.

Ski the Hagerman Pass Road SE and E several hundred yards around the curve from the Carlton Tunnel portal. Drop into Busk Creek at the east end of the curve. Ski through timber on the south side of Busk Creek and cross the creek at the 10,500-foot level. Ski down the north side of the Busk Creek valley into the open flats. Cross back over Busk Creek and continue down the drainage to intersect the Turquoise Lake Road. Follow the Turquoise Lake Road back around the north side of Turquoise Lake to the Turquoise Lake Trailhead.

SAFETY NOTES: Though the skiing on this trail is of the intermediate level, it is rated advanced because it is a long unmarked trail. Also note that this route has many miles of low-angle skiing. Thus, you should have lightweight equipment and good endurance. Get an early start. The route uses the Busk Creek valley rather than the lower Hagerman Pass Road to avoid exposure to avalanche paths on Bald Eagle Mountain. Do not attempt to cross the ice over Turquoise Lake.

SUMMER: These are good summer routes. The Hagerman Pass Road is fine for any high clearance 2-wheel drive vehicle, and it's fun on a bicycle. The old rail grade (option B) is a nice hike or bicycle route.

14.3

Fryingpan Drainage — Skinner Hut via Hagerman Pass Road

DIFFICULTY: Advanced
TIME: 12 hours up, 8 hours down
DISTANCE: 16 miles
ELEVATION GAIN: 2,785 feet; loss: 365 feet

TEXT MAP: pp. 196-197
10TH MTN MAP: Upper Fryingpan
USGS MAP: Homestake Reservoir, Nast

This alternate is a long route, but most of the trail is packed by snow machines. Use light touring gear and wax, with skins for the climb over Hagerman Pass. Carry a lightweight pack.

ROUTE DESCRIPTION: Park at the Hagerman Pass Road Trailhead. Use cross country wax for a long kick-and-glide up the Hagerman Pass Road. The road follows the old Colorado Midland rail grade and is quite obvious. One possible point of confusion is an intersection at 10,690 feet. Here the Hagerman Pass Road begins a climbing traverse through trees, yet maintenance snowcats and snowmobilers are more likely to be using the lower road into Ivanhoe Lake. If you pay attention it's easy to discern the two different roads.

The long traverse to Hagerman Pass is usually wind-scoured, but does pass below a few slopes with possible slide danger. To avoid the traverse, ski up the valley to the east end of Ivanhoe Lake, then climb a more direct route to the pass. Even this route may pose some risk during extreme instability, so beware. If your wax is working well it's possible to reach the pass without skins, but have them handy in case you need them. Most people skin up at about 11,400 feet.

From the Hagerman Pass summit follow the road as it takes a dropping traverse E to timberline. Stick to the road for a few hundred more yards, then follow a blue diamond marked route along the ridge E for 1/4 mile to the Skinner Hut. Take care not to ski the road past the Skinner Hut, as you cannot see the hut from the road.

You can shorten this route by skiing from the Elk Wallow Campground Trailhead. From the trailhead ski S for 1/4 mile across the bottom land to the point where the obvious power lines start up the mountainside. Put your skins on here and ski up the obvious road-cut that begins a few feet south of the power lines. After about a mile of snow-covered road you will reach Diemer Lake. At the north end of Diemer Lake, ski W up an obvious road-cut that climbs around the lake basin to a 10,031-foot saddle north of the lake. From the saddle ski the road SW for 3/4 mile to the main Hagerman Pass Road at Sellar Park, then follow the route above.

REVERSE ROUTE DESCRIPTION: From the Skinner Hut follow a blue diamond marked trail past the left side of the outhouse and ¼ mile W to intersect the Hagerman Pass Road. Follow the Hagerman Pass Road a few hundred yards to timberline. Above timberline the road traverses north-facing slopes to Hagerman Pass (11,925 feet). To avoid slide danger on this traverse, consider leaving the road at timberline and climbing the ridge south of the road. At the pass, if the snow is skiable, leave the road and enjoy a run down to Ivanhoe Lake. With light snow cover or difficult ski conditions it's best to use the road that traverses downhill NW from the pass. In either case follow Hagerman Pass Road down Ivanhoe Creek, then through Hell Gate, where the road traverses the side of a ridge. After Hell Gate the road is easy to follow around Sellar Park and to the Hagerman Pass Road Trailhead.

SAFETY NOTES: Use lightweight ski equipment for this long flat route. Carry skins for the climbing just below the pass. You must be fit and start early.

SUMMER: The Hagerman Pass Road is a minimally maintained dirt road. It's a fine hike, bicycle route, or auto tour (high clearance 2-wheel drive).

14.4

Skinner Hut to Betty Bear Hut via Hagerman Pass and Ivanhoe

DIFFICULTY: Intermediate	**TEXT MAP:** pp. 184, 196-197
TIME: 5 hours	**10TH MTN MAP:** Con. Div., U. Frypan.
DISTANCE: 4 ¼ miles	**USGS MAP:** Homestake Reservoir,
ELEVATION GAIN: 345 feet; loss: 865 feet	Nast

The standard connection between the Skinner Hut and Betty Bear Hut takes this 10th Mountain suggested route.

ROUTE DESCRIPTION: Follow reverse route 14.3 over Hagerman Pass. Take the road down the west side of the pass for ¼ mile to 11,800 feet. Leave the road here and take a dropping traverse SW to the Hagerman Tunnel portal (11,520 feet). Follow a snow-covered road SW then W from the portal as it traverses around the head of the drainage to an open saddle at 11,400 feet. Continue W from the saddle downhill 1 mile to Lily Pad Lake. Ski NW along the west side of the lake, then swing W for ⅛ mile through timber to Betty Bear Hut at 11,100 feet.

SAFETY NOTES: Visibility above timberline on Hagerman Pass can be limited in stormy weather. Calibrate your altimeter at the pass.

SUMMER: Use this route for a nice alpine hike. No summer tread connects Hagerman Pass with the tunnel road.

14.5

Skinner Hut to Uncle Bud's Hut via Glacier Creek and the Main Range/Colorado Trail

DIFFICULTY: Advanced
TIME: 8 hours
DISTANCE: 7 miles
ELEVATION GAIN: 1,690; loss: 1,930

TEXT MAP: pp. 184-185
10TH MTN MAP: Continental Divide
USGS MAP: Homestake Reservoir

Long and arduous, this route is the standard connection between the Skinner Hut and Uncle Bud's Hut.

ROUTE DESCRIPTION: Follow route 14.1 (reverse route) down Glacier Creek. At the 10,040-foot level in lower Glacier Creek take extra care to stick with the marked 10th Mountain route (blue diamonds). As the trail nears the creek, find the intersection of the Main Range/Colorado Trail with the Glacier Creek trail. This intersection is well marked, but many parties miss it because they don't pay attention to map and altimeter.

Follow the Main Range/Colorado Trail as it climbs out of Glacier Creek via an easterly traverse, then climbs N and NE through timber to timberline at 11,400 feet on the south ridge of Galena Mountain. The trail descends through glades from here to 11,200 feet, then takes a more gradual descent for ¼ mile past the south edge of a small lake. Pass this lake and climb a short hill to pass between the two Galena Lakes.

From Galena Lakes ski the Main Range/Colorado Trail through a flat marshy area and climb for ¼ mile to 11,240 feet. Swing E here through timber and make a short drop into Bud's Gulch, the watered drainage just west of Uncle Bud's Hut. Climb E up a short hill several hundred yards to the hut at 11,380 feet.

SAFETY NOTES: Use your map, compass, altimeter — and guidebook! Remember that wilderness trails are marked with tree blazes rather than blue plastic diamonds.

SUMMER: The Main Range/Colorado Trail is a fine hiking or horse route. Bicycles are not permitted in wilderness.

14.6

Skinner Hut to Uncle Bud's Hut via Busk Creek and Turquoise Lake Road

DIFFICULTY: Advanced
TIME: 12 hours
DISTANCE: 13 miles
ELEVATION GAIN: 1,680 feet; loss: 1,920 feet

TEXT MAP: pp. 184-185, 197
10TH MTN MAP: Con. Div., U. Frypan.
USGS MAP: Homestake Reservoir,
Mt. Massive

This alternate route is extremely long. It is most useful in the event of an unusually severe overnight snowfall — when descending Glacier Creek and breaking trail on the Main Range/Colorado Trail would be too dangerous and arduous. Cross country waxed lightweight equipment is best for this route.

ROUTE DESCRIPTION: Follow reverse route 14.2. As you ski around the north side of Turquoise Lake on the Turquoise Lake Road, identify your high point of 10,680 feet. Continue E down a gradual grade and level sections for 1 ¾ miles to 10,420 feet. Take a hard left here onto Road 107 and follow 10th Mountain suggested route 13.1 to Uncle Bud's Hut.

With adroit map work it's possible to ski N from the Turquoise Lake Road high point up the drainage to Uncle Bud's Hut. This alternative is problematic, however, because the trail is rarely broken and it's difficult to identify the exact point where you would leave the Turquoise Lake Road. Hence it is not recommended as an ascent for any but the most experienced parties.

SAFETY NOTES: Start early. The trail follows Busk Creek to avoid avalanche slopes that cross the road. Do not attempt to cross the ice over Turquoise Lake.

SUMMER: Busk Creek has no obvious summer tread. All the roads mentioned above are navigable with high clearance 2-wheel drive.

14.7

Lyle Peak from the Skinner Hut

DIFFICULTY: Advanced
TIME: 8 hours round trip
DISTANCE: 9 ½ miles round trip
ELEVATION GAIN: 1,309 feet round trip

TEXT MAP: pp. 184, 197
10TH MTN MAP: C. Div., U. Fryingpan
USGS MAP: Homestake Reservoir,
Nast

Tired of skiing through forests? Try this branch route.

ROUTE DESCRIPTION: Follow reverse route 14.3 to Hagerman Pass. From the pass simply ski or walk the Continental Divide N, skirting the southwest side of Divide Peak (12,259 feet) to a prominent saddle on the Continental Divide. From the saddle follow the Divide for 2 miles NW and N to the summit of Lyle Peak (12,489 feet). Return via the same route.

SAFETY NOTES: This route sticks to the ridge to avoid avalanche terrain. With spring "frozen corn" conditions, consider skiing the bowl on the east side of Hagerman Pass. This route is very exposed, so only attempt it in good weather.

SUMMER: Walk the Continental Divide for a fine high altitude trek.

Starting up the Glacier Creek trail to the 10th Mountain Skinner Hut.

14.8

Ski Tours from the Skinner Hut

DIFFICULTY: Intermediate to Advanced
TEXT MAP: pp. 184, 197
10TH MTN MAP: Continental Divide, Upper Fryingpan
USGS MAP: Homestake Reservoir

Indeed, the Skinner Hut sits in a spectacular location. Yet its ridgetop site precludes the easily accessed intermediate glade skiing that characterizes many other 10th Mountain Huts. Advanced and expert ski mountaineers will find plenty of options up on the Continental Divide.

ROUTE DESCRIPTIONS: For intermediate skiing your can make a few turns S down to the Hagerman Pass Road. Stay out of the tempting gully that drops S from the road—it leads into steep cliffy terrain. For a mellow scenic tour, simply ski down the ridge E from the back porch of the hut. Re-skin and climb back to the hut when you reach dark timber. Another scenic tour follows reverse route 14.3 up to Hagerman Pass. Wander a short distance up the Continental Divide N or S from the pass. Advanced skiers will enjoy skiing the slopes in the bowl dropping east from Hagerman Pass. Take care with avalanche terrain in this area.

SAFETY NOTES: Be aware of the steep cliffy terrain surrounding the Skinner Hut, especially off the north side of the ridge.

SUMMER: Hike the old Hagerman rail grade as shown on the USGS map. Bicycle or auto-tour Hagerman Pass Road (high clearance 2-wheel drive).

Chapter 15 • Betty Bear Hut

Completion of the Betty Bear Hut was a milestone for the 10th Mountain Trail Association. From the start an important 10th Mountain goal was to establish a group of huts that you could connect with one long ski tour.

ELEVATION: 11,100 feet
COUNTY: Pitkin
TEXT MAP: pp. 184-185, 196-197
10TH MTN MAP: Con. Divide, U. Frypan.
USGS MAP: Nast
TRAILHEADS: Road 505, Granite Lakes

With the Betty Bear Hut, even though the system is not a closed loop, you can start at either end of a huge 70-mile "U" and connect more than 10 huts for a great ski tour. Moreover, the 10th Mountain Trail was originally intended as a direct connection between Aspen and Vail, but complexities arose because of wildlife, private land, and ski resorts. As a result, the trail followed a circuitous route that never really connected Vail with Aspen. Now, that the Betty Bear Hut and Skinner Hut link the Aspen area huts with those to the east, you can ski between Vail and Aspen with no car shuttles. Betty Bear Hut was funded by Jack Schuss and Al Zesiger. The name honors their wives.

This hut is terrific for intermediate backcountry skiers. The long ski up the Fryingpan drainage on Road 505 (route 15.1) is a good run for waxed light tour skis (with a short "skin climb"), and the hut location lends itself to mellow walks with short descents. The trip over Hagerman Pass to the Skinner Hut (route 15.2) is rated intermediate, but has a good portion above timberline. To reach Margy's Hut, the Harry Gates Hut, or the Peter Estin Hut, you'll want to overnight in the Fryingpan valley. See Chapter 4 for information about lodging and connections to these huts.

15.1

Road 505 Trailhead — Betty Bear Hut via Road 505

DIFFICULTY: Intermediate
TIME: 7 hours up, 6 hours down
DISTANCE: 6 ¾ miles
ELEVATION GAIN: 2,020 feet; loss: 40 feet
TEXT MAP: pp. 196-197
10TH MTN MAP: Upper Fryingpan
USGS MAP: Nast

This 10th Mountain suggested route is the standard trail to Betty Bear Hut from the Fryingpan drainage. The bulk of the route uses snow-covered Road 505. This road is used by both skiers and snowmobilers, but it's wide enough for everyone.

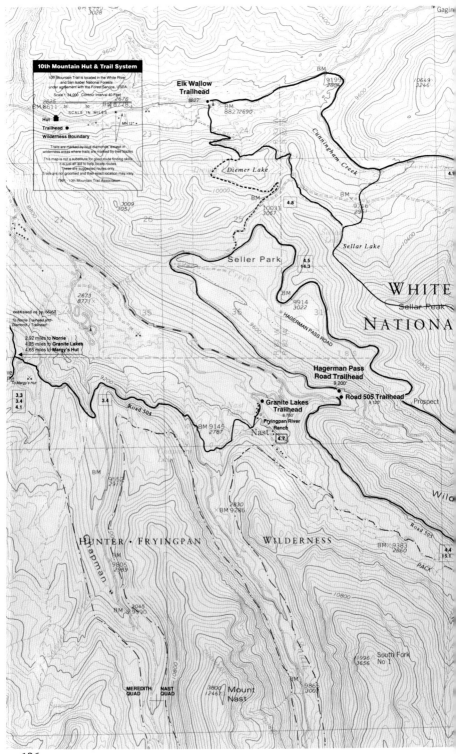

10th Mountain Hut & Trail System

10th Mountain Trail is located in the White River
and San Isabel National Forests
under agreement with the Forest Service, USDA.

Scale 1:34,000   Contour Interval 40 Feet

SCALE IN MILES

Hut

Trailhead

Wilderness Boundary

Trails are marked by blue diamonds, except in
wilderness areas where trails are marked by tree blazes.

This map is not a substitute for good route finding skills.
It is just an aid to help locate routes.
These are suggested routes only.
Trails are not groomed and their exact location may vary.

1991 10th Mountain Trail Association

Elk Wallow
Trailhead
8827

Diemer Lake

Cunningham Creek

Seller Lake

Seller Park

Sellar Peak

WHITE

NATIONAL

HAGERMAN PASS ROAD

Hagerman Pass
Road Trailhead
9,200'

Road 505 Trailhead
9,120'

Granite Lakes
Trailhead
8,760
Fryingpan River
Ranch

Nast

Road 504

Prospect

continued on pp. 66&65
To Norrie Trailhead and
Diamond J Trailhead

2.92 miles to **Norrie**
4.25 miles to **Granite Lakes**
4.65 miles to **Margy's Hut**

To Margy's Hut

HUNTER · FRYINGPAN   WILDERNESS

Hapman

Road 505

Wild

PACK

MEREDITH
QUAD

NAST
QUAD

Mount
Nast

South Fork
No 1

HOLY CROSS
WILDERNESS

DIVIDE

CONTINENTAL

Timberline Lake

BM
10499
3200

eff Gate

4.5
14.3

BM
10741
3274

Ivanhoe Creek

Hagerman Pass Road

11600

Virginia
Lake

14.7

continued on pp 184-185
To Turquoise Lake Trailhead
and Uncle Bud's Hut

Mountain

BM 10956
3339

10929 3331

Divide
12899 3737

30 miles to Skinner Hut
4.09 miles to Betty Bear Hut
6.37 miles to Uncle Bud's Hut
8.29 miles to Turquoise Lake

13.2
13.4
14.1
14.5

Ivanhoe Lake

Ivanhoe

Lily Pad Creek

Hagerman
Pass

Skinner Hut
11,620

1.30 miles to Skinner Hut
3.09 miles to Betty Bear Hut

16 miles to Betty Bear Hut
4.23 miles to Skinner Hut
6.78 miles to Road 505

2.11 miles to Betty Bear Hut
2.28 miles to Skinner Hut

OLD

RR

GRADE

Busk Creek

19 miles to Betty Bear Hut
miles to Road 505
2970

Betty Bear
Hut
3050 M 100
10035

Lily Pad
Lake

14.4
15.2

1.36 miles to Betty Bear Hut
3.03 miles to Skinner Hut

BM 11455
HOMESTAKE
RESERVOIR
QUAD
3759
2334
Busk-Ivanhoe

15.4

15.3

Route continues
to N Mount Massive
See text descriptions

14.2
14.6

197

ROUTE DESCRIPTION: Park at the Road 505 Trailhead on the Fryingpan—Hagerman Pass Road. Road 505 is easy to identify by the shape of the snow-covered roadbed, the metal gate at the start of the road, and a Forest Service road number stake with the numerals "505." Ski Road 505 as it climbs SE along the side of the Fryingpan drainage for 3 ½ miles to the road high point at the obvious concrete structure of the Granite Adit (9,990 feet). Enjoy the superb view of Mount Massive looming on the northeast side of the upper drainage. Continue on level road (with a few slight ups and downs) another mile to cross over Lily Pad Creek. This creek is inconspicuous as it has little flow and passes under the road through a culvert. The stub of the culvert is visible if you look over the downhill side of the road. Another good way to identify Lily Pad Creek is by paying attention to the two rock "gates" you pass through on Road 505. These "gates" are places where road-blasting left remnants of rock outcrops on the downhill side of the road. Lily Pad Creek is located about 100 feet past the second rock "gate."

Ski the road past Lily Pad Creek for several hundred feet. At this point the trail to Betty Bear Hut leaves the road and climbs NE up the side of the valley. With a lack of natural landmarks and your altimeter of little use because of the level road, this intersection of road and trail is a place where the blue diamond trail markers are essential. So look carefully.

Put on your climbing skins. Follow the marked trail as it makes several switchbacks up the valleyside, then parallels and gradually nears Lily Pad Creek. At 10,520 feet you'll break into an open area below the huge rock outcrop of Ivanhoe Point. Stay on the south (right) side of the creek and continue up the drainage as it swings S to 11,080 feet in another open area. Ski SW and enter the trees at the far southwest end of this open area, then continue SW for ⅛ mile through timber to Betty Bear Hut (11,100 feet). The hut sits at the edge of timber overlooking a southwest-facing clearing. If you miss the trail keep your eye on your altimeter. It is essential to not drop too low, and by no means try to make it down to the road from below the hut as the terrain is quite steep and rough.

REVERSE ROUTE DESCRIPTION: From Betty Bear Hut ski NE for ⅛ mile through timber, then continue NE across a clearing to Lily Pad Creek at 11,080 feet. Swing left and parallel the creek for 1 ¾ miles to timber at 10,520 feet. Diverge left (SW) from the creek here and follow several switchbacks down to the obvious cut of Road 505. This hillside can be dry early or late season, so be ready for possible hiking. Ski Road 505 NW for 4 ½ miles to the Road 505 Trailhead on the Fryingpan—Hagerman Pass Road.

SAFETY NOTES: With unusually unstable snow a few "bank sluff" avalanches could fall to Road 505. The first of these banks is just past the

Granite Adit, with another at 4.7 miles from the trailhead, and another at 5.3 miles. Skirt these banks as far to the opposite side of the road as possible, and pass below them one person at a time. Orienteering on this route is relatively easy, just take care to find where the marked trail leaves Road 505.

SUMMER: Road 505 is a good bet for all activities. Also, the Granite Lakes pack trail, located across the drainage from Road 505, is a fine hike or horse route into the Upper Fryingpan drainage. Start this trail at the Granite Lakes Trailhead.

15.2

Betty Bear Hut to Skinner Hut via Hagerman Pass

DIFFICULTY: Intermediate	**TEXT MAP:** pp. 184, 196-197
TIME: 5 ½ hours	**10TH MTN MAP:** Con. Div., U. Frypan.
DISTANCE: 4 ¼ miles	**USGS MAP:** Homestake Reservoir,
ELEVATION GAIN: 865 feet; loss: 345 feet	Nast

Use this 10th Mountain suggested route for the standard connection to the Skinner Hut.

ROUTE DESCRIPTION: From Betty Bear Hut ski for ⅛ mile through timber E to Lily Pad Lake. Ski SE then E around the lake to intersect a snow-covered road which leads through timber and an open area E to an open saddle at 11,400 feet.

Ski E from the saddle on a snow-covered road which traverses SE then E around the head of the Ivanhoe drainage about 1 mile to the Hagerman Tunnel portal (11,520 feet). The road ends at the portal. Take a climbing traverse NE from the portal for ⅜ mile to intersect the Hagerman Pass Road at 11,800 feet. The Hagerman Pass Road can be obscured by snow, but is sometimes marked by bamboo poles. This route is also marked with blue diamonds, but they are infrequent.

Climb the Hagerman Pass Road for ⅜ mile NE to Hagerman Pass (11,925 feet). Follow route 14.3 down to the Skinner Hut.

SAFETY NOTES: Much of this route is at or above timberline. Be ready for limited visibility.

SUMMER: Use this route for a good alpine hike. No summer tread connects the Hagerman Pass Road with the Hagerman Tunnel, but this connection is easy to walk.

15.3

Continental Divide and Busk-Ivanhoe Peak from Betty Bear Hut

DIFFICULTY: Advanced
TIME: 5 hours round trip
DISTANCE: 5 miles round trip
ELEVATION GAIN: 1,234 feet round trip

TEXT MAP: p. 197
10TH MTN MAP: Upper Fryingpan
USGS MAP: Homestake Reserv., Nast, Mt. Champ., Mt. Massive

This route is probably the best peak-climb accessible from Betty Bear Hut.

ROUTE DESCRIPTION: From Betty Bear Hut follow route 15.2 for ¾ mile to the upper end of a large open area (11,320 feet). Leave route 15.2 and continue SE to enter timber at 11,400 feet. Pass SE through the timber a short distance to timberline, then climb SE for ½ mile to the saddle (12,090 feet) just southwest of Busk-Ivanhoe Peak. Climb the ridge NE to the peak (12,334 feet). Descend via the same route.

SAFETY NOTES: You can encounter avalanche danger on any of the steeper slopes in this area. Follow wind-scoured ridges for safe travel.

SUMMER: Enjoy this as a fine alpine hike. Most of the route has no real trail, but the route-finding is easy.

15.4

North Mount Massive from the Fryingpan Drainage and Betty Bear Hut

DIFFICULTY: Expert
TIME: 15 hours round trip
DISTANCE: 14 miles round trip
ELEVATION GAIN: 5,300 feet round trip

TEXT MAP: pp. 196-197
10TH MTN MAP: Upper Fryingpan
USGS MAP: Nast, Mt. Champion, Mt. Massive

Mount Massive, the majestic 14,421-foot peak separating the Fryingpan drainage from the Leadville area, is a long ridge studded with 14,000-foot bumps. The highest bump is the true summit, but another bump to the north of the main summit is known as North Mount Massive. This summit can be climbed from the Fryingpan drainage, from either a high camp or from the Betty Bear Hut. In the latter case it would be a long day and should only be attempted by the strongest and most experienced mountaineers. With either start, it's best to attempt this route during spring snow season or hike it in the summer. Be sure to bring the appropriate USGS map with you for this trip.

Skiing North Mount Massive near Betty Bear Hut. Fryingpan drainage below.

ROUTE DESCRIPTION: From the Betty Bear Hut you must first descend
to the Fryingpan valley and Road 505. It's probably simplest to do this via
reverse route 15.1. But given good snow conditions (such as a spring snowpack), or in the summer, you could also take the route of the road that
leads downhill southeast of the hut site. Absolutely do not use this road
with a winter snowpack—it crosses prime avalanche terrain.

Either way, from the Road 505 terminus at 10,100 feet (or a bit higher if
you came down the road from the hut) continue up the Fryingpan drainage
to 10,890 feet. If you're on snow start with the left side of the valley rather
than the pack trail route shown on the USGS map, then vary your route to
stick to the clearings.

At 10,890 feet keep looking to your left and you'll see a very obvious cut
through the trees leading up to a wide, deep couloir. Climb this couloir to
11,650 feet. Here swing a bit right and climb an obvious couloir which
leads to the ridge. Follow the ridge to the summit. Descent is via the same
route.

SAFETY NOTES: Those with knee problems should forgo this route as a
hike, since the descent involves an arduous 3,000 vertical foot drop in elevation. Snow climbers and skiers will find the best conditions during the

spring season. In winter use the summer route and stick to windblown ribs to avoid avalanche danger. Take care with the many avalanche paths dropping into the Fryingpan River drainage. This would be a difficult route to do in one winter day from Betty Bear.

SUMMER: After snow melt-off, drive (or hike) to the end of Road 505 (see Chapter 1) and park near the valve station. Cross an obvious footbridge over the river, then hike a pack trail about 3 miles to the 10,800-foot level in the Fryingpan River drainage. Look up to the east and pick a likely looking flank for a hard hike/climb more than 3,000 vertical feet up to the Continental Divide ridge. Hike the ridge to the summit of North Mount Massive (14,320 feet). Descent is via the same route.

15.5

Ski Tours from Betty Bear Hut

DIFFICULTY: Intermediate to Advanced
TEXT MAP: pp. 184, 196-197
10TH MTN MAP: Continental Divide, Upper Fryingpan
USGS MAP: Nast, Mt. Champion, Homestake Reservoir, Mt. Massive

Because Betty Bear Hut is situated on a large flat-topped ridge, you won't find much downhill skiing close by the hut. Yet it's a beautiful location, and short forays will reward you with breathtaking vistas of the high peaks, or intimate views of icy ponds and quiet winter forests.

ROUTE DESCRIPTION: For a short tour you can orbit Lily Pad Lake. A longer jaunt leads NE from Lily Pad Lake and climbs to the summit of the ridge separating Lily Pad Creek from Ivanhoe Lake.

SAFETY NOTES: Even on short tours you should carry your pack with extra clothing, food, and survival gear.

SUMMER: Enjoy alpine hikes in any direction from Betty Bear Hut. Of particular note is a tundra walk on the Continental Divide (see route 15.4). Mountaineers should consider a hike/climb of North Mount Massive.

Chapter 16 • Janet's Cabin

L ocated at timberline in the Guller Creek drainage next to the Copper Mountain Ski Area, Janet's Cabin is a fine hut that attracts both novice and expert skiers. The hut was completed in 1990

ELEVATION: 11,610 feet
COUNTY: Summit
TEXT MAP: pp. 114-115, 144-145
10TH MTN MAP: Resol. Mt., Chi. Ridge
USGS MAP: Copper Mountain
TRAILHEADS: Vail Pass, Union Creek

by the Summit Hut and Trails Association, who owns the hut. Booking is by 10th Mountain. The lovingly crafted 3,000 square foot cabin is built with 10" Montana pine logs. Four bedrooms sleep a maximum of 20 guests. Heat is by wood stove, while sun-powered lighting, two propane cook stoves, and hutkeeper's quarters round out the amenities. Loungers will feel at home on the large front deck, where you can bake in the sun while you watch skiers descend from the high bowls.

Janet's Cabin is dedicated to the memory of Janet Boyd Tyler, a Vail resident and avid skier who passed away in 1988. According to her eulogy, "Janet was renowned for her quick smile and readiness to constantly rediscover the joy of life. She discovered her lifelong passion for skiing while attending school in New Hampshire. Early on, Janet met the challenges of the slopes, including (if the legends are true) Tuckerman's Ravine in the White Mountains. She dug into all her pursuits with the same enthusiasm she gave to skiing, and she often viewed life's challenges from a skier's perspective. Mountain views, fresh clear air, the beckoning of trees beside the trails, but most of all a good powder morning—these were all perceptions she carried every day. Janet's lifetime ski pass is now buried in the foundation of Janet's Cabin."

The standard trail to Janet's Cabin takes Guller Creek from the Copper Mountain Ski Area (route 16.1). Though this trail is easy, it still requires backcountry wherewithal. Experts will find more challenge by skiing to the hut from Vail Pass (route 16.2), and the "super expert" will have an interesting day challenging the high ridge from Union Peak (Union Mountain) to the hut (route 16.6). Though not officially part of the 10th Mountain hut and trail system, Janet's Cabin readily connects with Jackal Hut via Tim's Traverse (route 16.5), and with the Shrine Mountain Inn via Upper Stafford Creek (route 16.3).

16.1

Union Creek Trailhead — Janet's Cabin via Guller Creek

DIFFICULTY: Novice
TIME: 5 hours up, 3 hours down
DISTANCE: 4 ¾ miles
ELEVATION GAIN: 1,790 feet

TEXT MAP: p. 115
10TH MTN MAP: Resolution Mountain
USGS MAP: Vail Pass, Copper Mtn.

This trail up the Guller Creek drainage is the standard route to Janet's Cabin. Though rated novice, skiers on this route should be fully equipped and know their map reading.

ROUTE DESCRIPTION: Take care with the complicated start for this route. Begin at the Union Creek Trailhead at Copper Mountain Ski Area. From Union Creek you have two choices. The popular option is to ride K and L lifts to the top of the West Tenmile ski trail. You can get a one-ride lift ticket by presenting your 10th Mountain confirmation letter at the ticket window at Union Creek.

Ski about ¼ mile down the extreme west (left) side of the West Tenmile ski trail to 10,640 feet. An altimeter eliminates guesswork here. Watch carefully for a blue diamond marked trail that leaves the ski run (crosses the ski area boundary) at this elevation and heads W through the forest. Your other option is to put on your climbing skins and climb the ski runs to this same point. Stay to the side of the run so that you don't interfere with the downhill skiers.

In either case, after you leave the ski area follow an obvious trail-cut (take your skins off) as it traverses then drops W into the Guller Creek drainage to cross Jacque Creek and Guller Creek in an open area at 10,460 feet. From the crossing the trail stays on the north side of the creek for 2 miles to about 11,120 feet. Here the valley widens and becomes very low-angled. Switch to the south side of the creek here and continue up the drainage another mile to where the valley steepens and narrows. Put your skins on here.

Climb this steep section of the trail another ¼ mile to Janet's Cabin at 11,610 feet. The hut is just below the last timber a few hundred feet northwest of Guller Creek. If you find yourself above timberline, you have gone too high.

REVERSE ROUTE DESCRIPTION: Reverse the above route to the lower creek crossing at 10,460 feet. For the most fun put your skins back on here and continue to reverse your route back to the West Tenmile ski run. Then enjoy a downhill run to Union Creek.

As an alternative to the climb back to the ski run, you can continue down Guller Creek via an obvious trail. After a fast 2-mile downhill you'll intersect maintained ski touring trails. Climb the ski touring trails to your right (E) at the first opportunity and continue climbing E until you hit the first downhill ski run. Descend this run to Union Creek.

SAFETY NOTES: This trail has no avalanche danger. Though it's easier than most 10th Mountain Trails, it's still backcountry skiing—so be prepared.

SUMMER: The Guller Creek trail is fine for cycling, hiking, or horseback. Copper Mountain Resort has a comprehensive summer program that includes cycling. Call Copper Mountain for details.

16.2

Vail Pass Trailhead—Janet's Cabin via Upper Stafford Creek

DIFFICULTY: Advanced
TIME: 6 hours up, 5 hours down
DISTANCE: 5 ¾ miles
ELEVATION GAIN: 1,130 feet; loss: 100 feet

TEXT MAP: p. 115
10TH MTN MAP: Resolution Mountain
USGS MAP: Vail Pass, Copper Mtn.

This route is the most efficient ski connection between Vail Pass and Janet's Cabin. It also forms the bulk of the connection between Janet's and the Shrine Mountain Inn (route 16.3). Most of the route follows timberline, skirting high around several mountainsides. It's a more interesting trip than Guller Creek, with tremendous views and plenty of challenging navigation.

ROUTE DESCRIPTION: Start from the Vail Pass Trailhead. Put your skins on and ski S across West Tenmile Creek, then take a slightly climbing traverse S then SW into Wilder Gulch. Cross S through Wilder Gulch at the 10,600-foot level. Leave Wilder Gulch and climb 1 mile up the south ridge of Wilder Gulch to a shelf at 11,280 feet. Move S off the ridge here and take a traversing climb another mile to timberline at a small saddle and knob in the Stafford Creek drainage (11,640 feet).

Traverse the head of Stafford Creek by following an 11,600-foot contour, and gain an open saddle on the south ridge of the drainage at 11,680 feet. Take a slightly dropping contour SE from the saddle for ¼ mile down to Janet's Cabin at the head of Guller Creek. The hut is just below the last timber a few hundred feet northwest of Guller Creek. If you find yourself above timberline, you have gone too high.

REVERSE ROUTE DESCRIPTION: From the back steps of Janet's Cabin take a ¼-mile slightly climbing traverse N then NW to the open saddle (11,680 feet) on the ridge separating Guller Creek from Stafford Creek. Traverse the head of Stafford Creek via a 2-mile timberline traverse at 11,600 feet to a saddle and small knob at 11,640 feet. Drop N than E here for a short distance, then traverse to the ridge that separates Smith Gulch from Wilder Gulch. Follow the ridge down to 10,600 feet in Wilder Gulch, cross N through Wilder Gulch, then contour N another mile to Vail Pass.

SAFETY NOTES: Because much of this trail passes through open areas, do not depend on trail markers. Much of the terrain above timberline is exposed to avalanches. The correct trail avoids avalanche hazard by dipping in and out of the trees. Since the exact trail can be hard to find, skiers on this route should know how to identify avalanche hazard.

SUMMER: This is a good alpine hike. Lack of trail tread makes the route unsuitable for bicycles and horses.

16.3

Janet's Cabin to Shrine Mountain Inn via Upper Stafford Creek and Shrine Pass Road

DIFFICULTY: Advanced
TIME: 7 hours
DISTANCE: 8 ½ miles
ELEVATION GAIN: 796 feet; loss: 1,197 feet

TEXT MAP: p. 115
10TH MTN MAP: Resolution Mountain
USGS MAP: Copper Mtn., Vail Pass

This is the simplest and most reliable connection between Shrine Mountain Inn and Janet's Cabin. With good weather, strong groups can make a variation and follow a high route between the huts over Shrine Mountain by connecting route 16.4 with route 9.7.

ROUTE DESCRIPTION: Follow reverse route 16.2 to Vail Pass, then use route 8.1 to reach the Shrine Mountain Inn.

SAFETY NOTES: Because much of this trail passes through open areas, do not depend on trail markers. Much of the terrain above timberline is exposed to avalanches. The correct trail avoids avalanche hazard by dipping in and out of the trees. Since the exact trail can be hard to find, skiers on this route should know how to identify avalanche danger. The portion from Vail Pass to the Shrine Mountain Inn is easier, but even this could be dangerous in poor visibility during a storm.

SUMMER: The section to Vail Pass is a good alpine hike, but is unsuitable for bicycles and horses. Shrine Pass Road is a good cycling route. Hikers can explore Shrine Mountain and the surrounding drainages. Horse people can ride the road, but heavy car traffic could be a problem.

16.4

Janet's Cabin to Fowler/Hilliard Hut via Wilder Gulch

DIFFICULTY: Advanced	**TEXT MAP:** pp. 114-115
TIME: 9 hours	**10TH MTN MAP:** Resolution Mountain
DISTANCE: 8 miles	**USGS MAP:** Copper Mountain, Pando,
ELEVATION GAIN: 858 feet; loss: 968 feet	Vail Pass, Red Cliff

This scenic route includes a great deal of high altitude touring if you finish via Ptarmigan Hill. With poor weather, you can also take a low route that drops into Wearyman Creek from Wilder Gulch and follows a logging road to the Fowler/Hilliard Hut. This low route only has about 200 less vertical feet than the high route – and it's longer – so take the high route if you can.

ROUTE DESCRIPTION: Follow route 16.2 (reverse route) to the ridge between Smith Gulch and Wilder Gulch. Instead of dropping here, contour W into Wilder Gulch to intersect route 9.6 to the Fowler/Hilliard Hut.

SAFETY NOTES: Because much of this trail passes through open areas, do not depend on trail markers. Much of the terrain above timberline is exposed to avalanches. The correct trail avoids avalanche hazard by dipping in and out of the trees. In Wilder Gulch make whatever deviations you need to avoid potential bank sluffs. Be careful with the cornices on Ptarmigan Hill.

SUMMER: This is a good alpine hike. Lack of trail tread makes the route unsuitable for bicycles and horses.

16.5

Janet's Cabin to Jackal Hut via Tim's Traverse

DIFFICULTY: Expert	**TEXT MAP:** p. 144
TIME: 6 hours	**10TH MTN MAP:** Chicago Ridge
DISTANCE: 4 ½ miles	**USGS MAP:** Copper Mountain, Pando
ELEVATION GAIN: 1,230 feet; loss: 1,180 feet	

Do you want one of the finest "hut to hut" high tours? Try this alternate route.

ROUTE DESCRIPTION: From the front steps of Janet's Cabin, climb 430 vertical feet SW and S to Searle Pass (12,040 feet). Take the time at Searle Pass to identify Corbett Peak, which rises above the basin to the south. Ski across the basin (you might see markers for the Colorado Trail) and climb to the saddle on the ridge (12,460 feet) just north of Corbett Peak. Stay on the ridge and climb N to the first high point (12,600 feet), then drop off the ridge by following a rib which leads west to Pearl Peak.

Contour around the southerly side of Pearl Peak (or go over the summit to avoid avalanche danger) and descend the southwest ridge about a mile to the saddles and small bump (11,475 feet) that separate Cataract Creek to the south from Pearl Creek to the north. Intersect the marked 10th Mountain trail here that continues along the ridge west to the Jackal Hut. The hut is several hundred feet south of the ridge crest at 11,660 feet elevation.

SAFETY NOTES: Much of this route passes through avalanche terrain. You should carry avalanche rescue equipment and be expert with hazard avoidance. Consider skiing Tim's Traverse during a period of stable snow, such as a cold day during the spring corn-snow season.

SUMMER: Tim's Traverse is a good alpine hike. The section of Colorado Trail over Searle Pass and into the basin is good for all activities. The route from the basin over to Jackal Hut has no tread, so it's only good for hiking.

16.6

Copper Mountain Ski Area Summit — Janet's Cabin via High Route

DIFFICULTY: Expert
TIME: 6 hours
DISTANCE: 4 miles
ELEVATION GAIN: 892 feet; loss: 1,595 feet

TEXT MAP: p. 115
10TH MTN MAP: Resolution Mountain
USGS MAP: Copper Mountain

This fine high altitude ridge run is an alternate route that will appeal to expert ski mountaineers. It includes a climb of Jacque Peak, one of more than 700 Colorado peaks topping 13,000 feet elevation. Try this route late in the season when you can enjoy a corn-snow run down to the hut.

ROUTE DESCRIPTION: Drive to Copper Mountain Resort (see Union Creek Trailhead in Chapter 1). The route begins at the Copper Mountain Ski Area boundary on Union Peak (12,313 feet). It's best to use the ski lifts to reach this point. To do so, park at the transportation center on your left just after you enter Copper Mountain Resort. (Inquire about overnight parking). Take a shuttle to the Copper Mountain Center, purchase a lift ticket and grab a trail map, then ride the lifts to the summit of Union Peak.

From Union Peak exit the ski area boundary at the backcountry access gate (if this access is not obvious, inquire at the ski patrol building nearby). From the top of Union Peak, climb the ridge SW for ¾ mile and 892 vertical feet to the summit of Jacque Peak (13,205 feet). From Jacque Peak simply descend the ridge 1 ¾ miles W to Searle Pass. Leave the ridge at the pass and descend NW and W to Janet's Cabin. The hut is at 11,610 feet, just below timberline a few hundred feet northwest of Guller Creek.

REVERSE ROUTE DESCRIPTION: Due to the effort saved by riding ski lifts, this route is best done from Copper Mountain Ski Area to the hut. It's no problem to follow the route from the hut to the ski area—it's just more work. To do so simply reverse the route above.

SAFETY NOTES: This is adult mountaineering. Get a good weather report for your day on this high route. You should have expert knowledge of avalanche safety, be very fit, and be comfortable with high altitudes. Parts of the route are better hiked than skied, so be prepared for walking.

SUMMER: The climb up to Jacque Peak is a good hike/climb. Consider riding up the Copper Mountain ski lift to access this hike.

16.7

Ski Tours from Janet's Cabin

DIFFICULTY: Intermediate to Advanced
TEXT MAP: pp. 115, 144
10TH MTN MAP: Resolution Mountain, Chicago Ridge
USGS MAP: Copper Mountain

Janet's Cabin provides access to a vast area of high altitude terrain. Intermediate skiers will enjoy short forays into the low-angled bowls above the hut, as well as a bit of tree skiing below. Advanced skiers and experts can climb to Searle Pass or Sugarloaf Peak.

SAFETY NOTES: During times of low avalanche hazard, much of the terrain above Janet's Cabin is of low enough angle to be reasonably safe for skiing. Plenty of steeper pitches exist, as do drops off cornices and steep pitches into ravines. However smooth the snow looks, remember that hidden obstacles abound. Ski in control.

SUMMER: Try a hike on the Colorado Trail, or venture off-trail to the alpine bowls above the hut.

Appendix 1 • **Hut Data**

Hut	Built	Elevation	County	USGS map
Betty Bear Hut	1991	11,100	Pitkin	Nast
Diamond J Guest Ranch	1927	8,250	Pitkin	Meredith
Fowler/Hilliard Hut	1988	11,500	Eagle	Pando
Fryingpan River Ranch	1965	8,760	Pitkin	Nast
Harry Gates Hut	1986	9,700	Eagle	Crooked Creek Pass
Jackal Hut	1988	11,660	Eagle	Pando
Janet's Cabin	1990	11,610	Summit	Copper Mountain
Margy's Hut	1982	11,300	Pitkin	Meredith
McNamara Hut	1982	10,360	Pitkin	Thimble Rock
Peter Estin Hut	1985	11,200	Eagle	Crooked Creek Pass
Polar Star Inn	1987	11,040	Eagle	Fulford
Shrine Mountain Inn	1988	11,209	Eagle	Vail Pass
Skinner Hut	1990	11,620	Lake	Homestake Reservoir
10th Mt. Division Hut	1989	11,370	Lake	Homestake Reservoir
Uncle Bud's Hut	1989	11,380	Lake	Homestake Reservoir
Vance's Cabin	1988	10,980	Eagle	Pando

Appendix 2 • **Weather Forecasting**

RULES-OF-THUMB FOR FORECASTING WEATHER ON THE 10TH MOUNTAIN TRAILS

1. Steadily falling barometric pressure usually indicates a nearing storm. (You can evaluate this and number 2 with your altimeter.)

2. Steadily rising barometric pressure usually indicates clearing weather.

3. When barometric pressure is more than 30.10, rain or snow will probably end soon. (You can check this with most altimeters.)

4. When the temperature during a storm drops to less than 5 degrees F, snowfall will rapidly diminish.

5. Cirrus clouds can precede a storm by 24 hours or more. (A ring around the moon is caused by thin cirrus.)

6. Thickening and lowering clouds (usually coming from the west) indicate a nearing storm.

7. Thickening mountain wave clouds indicate increasing moisture and increasing winds aloft, and a possible nearing storm.

8. Mountain wave clouds and snow plumes on ridges indicate high winds at mountaintop levels.

9. Thinning and lifting clouds indicate clearing weather.

10. Frontal passage (the end of a storm) is often indicated by the lowest point of the barometric pressure curve (you can plot this from your altimeter), a wind shift, and a sudden appearance of ice-coated snow crystals or graupel.

11. Current weather reports on radio, especially NOAA Weather Radio on the VHF band, are your best sources for accurate forecasts while mountaineering.

FROM COMPUSERVE, A PUBLIC DOMAIN SOURCE

Appendix 3 • Sun & Moon Times

This table gives the approximate time and direction for sunrise, sunset, moonrise, and moonset. All times are in 24-hour format, and are for a level horizon (they'll be different for a valley floor). Direction is an azimuth, which is simply the degrees on your compass dial where the rise or set will occur (from geographic north, declination included). Moon phase is the percentage of a full moon, i.e., the date with .99 moon phase is the full moon.

Latitude: N 39.00   Longitude: W 106.00

NOTE: TIMES IN MST UNTIL NOTED

Date	Sunrise (azm)	Sunset (azm)	Moonrise(azm)	Moonset(azm)	Phase
15 DEC 1991	7:16 (105.3)	16:43 (225.8)	12:28 (64)	0:53 (263)	0.63
31 DEC 1991	7:23 (105.1)	16:52 (226.1)	3:43 (104)	13:30 (226)	0.15
15 JAN 1992	7:22 (102.5)	17:06 (228.7)	12:49 (45)	3:02 (284)	0.77
19 JAN 1992	7:21 (101.5)	17:10 (229.7)	17:20 (52)	7:02 (281)	0.99
31 JAN 1992	7:12 (97.6)	17:24 (233.7)	5:11 (107)	14:46 (225)	0.07
15 FEB 1992	6:57 (91.4)	17:41 (239.8)	14:52 (49)	4:49 (284)	0.90
17 FEB 1992	6:54 (90.5)	17:43 (240.7)	17:25 (63)	6:12 (272)	0.99
29 FEB 1992	6:38 (84.8)	17:57 (246.4)	4:25 (101)	14:35 (232)	0.12
15 MAR 1992	6:15 (77.3)	18:12 (254.0)	15:00 (59)	4:05 (275)	0.87
18 MAR 1992	6:10 (75.8)	18:15 (255.5)	18:40 (83)	5:43 (252)	0.99
31 MAR 1992	5:50 (69.2)	18:28 (262.1)	4:17 (81)	16:21 (254)	0.05

TIMES BELOW: MDT

Date	Sunrise (azm)	Sunset (azm)	Moonrise(azm)	Moonset(azm)	Phase
15 APR 1992	6:27 (61.9)	19:42 (269.3)	18:29 (87)	5:11 (248)	0.97
16 APR 1992	6:26 (61.5)	19:43 (269.8)	19:40 (94)	5:43 (241)	0.99
30 APR 1992	6:07 (55.4)	19:57 (275.8)	4:35 (63)	18:13 (271)	0.04
15 MAY 1992	5:51 (50.0)	20:11 (281.2)	19:38 (102)	4:50 (231)	0.99
31 MAY 1992	5:41 (46.0)	20:24 (285.2)	4:59 (45)	20:21 (287)	0.00
14 JUN 1992	5:38 (44.2)	20:32 (287.0)	20:24 (107)	5:00 (224)	0.99
15 JUN 1992	5:38 (44.1)	20:32 (287.0)	21:11 (105)	5:54 (224)	0.99
30 JUN 1992	5:42 (44.4)	20:34 (286.7)	5:47 (46)	20:56 (283)	0.00
13 JUL 1992	5:50 (46.4)	20:30 (284.7)	19:51 (104)	4:43 (226)	0.99
15 JUL 1992	5:51 (46.8)	20:29 (284.3)	20:59 (95)	6:41 (233)	0.99
31 JUL 1992	6:05 (51.3)	20:16 (279.8)	8:24 (68)	21:20 (259)	0.05
12 AUG 1992	6:15 (55.7)	20:03 (275.3)	19:31 (92)	5:33 (236)	0.99
15 AUG 1992	6:18 (57.0)	19:59 (274.1)	20:47 (73)	8:27 (255)	0.94
31 AUG 1992	6:33 (64.1)	19:36 (267.0)	10:53 (95)	21:29 (233)	0.18
11 SEP 1992	6:42 (69.4)	19:19 (261.7)	18:52 (75)	6:21 (252)	0.99
15 SEP 1992	6:46 (71.4)	19:12 (259.7)	20:45 (52)	10:18 (277)	0.87
30 SEP 1992	7:00 (78.9)	18:48 (252.2)	11:55 (106)	21:35 (225)	0.23
10 OCT 1992	7:09 (83.8)	18:33 (247.2)	17:46 (65)	6:09 (263)	0.99
15 OCT 1992	7:14 (86.2)	18:25 (244.8)	20:58 (45)	11:16 (286)	0.83

TIMES BELOW: MST

Date	Sunrise (azm)	Sunset (azm)	Moonrise(azm)	Moonset(azm)	Phase
31 OCT 1992	6:31 (93.5)	17:04 (237.6)	11:59 (101)	22:12 (232)	0.35
10 NOV 1992	6:42 (97.4)	16:54 (233.7)	17:03 (47)	7:04 (282)	0.99
15 NOV 1992	6:48 (99.2)	16:50 (231.9)	22:10 (56)	11:30 (277)	0.68
30 NOV 1992	7:04 (103.3)	16:43 (227.8)	11:30 (88)	22:54 (246)	0.36
9 DEC 1992	7:12 (104.8)	16:42 (226.3)	16:36 (45)	6:53 (286)	0.99
15 DEC 1992	7:17 (105.4)	16:43 (225.7)	23:31 (75)	11:13 (259)	0.61
31 DEC 1992	7:23 (105.0)	16:52 (226.1)	11:14 (66)	**:**	0.46
1 JAN 1993	7:24 (104.9)	16:53 (226.2)	11:41 (61)	0:28 (268)	0.56
7 JAN 1993	7:24 (104.0)	16:58 (227.1)	16:25 (48)	6:30 (285)	0.99
15 JAN 1993	7:22 (102.3)	17:07 (228.9)	0:46 (94)	11:26 (234)	0.43
31 JAN 1993	7:12 (97.3)	17:25 (234.0)	11:22 (49)	1:15 (281)	0.58
6 FEB 1993	7:06 (94.9)	17:32 (236.3)	17:40 (61)	6:33 (273)	0.99
1 MAR 1993	6:37 (84.4)	17:57 (246.8)	10:50 (46)	1:02 (285)	0.51
7 MAR 1993	6:28 (81.4)	18:04 (249.8)	17:42 (72)	5:37 (262)	0.99
15 MAR 1993	6:16 (77.4)	18:12 (253.9)	1:36 (105)	11:22 (226)	0.43
31 MAR 1993	5:50 (69.3)	18:27 (261.9)	11:42 (51)	1:31 (282)	0.56

213

TIMES BELOW: MDT

Date	Sunrise (azm)	Sunset (azm)	Moonrise(azm)	Moonset(azm)	Phase
6 APR 1993	6:41 (66.3)	19:33 (264.9)	19:59 (91)	6:14 (244)	0.99
15 APR 1993	6:28 (62.1)	19:42 (269.2)	3:07 (92)	14:09 (241)	0.31
30 APR 1993	6:07 (55.5)	19:57 (275.7)	13:57 (66)	2:28 (268)	0.64
5 MAY 1993	6:02 (53.6)	20:01 (277.7)	19:59 (100)	5:24 (234)	0.99
15 MAY 1993	5:52 (50.1)	20:11 (281.1)	2:30 (77)	14:51 (257)	0.28
31 MAY 1993	5:41 (46.0)	20:24 (285.2)	16:28 (92)	2:41 (243)	0.82
3 JUN 1993	5:40 (45.5)	20:26 (285.7)	19:54 (104)	4:47 (228)	0.99
15 JUN 1993	5:38 (44.2)	20:32 (287.0)	2:21 (57)	16:31 (277)	0.18
30 JUN 1993	5:42 (44.4)	20:34 (286.7)	17:41 (104)	2:40 (229)	0.88
4 JUL 1993	5:44 (44.8)	20:33 (286.3)	21:03 (98)	6:27 (231)	0.99
15 JUL 1993	5:51 (46.7)	20:29 (284.4)	2:11 (48)	17:15 (284)	0.15
31 JUL 1993	6:04 (51.2)	20:17 (279.9)	19:01 (99)	4:16 (229)	0.96
1 AUG 1993	6:05 (51.5)	20:16 (279.5)	19:37 (95)	5:18 (233)	0.99
15 AUG 1993	6:18 (56.9)	19:59 (274.2)	3:48 (51)	18:22 (277)	0.05
31 AUG 1993	6:32 (64.0)	19:36 (267.1)	19:09 (81)	6:09 (247)	0.99
15 SEP 1993	6:46 (71.2)	19:13 (259.8)	6:11 (73)	18:42 (254)	0.00
28 SEP 1993	6:58 (77.7)	18:52 (253.3)	17:39 (77)	5:01 (251)	0.96
30 SEP 1993	7:00 (78.8)	18:49 (252.3)	18:33 (65)	6:55 (263)	0.99
15 OCT 1993	7:14 (86.1)	18:26 (245.0)	7:28 (91)	18:27 (237)	0.00
29 OCT 1993	7:29 (92.5)	18:07 (238.6)	17:34 (57)	6:42 (272)	0.99

TIMES BELOW: MST

Date	Sunrise (azm)	Sunset (azm)	Moonrise(azm)	Moonset(azm)	Phase
15 NOV 1993	6:48 (99.1)	16:50 (232.0)	8:44 (104)	18:39 (227)	0.04
28 NOV 1993	7:02 (102.8)	16:43 (228.3)	16:28 (48)	6:26 (282)	0.99
15 DEC 1993	7:16 (105.4)	16:43 (225.8)	9:02 (98)	19:31 (234)	0.07
28 DEC 1993	7:23 (105.3)	16:50 (225.8)	16:59 (49)	6:56 (283)	0.99
1 JAN 1994	7:24 (105.0)	16:53 (226.2)	21:22 (69)	9:35 (265)	0.83
15 JAN 1994	7:22 (102.4)	17:06 (228.8)	9:12 (80)	21:20 (254)	0.14
26 JAN 1994	7:16 (99.1)	17:19 (232.1)	16:50 (55)	6:18 (278)	0.99
31 JAN 1994	7:12 (97.4)	17:24 (233.9)	22:38 (87)	9:16 (247)	0.77
15 FEB 1994	6:56 (91.2)	17:42 (240.1)	9:06 (60)	22:56 (273)	0.23
25 FEB 1994	6:43 (86.5)	17:53 (244.8)	17:57 (70)	6:05 (264)	0.99
1 MAR 1994	6:37 (84.5)	17:57 (246.7)	22:45 (96)	8:29 (238)	0.81
15 MAR 1994	6:16 (77.5)	18:12 (253.7)	7:39 (58)	1:43 (276)	0.10
26 MAR 1994	5:59 (71.9)	18:22 (259.3)	17:55 (81)	5:08 (254)	0.99
31 MAR 1994	5:51 (69.4)	18:27 (261.8)	23:49 (103)	8:46 (228)	0.74

Date	Sunrise (azm)	Sunset (azm)	Moonrise(azm)	Moonset(azm)	Phase
15 APR 1994	6:28 (62.2)	19:42 (269.1)	9:17 (49)	**:**	0.19
25 APR 1994	6:14 (57.7)	19:51 (273.6)	20:11 (96)	5:55 (238)	0.99
30 APR 1994	6:08 (55.6)	19:56 (275.6)	0:22 (101)	10:37 (232)	0.68
15 MAY 1994	5:52 (50.2)	20:10 (281.1)	9:55 (53)	**:**	0.22
24 MAY 1994	5:45 (47.6)	20:18 (283.6)	20:08 (102)	5:16 (231)	0.99
31 MAY 1994	5:41 (46.1)	20:23 (285.1)	0:49 (84)	12:34 (249)	0.53
15 JUN 1994	5:38 (44.2)	20:32 (287.0)	12:00 (72)	**:**	0.38
22 JUN 1994	5:39 (44.0)	20:34 (287.1)	19:55 (102)	4:53 (228)	0.99
30 JUN 1994	5:42 (44.4)	20:34 (286.7)	0:17 (70)	13:17 (264)	0.50
15 JUL 1994	5:51 (46.7)	20:29 (284.4)	13:14 (89)	**:**	0.47
22 JUL 1994	5:57 (48.4)	20:25 (282.7)	20:10 (95)	5:50 (234)	0.99
31 JUL 1994	6:04 (51.1)	20:17 (279.9)	0:24 (54)	14:51 (279)	0.38
15 AUG 1994	6:18 (56.8)	20:00 (274.3)	15:32 (102)	0:36 (230)	0.67
20 AUG 1994	6:22 (58.9)	19:53 (272.2)	19:19 (87)	5:45 (241)	0.99
31 AUG 1994	6:32 (63.8)	19:37 (267.2)	1:17 (49)	16:03 (281)	0.15
15 SEP 1994	6:46 (71.1)	19:13 (259.9)	16:43 (93)	2:33 (235)	0.83
19 SEP 1994	6:49 (73.1)	19:07 (257.9)	18:52 (72)	6:39 (256)	0.99
30 SEP 1994	6:59 (78.6)	18:49 (252.4)	1:58 (57)	15:56 (271)	0.23
15 OCT 1994	7:14 (86.0)	18:26 (245.1)	16:24 (79)	3:33 (249)	0.87
18 OCT 1994	7:17 (87.4)	18:22 (243.7)	17:54 (63)	6:28 (266)	0.99

TIMES BELOW: MST

Date	Sunrise (azm)	Sunset (azm)	Moonrise(azm)	Moonset(azm)	Phase
31 OCT 1994	6:31 (93.3)	17:05 (237.8)	3:01 (77)	15:11 (251)	0.10
17 NOV 1994	6:50 (99.7)	16:49 (231.4)	16:38 (53)	6:12 (277)	0.99
30 NOV 1994	7:03 (103.2)	16:43 (227.9)	4:10 (93)	15:02 (236)	0.07
17 DEC 1994	7:18 (105.5)	16:44 (225.7)	16:49 (49)	6:44 (282)	0.99
31 DEC 1994	7:23 (105.1)	16:52 (226.1)	6:21 (101)	16:32 (230)	0.00
1 JAN 1995	7:24 (105.0)	16:53 (226.2)	7:17 (100)	17:40 (233)	0.00
16 JAN 1995	7:22 (102.2)	17:07 (229.0)	17:27 (55)	6:53 (277)	0.99
31 JAN 1995	7:12 (97.4)	17:24 (233.8)	7:19 (89)	18:42 (245)	0.00
15 FEB 1995	6:56 (91.3)	17:42 (240.0)	18:19 (68)	6:39 (266)	0.99
28 FEB 1995	6:39 (85.2)	17:56 (246.1)	5:50 (86)	17:29 (248)	0.00
16 MAR 1995	6:15 (77.1)	18:12 (254.1)	18:13 (77)	5:43 (257)	0.99
31 MAR 1995	5:51 (69.5)	18:27 (261.7)	5:59 (66)	19:22 (268)	0.00

Appendix 4 • Directory

CENTRAL RESERVATIONS

10th Mountain Trail Association (use this for huts)
1280 Ute Avenue
Aspen CO 81611
(303)925-5775

Aspen Central Reservations
(303)925-9000

Copper Mountain Resort
(800)458-8386

Vail Central Reservations
(303)476-5677

PRIVATE RESERVATIONS

Delaware Hotel (Leadville)
(719)486-1418

Diamond J Guest Ranch (Fryingpan Valley)
(303)927-3222

Fryingpan River Ranch (Fryingpan Valley)
(303)927-3570

Pilgrim's Inn (Red Cliff)
(303)827-5333

Shrine Mountain Inn Restaurant (Shrine Pass)
(303)476-6548

Timberline Motel (Leadville)
(719)486-1876

SHUTTLE SERVICES

Dee Hive Transportation (Eastern huts)
(719)486-2339

High Mountain Taxi (Aspen)
(303)925-8294

Resort Express (Copper Mountain and Vail)
(303)468-7600

Timberline Ski Tours (Western huts)
(303)920-3217

GUIDES

Aspen Alpine Guides
(303)920-8525

Elk Mountain Guides
(303)927-9377

Paragon Guides
(303)949-4272

USGS MAPS

USGS
Bx 25286 Denver Federal Center
Denver CO 80225

WEATHER

(900)932-8437

AVALANCHE CONDITIONS

Aspen: (303)920-1664
Denver/Boulder: (303)236-9435
Summit County: (303)668-0600
Minturn: (303)827-5687

FOREST SERVICE

San Isabel National Forest
(719)486-0752

White River National Forest
(303)945-2521

COUNTY SHERIFF

In the event of an emergency, call 911 from any phone. If 911 does not
work, call directory assistance and ask for the County Sheriff number.

LOCAL STORES

ASPEN
The Hub of Aspen (303)925-7970
Ute Mountaineer (303)925-2849

CARBONDALE
Life Cycles (303)963-1149

GLENWOOD SPRINGS
Summit Canyon Mountaineering (303)945-6994

LEADVILLE
Bill's Sport Shop (719)486-0739
10th Mountain Sports (719)486-2202

VAIL/AVON
Christi Sports (303)949-0241
Vail Mountaineering (303)476-4223

Bibliography

Barnett, Steve. *Cross Country Downhill*, 3rd ed. Seattle: Pacific Search Press, 1983.

Burton, Hale. *The Ski Troops*, New York: Simon and Schuster, 1971.

Danielson, Clarence L. and Ralph W. Basalt. *Colorado Midland Town*, Boulder: Pruett, 1965, 1971.

Dawson, Louis W. *Colorado High Routes*, Seattle: The Mountaineers, 1986.

Kelner, Alexis and Hanscom, David. *Wasatch Tours*, Salt Lake City: Wasatch Publishers, Inc., 1976.

LaChapelle, Edward R. *The ABC of Avalanche Safety*, 2nd ed., Seattle: The Mountaineers, 1985.

Ohlrich, Warren H. *Aspen/Snowmass Cross Country Ski Trails*, Aspen: WHO Press, 1989.

Ohlrich, Warren H. *Aspen/Snowmass Trails*, Aspen: WHO Press, 1988.

Parker, Paul. *Free-Heel Skiing*, England: Diadem Books, 1988.

Peters, Ed. *Mountaineering, the Freedom of the Hills*, 4th ed., Seattle: The Mountaineers, 1982.

Perla, Ronald and Martinelli, M. *Avalanche Handbook*, Washington, D.C.: U.S. Department of Agriculture #489, 1976.

Shoemaker, Len. *Pioneers of the Roaring Fork*, Denver: Sage Books, 1965.

Tejada-Flores, Lito. *Backcountry Skiing*, San Francisco: Sierra Club Books, 1981.

Watters, Ron. *Ski Camping*, San Francisco: Solstice Press/Chronicle Books, 1979.

Williams, Knox and Armstrong, Betsy. *The Snowy Torrents–Avalanche Accidents in the United States 1972- 1979*, Jackson, Wyoming: Teton Bookshop Publishing Company.

Williams, Knox and Armstrong, Betsy. *The Avalanche Book*, Golden, Colorado: Fulcrum, Inc., 1986.

Index

Minturn, 40-41
Montgomery Flats, 34, 68, 71, 78-80
Mosquito Range, 167, 176, 182
Mountain Haven, 35
Mount Massive, 73-74, 172, 198, 200
Mount of the Holy Cross, 100, 113
Mount Sherman, 182
Mount Yeckel, 55, 63-64
Muckawanago, 70-71
Muckawanago Creek, 70
Mushroom Bowl, 117

N

Nast Lake, 35, 71
Newcomer Spring, 100, 103, 109
Newcomer Spring Trail, 95, 107
New England Traverse, 108
New York Mountain, 102-3, 106, 110
Nolan Creek, 103, 107
Norrie Colony, 35
Norrie Trailhead, 34-35, 58, 60, 65, 68, 71, 74
North Fork Road, 35-36, 73-74, 80, 165
North Fork West Tennessee Creek, 161, 164-67, 177
North Maroon Peak, 124
North Mount Massive, 200-2

P

Pando, 41, 127, 143
Pando Trailhead, 41-42, 125-30, 143, 146
Peak 12,234, 64
Pearl Creek, 124, 137-38, 143, 146-53, 209
Pearl Peak, 153, 209
Peter Estin Hut, 7, 72, 78, 83-86, 91-101, 109, 195, 211
Peterson, Pete, 161
Piney Gulch, 154-57, 160
Polar Star Inn, 7, 99, 102-11, 211

Porcupine Creek, 168, 177
Porcupine Gulch, 168, 176-77
Ptarmigan Hill, 121, 124, 128-30, 133-34, 137-41, 149, 208
Ptarmigan Hill Traverse, 128-29
Ptarmigan Pass, 121, 128-30, 133-34, 137, 149
Ptarmigan Ridge, 121, 133
Ptarmigan Shoulder, 128-29

R

Ranch Creek, 139, 142, 146-47, 153
Ranch Creek Road, 146-47
Red Cliff, 40-41, 113, 119, 122, 132
Red Cliff Trailhead, 40, 118-19, 130-33
Red Mountain, 44
Red Tables, 73
Resolution Bowl, 138-40
Resolution Creek, 124-29, 138-39, 143, 146, 150-51
Resolution Mountain, 124-28, 131, 138, 140, 150-51
Resolution Narrows, 125-27, 131, 150
Resolution Road, 41, 127-29, 138-43, 146, 150-51
Resolution Saddle, 125-27, 131, 150
Road 505, 36, 69, 72, 195, 198-202
Road 505 Trailhead, 36, 69, 72, 195, 198
Roaring Fork River, 32-33

S

Sawatch Mountains, 73
Sawmill Park, 52-53, 56, 59-64
Schuss, Jack, 142, 195
Searle Basin, 137
Searle Pass, 153, 209-10
Sellar Lake, 72-73
Sellar Park, 189-90
Sellar Peaks, 73-74
Sherwood Forest, 20, 85, 98

Shrine Mountain, 113, 116, 120, 135, 207-8
Shrine Mountain Inn, 112-124, 135-36, 203, 206-7, 211, 216
Shrine Mountain Ridge, 113, 121, 124, 135-36
Shrine Mountain Saddle, 120, 135
Shrine Pass, 113, 116-123, 136-37
Shrine Pass Road, 40-41, 112-13, 116-19, 122-23, 130-33, 136-37, 207-8
Siberia Peak, 39, 117-18
Silver Creek, 57-58, 78
Ski Cooper, 42, 156-59, 169
Skinner, William Wood, 182
Skinner Hut, 69-72, 172, 175, 178, 182-95, 199, 211
Slab Park, 53-54
Slide Creek, 165
Slide Lake, 166, 170-71
Slim Jim Gulch, 81, 83, 89-90, 98
Smith Gulch, 139, 207-8
South Camp Hale Trailhead, 41-42, 146-48, 155-56
South Fork Fryingpan River, 60-61
Spine Creek, 82, 84, 93, 97
Spring Creek Fish Hatchery, 34, 81
Spring Creek Trailhead, 34, 68-69, 80-81
Spruce Creek, 49-52, 55-57, 62
Spruce Creek Trail, 52, 56
Squaw Creek, 108-9, 111
Squaw Creek Saddle, 108-9
Squaw Creek Trail, 111
Stafford Creek, 139, 206-7
St. Kevin Creek, 168, 174
St. Kevin Gulch, 168, 174, 181
St. Kevin Lake, 179
Sugarloaf Peak, 210
Summit Hut and Trails Association, 203
Sylvan Lake, 37, 69, 78-81
Sylvan Lake Road, 37-38
Sylvan Lake Trailhead, 37-38, 82-83, 92-93

T

Tagert, Billie, 5
Taylor Hill, 152, 154-57, 159-60
Tellurium Lake, 89
Tellurium Park, 75, 88-90
Tellurium Park Loop, 87, 90
Tennessee Park, 42
Tennessee Pass, 5, 41-42, 154, 159, 164, 166, 169
Tennessee Pass ski touring trails, 164, 168
Tennessee Pass Trailhead, 42, 156-57, 161, 164-65
10th Mountain Bridge, 45, 49
10th Mountain Division, 5, 41, 116, 161, 172, 182
10th Mountain Division Hut, 159, 161-72, 176, 211
10th Mountain Trail Association, 5-6, 8, 16, 195, 216
Timber Creek, 116
Timberline Lake, 175, 183, 187
Timberline Lake Trail, 178, 183
Tim's Traverse, 137, 149, 152, 203, 208-9
Toklat Chalet, 6
Triangle Creek, 106
Turkey Creek, 40, 113, 116, 119, 122, 136
Turquoise Lake, 43, 171-74, 183, 187-88, 192
Turquoise Lake Road, 174-75, 178, 183, 186-88, 192
Turquoise Lake Trailhead, 43, 173-74, 183, 187-88
Twin Meadows, 36, 55, 58-61, 68, 71-72
Twin Meadows Road, 59
Two Elk Creek, 117-18
Two Elk Pass, 117
Tyler, Janet Boyd, 203

U

Uncle Bud's Hut, 161, 167-68, 171-81, 191-92, 211
Union Creek, 40, 205-6
Union Creek Trailhead, 40, 205, 209
Union Mountain, 203
Union Peak, 203, 209-10
Upper Fryingpan drainage, 36, 65, 71, 199
Upper Stafford Creek, 122, 203, 206-7
Upper Town, 103, 106-7
Upper Van Horn Park, 48-49
Upper Van Horn Saddle, 48

V

Vail, 5-6, 37-41, 112, 117-18, 195, 203, 216
Vail Pass, 39, 116, 118, 122-23, 134, 139, 203, 206-7
Vail Pass Trailhead, 39, 112-13, 116, 123, 133-34, 206
Vail Ski Area, 117-18
Vail Trailhead for the Commando Run, 39, 116-17
Vance's Cabin, 142, 148, 151-52, 154-60, 164, 169, 211
Van Horn Park, 45, 48

W

Wearyman Creek, 119-21, 124, 130-36, 140, 208
Wearyman Creek Road, 122, 130, 133, 136-37
Wearyman Saddle, 134
West Brush Creek Road, 37, 82, 93
West Face of Yeckel, 63
West Lake Creek Road, 39
West Lake Creek Trailhead, 38, 103, 108-9
West Sellar Peak, 73
West Tenmile Creek, 113, 119, 122, 133-36, 206

West Tenmile ski trail, 205
West Tennessee Creek, 165-67, 177
White Quail Gulch, 107, 110
White River National Forest, 8, 113, 119, 136, 217
Widow Gulch, 44
Wilder Creek, 121, 133
Wilder Gulch, 129, 133-34, 139, 206-8
Williams Mountains, 54, 91
Winter, Bud, 172
Woods Lake Road, 81-85
Woody Creek, 48-53, 56-57, 62
Woody Creek Road, 33, 52
Woody Creek Trail, 52, 62
Wurts Ditch Road, 42, 165-66

Y

Yeckel Bowl, 63
Yeoman Park, 38, 92, 107
Yeoman Park Campground, 103
Yeoman Park Trailhead, 38, 94-96, 100, 103, 106-7

Z

Zesiger, Al, 142, 195